Marketing tourism places

Edited by Gregory Ashworth and
Brian Goodall

ROUTLEDGE
London and New York

First published 1990
by Routledge
11 New Fetter Lane, London EC4P 4EE

Simultaneously published in the USA and Canada
by Routledge
a division of Routledge, Chapman and Hall, Inc.
29 West 35th Street, New York, NY 10001

© 1990 Gregory Ashworth and Brian Goodall

Printed and bound in Great Britain by
Biddles Ltd, Guildford and King's Lynn

British Library Cataloguing in Publication Data

Marketing tourism places.
  1. Tourism. Marketing
  I. Ashworth, Gregory J. *1943–* II. Goodall, Brian
  1937–
  658.8′09′91

  ISBN 0-415-03810-3

Library of Congress Cataloging in Publication Data

Marketing tourism places / edited by Gregory J. Ashworth and Brian
  Goodall.
      p.   cm.
   Bibliography: p.
   ISBN 0-415-03810-3
   1. Tourist trade. 2. Marketing. I. Ashworth, G.J. (Gregory
John) II. Goodall, Brian.
G155.A1M298   1990
338.4′791–dc20   89-10530
                                          CIP

CONTENTS

Contents

Contents

Contents

Contents

TABLES

Tables

FIGURES

Figures

CONTRIBUTORS

Dr. Gregory ASHWORTH*

Reader, Faculty of Spatial Sciences, Rijksuniversiteit Groningen

drs. Jan BERGSMA

Lecturer, Sektor Toerisme en Rekreatie, Nationale Hogeschool voor Toerisme en Verkeer, Breda

Ms. Ann CLEWER

Lecturer in Management Science, Econometrics and Social Sciences, University of Kent, Canterbury

Professor Brian GOODALL*

Professor and Head of Department of Geography and Consultant Director of the NERC Unit for Thematic Information Systems, University of Reading

drs. Theo Z. de HAAN

Research Officer, National Research Institute for Recreation and Tourism, Breda

* Editors

Contributors

Dr. Myriam C. JANSEN-VERBEKE	Lecturer, Department of Geography, Catholic University of Nijmegen and Nationale Hogeschool voor Toerisme en Verkeer, Breda
Peter KENT	ESRC Postgraduate Student, Departments of Economics and Geography, University of Reading
drs. Ed C. van der KNIJFF	Economic Research Officer, Department of Research, Province of Friesland, Leeuwarden
Professor Luiz MOUTINHO	Professor of Marketing, University College of Wales, Cardiff
Alan PACK	Lecturer in Management Science, Econometrics and Social Statistics, University of Kent, Canterbury
Ms. Gill PATTINSON	Marketing Manager, Thames & Chilterns Tourist Board, Witney
Mark RADBURN	Lecturer, Department of Catering and Tourism Studies, Herefordshire Technical College, Hereford
Dr. M. Thea SINCLAIR	Lecturer in Economics, University of Kent, Canterbury
Michael J. STABLER	Lecturer in Economics, University of Reading

Professor Henk VOOGD

Professor, Faculty of Spatial Sciences, Rijksuniversiteit Groningen

Dr. Friedrich ZIMMERMANN

Lecturer, Department of Geography, University of Klagenfurt

The tourism industry has reached the stage of maturity. Tourists today are more experienced and therefore increasingly discerning in their choice of holidays, in terms of both destinations and activities. Indeed their expectations of their holiday environment have often been heightened by the tourism industry itself. The industry, however, is a fiercely competitive one, with many destinations competing to attract the potential tourists. Gone are the days when a destination could simply make known its attractions and sit back and await the arrival of visitors. Today tourists have to be enticed: the destination's place product must be marketed effectively. The new-found maturity of the tourism market does not rule out continuous and extensive change since destinations have reacted to increased competition with high levels of investment and new place products in order to maintain and increase market share and in an attempt to capture new market segments. Destinations are 'coming of age' in a marketing context, acknowledging that place products have to be sold, implying greater emphasis on marketing techniques such as positioning and branding.

This book is based on the theme of the third international tourism workshop organised by the Geographical Institutes of the Universities of Groningen (The Netherlands) and Reading (United Kingdom) which was held in Groningen from 3 to 6 October 1988. The theme was selling tourism places or destinations. Contributors to the workshop were invited from both academic institutes and the tourism industry to provide a multidisciplinary and professional consideration of the theme. The contributions addressed various aspects of the theme 'selling tourism places': they ranged from the theoretical base to the empirical evaluation of actual campaigns. Following presentation and discussion at the workshop contributors went away and wrote their papers to incorporate the workshop discussions. These papers have been organised and linked by the editors in a progression from theoretical considerations, through the shaping of the place product, to the organisations involved in selling such places. The editors anticipate that the resulting book will appeal to a wide readership of academics, professionals and students with interests in tourism.

As always the editors would wish to thank not only their academic and professional colleagues who have contributed to this book but also the financial support of the University of Groningen which made it possible to invite colleagues from other institutes. In particular we must thank most sincerely those other colleagues who have been indispensable in the production of this book: Rosa Husain for preparation of the camera-ready typescript and Sheila Dance and Joy Liddell for preparation of the diagrams.

G.A.   B.G.

Chapter 1

CAN PLACES BE SOLD FOR TOURISM?

Gregory Ashworth and Henk Voogd

INTRODUCTION

Can places be sold for tourism? This question appears to have a self-evident positive answer. Ever since Leif Ericson recruited settlers for his 'Green' land, places have been promoted by means of the projection of favourable images to a potential market of users by those who have an interest in attracting them. More recently, however, the idea of selling places, or **geographical marketing** (as defined by Ashworth & Voogd, 1987b), has received growing attention by public authority planners and decision-makers as a form of place management.

Place marketing, and especially place promotion, accounts for an increasing share of both municipal budgets and attention from academics from a number of disciplines, with the new, or at least newly respectable, study of 'Marketing Science' in the vanguard. 'Selling places' (cf. Burgess, 1975) has become an accepted part of the function of public authority place management, although not without the misgivings of many (Clarke, 1986). Places are 'sold' in a large number of potential consumer markets and by private as well as public sector organisations. The concern of this chapter and many chapters in this book, however, is the 'selling' of tourist destinations by public agencies with broader civic responsibilities. It is in this area that the difficulties of transferring and adapting ideas and techniques developed for the sale of goods and services by commercial firms for measurable intermediate financial profit, become most apparent.

The aim of this chapter is to address the theoretical and conceptual assumptions implicit in such approaches. It begins with a brief empirical exercise, in which the obvious relationship between promotional activities and tourist visitors is illustrated. The possible theoretical consequences

1

of this relationship will be subsequently discussed. Attention is paid to marketing planning as a kind of public sector place management and to the concept of a tourism destination as a marketable product. In addition, the question will be raised whether a tourist can be compared with a 'place customer'. Finally, the central importance of the price mechanism within marketing, including marketing tourism places, is raised.

TOURISM PROMOTION AND TOURIST USE

Marketing, and especially its promotional aspects, is based on the assumption that there is some relationship between the amount of promotion and the number of visitors (or 'customers'). The same assumption holds for place marketing. It is therefore interesting to investigate this relationship in more detail. For this reason the advertisements in the weekend editions of three Dutch national newspapers (viz. De Volkskrant, Trouw, and Parool) have been examined over a certain period (i.e. from 9 July to 17 September 1988) in order to obtain an idea about the differences in promotional activities towards domestic tourists between the Dutch provinces. In total 1,773 advertisements were counted which addressed one or more aspects of the tourism 'product' of a province and/or town or region within the province. The majority of the advertisements was devoted to the promotion of tourist accommodation (e.g. hotels, apartments, camp sites): among other subjects were the promotion of horse riding, sailing and sea fishing opportunities.

The results are presented in Fig. 1.1. It shows that the highest percentage of advertisements relate to places in the provinces of North Holland and Limburg, followed by Friesland and Drenthe. However, the high figures for North Holland and Friesland are to a considerable extent determined by the Wadden Islands. North Holland includes the island of Texel, whereas Vlieland, Terschelling, Ameland and Schiermonnikoog belong to the province of Friesland.

It is interesting to compare this level of promotional activity with some figures about the tourists that visit the various provinces. This is done in Fig. 1.2, which includes both the percentage of tourism advertisements and the

Figure 1.1: Tourism advertisements in weekend editions of Dutch national newspapers, 9 July - 17 Sept. 1988

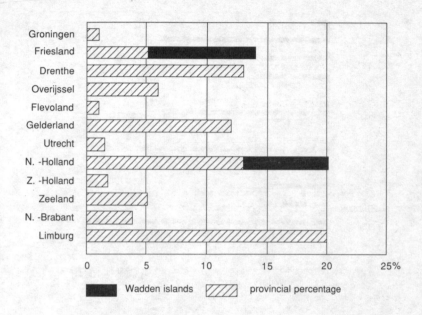

provincial percentage of short and long holidays for 1985 (Central Bureau of Statistics, 1987). This illustrates that there is some relationship between promotion and number of visitors. The provinces with hardly any advertisements (e.g. Groningen, Flevoland) attract relatively few tourists, whereas the provinces with more advertisements also have more people for a short holiday (Limburg) or a long holiday (Gelderland, Friesland). However, it is also obvious from Fig. 1.2 that no one-to-one relationship exists: for instance, the many advertisements for North Holland are not entirely reflected by the number of tourists in 1985.

On the basis of Fig. 1.2, we may distinguish four provinces with a higher 'advertisement rate' than tourist visitors: Friesland, Drenthe, North Holland and Limburg. Seven provinces show the opposite picture, viz. relatively less advertisements and a higher 'tourist rate': Overijssel, Flevoland, Gelderland, Utrecht, South Holland, Zeeland and North Brabant.

3

Figure 1.2: Tourism advertisements compared with long and short holidays in 1985 by province

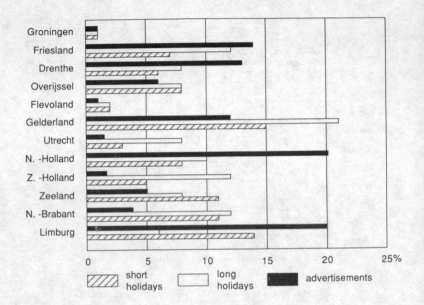

Of course, the present data do not allow more detailed conclusions. This rough exercise is only meant as an incentive to a further study of tourist behaviour in relation to place promotion, and vice versa, but it does demonstrate that the assumption of even simple relationships needs further examination. In particular the simple question is posed as to why some provinces appear to be more effective in their marketing activities than others. Such questions are addressed by many of the subsequent chapters in this book.

MARKET PLANNING AS PUBLIC SECTOR PLACE MANAGEMENT

Places have been managed on the basis of a large number of different philosophies, in pursuit of a wide variety of goals, but in order to emphasise some of the differences in approach, three such philosophies, relevant to tourism and commonly found among public local authorities, are compared in Table 1.1.

Table 1.1: Some public authority planning philosophies

Dominant Philosophy	Orientation	Goal	Example	Values	Determined by
preservation	object	protection	monuments	cultural	preservers
physical regulation	spatial patterns	conflict resolution	urban conservation	legal norms	professional planners etc., politicians
redistribution	needs	equity	recreation	social	
marketing	customer	sales development	tourism promotion	market	user

The implications of a marketing philosophy can be best appreciated if it is compared with a cursory summary of some other possible approaches to tourism planning. A preservationist philosophy regards the protection of the natural and built environment from threats to it as a public trust. The place as a tourism resource, whether preserved and renovated historic city or protected landscape, is treated defensively and success is measured in terms of its maintenance. Most public physical planning has concentrated on places as spatial patterns of morphological forms and interacting functions, which must be channelled and controlled so that conflicts can be avoided or a desirable balance between functions achieved. Tourism is, in this case, one function within the multifunctional place to be managed on the basis of professionally determined norms and political decisions about the role it should play in the wider spatial setting for the attainment of municipal goals.

The adoption of the last listed public planning philosophy, viz. 'marketing', is, in a superficial sense, deceptively easy to accomplish. At the shallowest level it is merely a matter of substituting a new terminology and renaming the various procedures of the planning process. Tourism supply becomes the tourism product to be 'positioned' in relation to competing products, demand becomes the customers, which need 'segmentation' according to product purchasing behaviour, and management becomes market planning undertaken in a 'development' or 'promotion' department. At a deeper level the transfer is attained by regarding marketing as the adoption of a new set of planning procedures that claim to be customer or client orientated (see Ashworth & Voogd, 1987b, or Hebestreit, 1977, for what amounts to a procedural manual for tourism marketing). Some of the most obvious examples in tourism are to be found in the British Tourism Development Action Programmes or the, in many ways very similar, Dutch Tourism and Recreation Development Plans (Kerstens, 1983; Ashworth & Bergsma, 1987). In both of these 'feasibility' studies, existing and potential demand conditions are compared with 'product analyses', i.e. inventories of the facilities and attractions of places, in the light of such demands and in comparison with competing places. Deficiencies are thus highlighted and dealt with by a mixture of new investments on the supply side and market promotion on the demand side.

Whether such tourism plans are just 'old wine in new bottles', they regard market planning as a set of procedures. A further and usually much more difficult step for many public authorities is to substitute market responsiveness for what could be termed the professional normative responses, which are intrinsic to the nature of bureaucracies. In particular much of the land use planning developed in post-war Western Europe (Burtenshaw et al., 1981) attempts to manage tourism by appeals to norms derived from contemporary professional conventional wisdom, and enshrined in legislation or 'good practice' so as to determine 'carrying capacities', 'conforming land uses', 'acceptable functional mixes' and the like. Market planning as an organisational philosophy does not so much arrive at different answers to these sorts of problems of place management as largely ignore the questions and substitute quite different ones, and equally important, quite different methods of obtaining answers for them. It is these differences that will be examined in more detail below.

IS A TOURISM DESTINATION A PRODUCT?

Tourism destinations can undoubtedly be treated as products. They are logically the point of consumption of the complex of activities that comprises the tourism experience and are ultimately what is sold by place promotion agencies on the tourism market. The potential holidaymaker in that sense is buying at the travel agents the product 'Benidorm' in preference to one labelled 'Sitges', and it makes no difference to this definition that only a selected portion of the town, a particular set of facilities and services, is being purchased. As with a more easily delimitable good or service the attributes purchased by the customer do not have to amount to a full technical inventory of all possible attributes of the object on sale. The National Marketing Plan for Historic Environments, produced by the Netherlands Research Institute for Tourism (1988), for example treats historic artefacts and associations as important tourism products and Kirby (1985) argues that leisure as a whole could be treated as a 'commodity'.

There are, however, a number of fundamental differences between a place as a tourism destination and a marketable good or service purchased directly by customers of the tourism industry, such as the hire of hotel space or purchase of souvenirs. Jansen-Verbeke (1988) combines these two product definitions in her concept of the **Tourist Recreation Product** (TRP). Such a TRP is treated simultaneously in the selected worked examples, as both the inner city as a whole and also the 'commodities' of which it is composed. Four points need further investigation:

(i) The problem of defining and subsequently delimiting a place as a product has been raised previously (see Ashworth's 1985 discussion of towns as tourism resources), but such difficulties as defining, delimiting and thus planning for the tourist's Benidorm as opposed to other varieties of the same product, or more accurately other products of the same name, are practical rather than conceptual and are thus open to solutions of working practice, not relevant to the discussion here. However, the series of studies of the Tourist-Historic city (Ashworth & de Haan, 1986) which attempted to define and delimit on the ground the historic attractions of the city as defined by use in tourism, revealed a particular difficulty. Places, in this case tourism towns, both contain tourism facilities and attractions and simultaneously <u>are</u> such a facility and an attraction. The place is both the product and the container of an assemblage of products. This in turn has implications for the promotion and management of such places.

(ii) The distinction mentioned above leads to two further qualities of places as products which have a particular influence upon how such places can be marketed. The tourism product consumed at a particular place is assembled from the variety of services and experiences obtainable there, but this assembly is conducted largely by the consumer rather than the producer. Even when some important items are sold together in packages determined by the tourism producers or intermediaries, each individual holiday will still largely consist of a consumer selection of products which will be necessarily unique. This situation is quite different from that found in the marketing of most goods and services, whether in the private or public sector. Clearly, a consequence of this situation is that the place product is marketed by destination agencies without any clear idea of the nature of the product being consumed.

(iii) Another consequence of the delimitation problem is that of spatial scale, a characteristic possessed by places but not by other types of product. A place is inevitably one component in a hierarchy of spatial scales. This is more than the inevitable parochial viewpoint of a geographer accustomed to hierarchical spatial modelling: it is central to the nature of the tourism product and how it is marketed. The potential holidaymaker buying Benidorm, may equally be purchasing other levels in the hierarchy, the hotel and its grounds, the tourism sea front zone, the Costa Brava, Spain and even the Mediterranean. One conclusion of the study of the Languedoc coast (see Chp.9) is that there are major scale discrepancies in the definition of the product by those concerned with shaping, marketing and managing it. Here, as in many such tourism areas, the choice of scale for the definition of the tourism product is determined by the nature of local government boundaries at different scales. Thus arbitrary political boundaries, and the division of public functions within the local government hierarchy, assume a greater significance in shaping the product than the intrinsic characteristics of the place or the perceptions and behaviour of the customer. Are national, regional and local tourism promotion agencies selling different products or parts of the same products? Would a differently structured hierarchy create a different product?

(iv) Finally, and probably of greatest significance to the introduction of marketing techniques into local authority planning: places are **multi-sold**. There are few parallels in the commercial marketing of goods and services to the situation in place marketing, where precisely the same physical space, and in practice much the same facilities and attributes of that space, are sold simultaneously to different groups of customers for different purposes. The earlier reference to the analysis of the concept of the historic city, for instance, draws the clear distinction between the sale of facilities in such a city (visits to attractions, museums and the like, as well as the sale of supporting services such as catering and accommodation) and the sale of the city as a whole (see Berkers et al., 1986, for an account of the practical consequences of this distinction for management policy in the city of Norwich). In the latter, but not in the former definition, there is no question of exclusiveness: the historic city is sold at the same time as a shopping city, the residential city, the sporting city or many other 'cities' to the same or quite different customers. This is not quite the same as the misleadingly similar and well-known marketing situation where individual units of the same good or service can be marketed to different customers as different products. In place marketing it is the same place, and not subdivisions of it, that is the product. This raises the curious marketing situation where the sale of the product in no way diminishes the stock of the product held by the producer, at least until some capacity limit is reached. If this line of thought is continued then many of the characteristic problems and working solutions of 'traditional' land use regulatory planning return in a different guise. Although the sale of different 'cities' does not necessarily result in a situation of zero-sum gain nevertheless multi-selling of the same physical space can result in precisely the same land use conflicts long familiar to local authority physical planning departments (Ashworth & Voogd, 1987b). Regulatory planning thus finds a continuing need for its techniques but within a quite different planning framework.

Can Places be Sold for Tourism?

IS THE TOURIST A PLACE CUSTOMER?

Again the search for answers to this question seems to be both familiar in marketing and to offer few intrinsic difficulties. The customer has only to be defined, identified and categorised in terms of the relationship to the product. The market can be segmented in this precise technical sense (Ashworth & Voogd, 1988). However, a number of difficulties can be identified:

First, the fact that tourists as place consumers have extremely varied patterns of holiday behaviour, intensities of use of the product, previous histories of experience of the product and sets of motives for the visit poses no conceptual problem. Although such variables are arguably more varied than is the case with many marketed goods and services, they can nevertheless be accommodated within the existing techniques of market analysis. They become variables in the construction of so-called 'AIO' (attitudes, interests, opinions) clusters. A number of commentators on the nature of tourism demands have stressed the range of individual perceptions of tourist destinations (Crompton, 1979) and the role of individual fantasy (Dann, 1976). But the fact that individual consumers experience the same product quite differently is not unique to tourist destinations nor an insuperable obstacle to treating the tourist as a customer.

Second, it can be argued that tourism demand contains such a large latent or option element that the market cannot be adequately equated with participation. The tourism market, at least at the level of the individual tourist destination, is supply-led to an extent that renders an approach from consumption superfluous. But although this may present theoretical problems to an analysis based on supply and demand as independent variables, it has little effect on a marketing approach that makes no such assumption, and the main residual difficulty is only one of demand measurement.

Third, the most fundamental difficulty stems from the equivalent on the consumption side to the multi-sold product. The tourist destination is multi-bought with only non-exclusive rights of consumption of places being purchased. The holidaymaker is consuming one place while the shopper, resident and worker are consuming another, which occupies the same physical space and may be composed of the same facilities on that space. The situation is however even more complex than this. It is not merely that different groups of consumers are purchasing different 'places' even within the same trip. A number of studies of actual tourist purchasing behaviour in tourist destinations have tried to come to terms with this phenomenon. Jansen-Verbeke's studies (1986, 1988) of visitors to the inner city have confronted this problem of identification of a separate tourism market, as have the studies of the concept of 'user' of tourist places (Ashworth & de Haan, 1986). Both arrive at the similar conclusion that the tourist can only be identified at the point of consumption on the basis of individual motivation at that moment. The tourist is thus logically a place consumer but the identification and measurement of this market will pose particular difficulties.

CAN TOURISM PLACES BE MANAGED THROUGH MARKET PLANNING?

The answer to the simpler question of how can places be managed through market planning has already been provided by a number of accounts of procedures and techniques of public sector planning using marketing approaches (for example, Ashworth & Voogd, 1987a). Similarly, there is no need to repeat here the well-known conceptual basis for the application of marketing approaches to non-profit enterprises, to social goals or to the marketing of attitudes and ideas, other than direct consumer behaviour. Tourist destination management has long been an example of public-private partnership (see Brown, 1988 for examples that are almost a century old) and the application of market planning does not imply any alteration in the balance of these responsibilities nor any change in the nature of public authority goals in the management of tourism places.

Instead of pursuing these types of argument, two difficulties in answering the question can be raised:

(i) There are many organisational problems. The organisational suitability of public sector working methods, personnel and general ethos for adopting marketing approaches, has been questioned elsewhere, in particular Torkildsen's (1983) claim that local authorities are

11

intrinsically 'product' rather than client orientated will be important here. However, the important but very simple point being raised here is that in the management of tourism places those responsible for product promotion are not the same as those concerned with production and operation of the components. There are of course many detailed exceptions to this comment, but in general the promotion of the tourism services on offer within the place are managed by private sector enterprises. Even when the product is produced and managed by public authorities (such as historic attractions, museums, national parks and nature reserves), they are generally the responsibility of quite separate branches of state within a strongly departmental government structure. In few other sectors of the economy is the product managed by such a variety of enterprises and the promotion of the product in the hands of an agency that has no direct part in its production. Similarly there is the same discrepancy between the promotion of the product to the market and the reception and management of the customers attracted by such promotion. Local promoters, as Jansen-Verbeke (1986) has confirmed in a sample study in The Netherlands, largely accept the tourism product as given, and assume only a minimal role in the management of place consumers.

(ii) The second difficulty is again simple but in need of emphasis. Namely, the instruments available for managing tourism places through market planning are weak. This is in part a consequence of the problems raised above of the definition, delimitation and measurement of both the product and the customer market. It is also a result of the generally undifferentiated, untargeted nature of most place promotional exercises, as demonstrated by Koster's (1988) critique of such exercises in the Dutch tourism context, and the lack of effective behaviour in tourism places (Nolan, 1976). It is just wishful thinking to claim that marketing approaches are a form of place management when their role in either attracting visitors or controlling their holiday behaviour is at best indirect and at worst barely existent. Whatever criticisms can be directed at the other philosophies of place management listed earlier, there is no doubt that they are operationalised through sets of instruments that actually regulate the functioning of tourism places. The absence of such place management instruments is perhaps most evident in the lack of quality control over the destination or place product, which can have serious consequences within tourism.

HOW MUCH ARE WE SELLING TOURISM PLACES FOR?

The identification and discussion of difficulties is not a denial of the potential advantages of an approach. On the contrary, poor market planning of which there are numerous examples in tourism place promotion, will only serve to discredit the approach as a whole and prevent these potentials being realised.

The central core of marketing is voluntary exchange. In this case a place, however defined in terms of a set of tourism experiences associated with that place, is freely exchanged in return for a price, within a competitive market with other such places. Pricing is central to the whole process, as a regulatory mechanism linking producer and consumer, and defining the relationships between producers. This is self-evident in the commercial sphere, but such a pricing mechanism is either non-existent or only partially developed in public sector tourism place management. In most cases the price of the tourism place is indirect, intangible and spread over such a large variety of consumers and non-consumers as to be an ineffective regulatory instrument, or just unknown by producer and consumer alike. Marketing without pricing is an unreal exercise.

That is not of course to imply that the exchange must be monetary and directed only to short-term profit maximisation for the producer. There is 'social exchange' (Torkildsen, 1983), using other units of account, in which both payment and receipt can be diffused beyond the individual customer and individual producer, and the goals of the enterprise can be assessed on the basis of factors other than financial return. It is also not assigning prices, whatever units of measurement are used, to the tourism attributes of places. Either working solutions to such difficulties are found or marketing approaches are masquerading in an area to which they cannot make a contribution. The place must be priced if it is to be sold. Objectives must be established, which in public authorities are necessarily and correctly broad, means of measuring

13

the tourism product devised, and the costs, benefits and profits of the exchange quantified. For without quantification, how can success in achieving the initial objectives be assessed?

CAN PLACES BE SOLD FOR TOURISM?

The application of marketing approaches to the management of places, and in particular selling places to tourists, can provide an effective development instrument. Such applications, however, if they are to be more than a 'biased and limited approach' (Jansen-Verbeke, 1988), involving only the substitution of a fashionable terminology, contain implicit assumptions and more explicit implications which deserve more attention than they have received. This is necessary, not so much as a defence of other public planning philosophies but for the effective operation of marketing approaches. Places can be sold and tourists can be treated as place consumers, but this selling and purchasing of places will only be effective if tourist destinations and tourists are recognised as being different in a number of fundamental respects from the products and customers in the commercial sector for which marketing science was originally evolved.

Currently, most public sector tourism place marketing is the attempt to sell an unpriced product, in largely unknown quantities, for a profit measured only in terms of receipts. If the marketing approach is a 'password for entering a new experimental field' (Jansen-Verbeke, 1988) then those experiments must surely concentrate on shaping a pricing mechanism without which the 'password' is just ephemeral, fashionable jargon.

REFERENCES

Ashworth, G.J. (1985) The evaluation of urban tourist resources, pp 37-44 in G J. Ashworth & B. Goodall (Eds), The Impact of Tourist Development on Disadvantaged Regions, Sociaal-Geografische Reeks 35, GIRUG, Groningen
Ashworth, G.J. & Bergsma, J. (1987) New policies for tourism: Opportunities or problems, Tijdschrift voor Economische en Sociale Geografie, 78 (2) 151-156

Ashworth, G.J. & de Haan, T.Z. (1986) Uses and users of the tourist-historic city, Field Studies Series 8, GIRUG, Groningen

Ashworth, G.J. & Voogd, H. (1987a) The marketing of European heritage as an economic resource, pp. 38-40 in J.J.M. Angenent & A. Bongenaar (Eds), Planning Without a Passport; the Future of European Spatial Planning, Netherlands Geographical Studies/SISWO, Amsterdam, vol. 44

Ashworth, G.J. & Voogd, H. (1987b) Geografische Marketing, een bruikbare invalshoek voor onderzoek en planning, Stedebouw & Volkshuisvesting, 3, 85-90

Ashworth, G.J. & Voogd, H. (1988) Marketing the City; concepts, processes and Dutch applications, Town Planning Review 59(1) 65-80

Berkers, M.; de Boer, G.; van Doorn, G.; Glas, R.; Jense, H.; Koopman, K.; Oosc, L. & Renkema, J. (1986) The planning and management of the British historic city, Field Studies Series 9, GIRUG, Groningen

Brown, B.J.H. (1988) Developments in the promotion of major seaside resorts, pp.176-186 in B. Goodall & G.J. Ashworth (Eds), Marketing in the Tourism Industry, Croom Helm, Beckenham

Burgess, J.A. (1975) Selling places, Regional Studies 16(1) 1-17

Burtenshaw, D., Bateman, M. & Ashworth, G.J. (1981) The City in West Europe, Wiley, Chichester

Central Bureau of Statistics (1987) Staatsuitgeverij, The Hague

Clarke, A. (1986) Local authority planners or frustrated tourism marketeers?, The Planner, 72(5) 23-26

Crompton, J.L. (1979) An assessment of the image of Mexico as a vacation destination, Journal of Travel Research 17 (4) 18-23

Dann, G. (1976) The holiday was simply fantastic, Tourism Review, 31 (5) 19-23

Hebestreit, D. (1977) Touristik Marketing, Springer Verlag, Berlin

Jansen-Verbeke, M. (1986) Inner city tourism: resources, tourists, promoters, Annals of Tourism Research 13, 79-100

Jansen-Verbeke, M (1988) Inner cities and urban leisure resources in The Netherlands, in I. Henry (Ed), Leisure and Urban Processes, Methuen, London

Can Places be Sold for Tourism?

Kerstens, P. (1983) Marketing benadering in toeristisch recreatieve ontwikkelingsplannen, Recreatie 5, 12-18

Kirby, A. (1985) Leisure as commodity: the role of the state in leisure provision, Progress in Human Geography 9, 64-84

Kosters, M.J. (1988) Changing tourism requires a different management approach, pp 198-212 in B. Goodall & G.J. Ashworth (Eds), Marketing in the Tourism Industry, Croom Helm, Beckenham

Netherlands Research Institute for Tourism (1988) Marketing van de Historische Omgeving, NRIT Breda

Nolan, D.S. (1976) Tourist's use and evaluation of travel information sources, Journal of Travel Research, 14, 6-8

Torkildsen, G. (1983) Leisure and Recreation Management, Spon, London

I

THEORY AND CONCEPT

Tourists were likened to **place consumers** and tourist destinations to **place products** in Chapter 1 by Ashworth and Voogd, who also posed questions about the pricing of place products. If destinations are also regarded as suppliers of place products a straightforward demand-supply relationship would appear to hold. Since, in most destinations, the supply of attractions and facilities (which together make up a particular place product) is dominated by many small enterprises, it would also appear that conditions of pure competitition exist under which price is determined by the market interaction of many consumers and many suppliers.

However, the place at which consumer demand is effective in the first instance is the tourist-origin region and this is different from the place of consumption of the product, namely the tourist destination. Of course, this destination is also the place of supply of the product. Therefore to consume place products tourists have to travel from their regions of normal residence to the suppliers' location where they will holiday, conduct business, attend conferences, visit friends, etc. Thus, the market in which place products are traded is not a single, simple entity. Moreover the requirement for tourists to travel in order to consume place products suggests that a place product may be viewed differently in tourist-origin areas and tourist destinations: inclusive of travel in the former but exclusive of travel in the latter.

If places are to be sold successfully for tourism they must identify clearly what they have to offer, <u>viz</u>. the place product, which persons will have the time, money and desire to visit the place, <u>viz</u>. the target market(s), and the best ways to convince prospective tourists to visit that place, <u>viz</u>. place marketing. Interaction between tourist origins and destinations has formed the basis for much theoretical and empirical research in tourism: travel and place have been the key

19

elements in the modelling of tourism. Such research has emphasised the volume and direction of tourist flows with explanation directed towards the tourists' characteristics and the relative attraction of destinations. It has given little attention, however, to the nature of the place product and to the role of the tourism industry in determining product supply. An approach which demonstrates not only the linking of tourist origins and destinations but also the interactions between tourists, the tourism industry and place products is needed. The opportunity sets concept is one such approach which is of particular value in identifying the nature of the place product from the viewpoints of the tourist, the tourism industry and the destination whilst maintaining awareness of the importance of origin-destination interactions.

Place products can be arranged in opportunity sets which comprise, for example, holiday opportunities available at a given point in time to a variety of destinations. There is a common, overall set which embraces all place products (holidays, conventions, business meetings, etc.) offered at a point in time. This may be disaggregated in various ways according to whether the viewpoint taken is that of the tourist, the destination area or the tourism industry.

The distinction on the supply side between the tourism industry and the tourist destination is an important one: the product of the industry and that of the destination overlap but are not necessarily identical. Given the separation of tourist origins and destinations, firms which are part of the tourism industry may locate either in origin or destination areas. In destinations they are most likely to supply only part of the place product, such as attraction or facility components, whereas in origin areas firms, most notably tour operators, offer a **tourism product** which combines the place product with the necessary travel element, e.g. package holidays or inclusive tours. Tourists choosing a holiday from their home base are therefore likely to select from opportunity sets comprising tourism products rather than place products, notwithstanding the fact that these tourism products offer a very wide range of destinations. Every tourism product contains one or more place products. For destination areas their place product will be a part of tourism products in many separate markets in different tourist-generating regions.

Applying the opportunity set concept from the viewpoint of the tourism industry, Stabler emphasises the role of intermediaries, especially tour operators, in determining the nature and range of tourism products (and therefore place products) offered for sale in tourist-generating areas. It is clear that tour operators pursuing objectives such as profit, sales or market share maximisation, market their tourism products in a way which does not necessarily bring the fullest benefit to individual destinations, the place product suppliers. Potential tourists seeking a holiday may differ in the ways in which they regard the tourism product and the place product. For some the type of holiday, i.e. the tourism product, is most important whereas for others place, and therefore the place product, is the more significant factor - Kent demonstrates the tourist's holiday choice process within the opportunity set framework whilst acknowledging this distinction.

Firms based in tourist-origin areas offer tourism products which cover many place products and consumers therefore enjoy choice from a wide variety of destinations or place products, irrespective of the importance of place in their selection criteria. However, the individual destination represents a single place product (which may include several holiday activities) but no firm within a destination exercises overall control of the place product: each firm controls just part of that product, e.g. a hotel, marina, amusement arcade, souvenir shop, etc. Destination area tourism agencies which shoulder much of the responsibility for external marketing of the place product to consumers in tourist-generating areas are not product suppliers in the usual sense of the term. Goodall, therefore, in viewing opportunity sets from the destination viewpoint emphasises the interaction of the two supply-side applications of opportunity sets to destinations and to the tourism industry. Understanding the structure of the tourism industry and the roles of its component firms and agencies is essential to an understanding of the transition from place products at the destination to tourism products as purchased by consumers in tourist-generating areas.

The opportunity set analyses concentrate on products, holiday opportunities in particular, and the disaggregation of supply-side opportunity sets acknowledges that neither tourism nor place

products are homogeneous. The product mix, and
particularly the place product or destination mix,
will influence the price at which a holiday can be
sold. Price is not simply the sum of the prices of
the individual components and Sinclair et al.
demonstrate, by means of an hedonic price analysis
of inclusive tours to a given destination, the
extent to which place product attributes, such as
hotel facilities and resort images, influence the
asking price of inclusive tours relative to
attributes of the tourism product associated with
the tour operators' images.

For successful marketing the product must be
the right one and this holds true for place
products. If this is not the case the place
product will not command the best possible price
and destination areas will have difficulty
marketing their product to tourists and tour
operators. However, the fragmented nature of the
tourism industry within destination areas - with
individual firms often working independently of
each other, even where supplying similar components
of the place product - means that coordinated and
cooperative development and promotion of the place
product by a destination area's private sector is
difficult. Moutinho investigates the factors which
small firms in the tourism industry see as
important to their business future and discusses
possibilities for cooperation between firms and
with public sector tourism agencies in product
improvement and marketing.

These chapters move progressively from a
largely theoretical discourse on the tourism
product, and ways in which it may be disaggregated,
to conceptual matters pertaining to the pricing and
marketing of tourism products. Overall they echo
Ashworth and Voogd's conclusions concerning
problems of identification of place products per se
and of the latter as part of broader tourism
products. They also suggest the need for an
understanding of the structure of the tourism
industry, in both tourist-origin and destination
areas, and its role in determining the nature of
the products marketed.

Chapter 2

THE CONCEPT OF OPPORTUNITY SETS AS A METHODOLOGICAL
FRAMEWORK FOR THE ANALYSIS OF SELLING TOURISM
PLACES: THE INDUSTRY VIEW

Mike Stabler

INTRODUCTION

The concept of opportunity sets, originally
employed in studies of retailing (Marble & Bowlby,
1968) has been applied to a limited extent in
tourism research being confined to consumers only.
Woodside, Ronkainen and Reid (1977) and Woodside
and Sherrell (1977), in projects on travel
marketing and vacation choice, have utilised sets
of their own specification and Ulm and Crompton
(1987) have made reference to these in modelling
consumer destination choice decisions. Goodall et
al. (1988) and Stabler (1988) have extended the
notion of opportunity sets by constructing a model
designed to demonstrate the interrelationships
between tourists, the industry and the product.
They have argued that these interrelationships need
to be identified and understood before the
structure of the industry and the impact of tourism
can be explained. However, the exposition of the
concept has not specified, other than by referring
to the types of holiday, for example inclusive
tours, the content or magnitude or spatial context
of the sets.

This chapter therefore, will examine in more
detail the industry view of opportunity sets.

THE CONCEPT OF OPPORTUNITY SETS

Opportunity sets are the holiday opportunities
which exist at any given point in time. The total
opportunity set comprises all possible holidays
both commercial and non-commercial which are
available. These holiday opportunities can be
classified along different dimensions such as one
or more combinations of; type of activity, season,
location, organisation or structure, accommodation
type, motive.

Within the total opportunity set are encompassed the industry (IOS), consumer or tourist (C/TOS) and destination area (DAOS) opportunity sets. Considered from the standpoint of each of the three sectors, their opportunity sets can be referred to as subjective because they reflect the perspectives of those within them. However, it is possible to conceive of sets from a viewpoint outside these sectors based on different criteria. For example, tour operators will tend to emphasise those attributes and facilities of a particular destination which, in the holiday choices offered, assist them to achieve their own aims, whereas a destination area tourism agency may well give a different impression, using a different categorisation and analysis of resources. Clearly, their respective opportunity sets overlap. Figure 2.1 demonstrates the interrelationships between these tourism sectors in the form of a model of the consumer-industry links. The analysis of the sets shown in Fig. 2.1 can be at either an aggregated or disaggregated level. In examining the general pattern of holiday opportunities available through the industry and as perceived and demanded by consumers, an aggregative approach would be appropriate. However, in identifying the choice process of a specific holiday by a single consuming unit the figure can be interpreted at a disaggregated level (see Chp. 3).

The tourism industry is interpreted here as the intermediaries, i.e. tour operators, travel agents and carriers offering holidays in generating or origin areas. Later, in examining opportunity sets in a spatial context, it is redefined to include supply-side organisations in destination areas.

Industry opportunity sets

The **industry set** as depicted in the top half of the **total opportunity set** of Fig. 2.1 consists of an **inclusive tour (IT) set** nested entirely within the industry set. The area outside the IT set but within the industry set constitutes the **non-inclusive tour set**. Given the various dimensions on which holidays can be classified as set out above, it should be appreciated that the presentation of IT and non-IT sets is purely illustrative. Other industry opportunity sets could be embodied within and overlapping the others as is

Figure 2.1: A diagrammatic representation of tourism opportunity sets

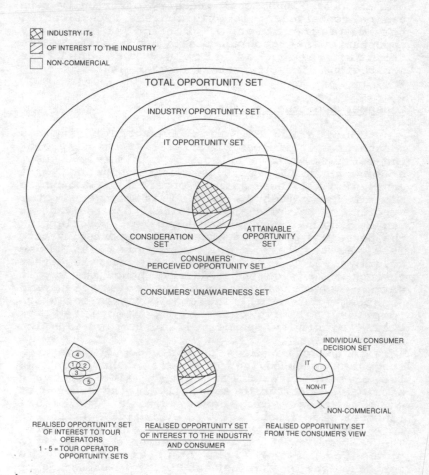

shown for tour operators, i.e. **company opportunity sets,** in the left hand reproduction of the **realised opportunity set** below the main diagram.

One aspect of the industry set (not shown in the figure) is that it can vary with location both intra- and internationally. Intra-nationally, tour operators in marketing holidays may take account of regional and sub-regional variations in the pattern of demand arising from socio-economic differences. Likewise, there are variations internationally in d'emand for ostensibly the same type of holiday reflecting national characteristics and preferences. Thus **local industry opportunity sets** can be conceived of in origin areas necessitating the disaggregation of the total industry opportunity set geographically, for example the identification of distinct regional, or sub-regional industry sets (see Chp. 14).

Consumer opportunity sets

Considering Fig. 2.1 from the consumer's perspective it is possible to derive the nature of the set from which a holiday is ultimately chosen. A consumer will have a **perceived opportunity set** containing all those holiday opportunities known to him or her which is nested within the total opportunity set. The area outside the perceived set can be designated an **unawareness set**. Overlapping the perceived set is an **attainable opportunity set**. This, as the term suggests, represents those holidays which a consumer is able to take either through or outside the industry, hence the way it encompasses part of both the commercial and non-commercial sets. The **consideration set** which comprises holidays currently contemplated, is wholly within the perceived set but overlaps the attainable set.

Though other kinds of consumer set have been suggested as embodying consumers' behaviour, the two of most interest are the consideration and attainable opportunity sets. It is the overlap of each of these which constitutes an individual consumer's **realisable set**, i.e. holidays which are both actively under consideration and attainable. The realisable set from the consumer's viewpoint is presented in the right hand diagram of the reproductions of that set in Fig. 2.1. Depending on the consumer, the realisable set will include few or many holidays which might be taken. In order to bring the number of possible holidays down to a level from which the consumer can make an informed final selection, a **choice set** within which a **decision set** is nested can be conceived of inside the realisable set. In effect this disaggregation from the perceived opportunity set down to the decision opportunity set is a sequential decision-making process, perhaps with feedbacks to a set at a higher level in the event of a reappraisal of the choice of holiday, for example as a result of a change in personal circumstances or because a desired holiday is fully booked.

The link between the consumer and the industry is indicated by the hatched and cross-hatched area of the realised opportunity set, i.e. that resulting from the overlap of the consumer's consideration and attainable sets with the industry opportunity set, shown in Fig. 2.1 in the main diagram, and the reproduction below it. Clearly it is in the industry's interest that the overlap of its opportunity set with the consumer's realisable opportunity set, the whole area as indicated in the right-hand reproduction in Fig. 2.1, should be as large as possible.

Destination opportunity sets

Destination area opportunity sets are holiday possibilities in a particular area which may be a country, region or resort depending on the level of aggregation at which such sets are being considered. The resources and attributes of destinations ultimately delineate the nature and range of holidays taken by tourists whether offered by the industry or not. Important factors affecting the demand for specific destinations will be the price level, exchange rates, the attitude of residents and the political structure as well as the physical and cultural resources and attributes. These factors allow delimitation of the **destination area opportunity set.** The total opportunity set must be fully covered by a family of destination area opportunity sets, which can be environmentally or locationally specific (see Chp. 4).

If the subjective sets reflecting, respectively, the perceptions or aims of potential tourists, the intermediaries and organisations and residents in the destinations themselves do not coincide, there are important implications for the three tourism sectors. A smaller realised set will almost certainly result from consumer and industry subjective sets, which might be that on which tourists and intermediaries in origin areas base their decisions, compared with the objective set which depicts the full potential of destinations. This of course is not certain as tourists and intermediaries are likely to obtain their perceptions from sources other than just the images projected by destination area agencies. Moreover, the intermediaries' view of destinations is coloured by business considerations such as access, the cost and capacity of transport and accommodation, facilities and services. Thus, industry opportunity sets, particularly for destinations catering for the mass IT market, will encompass quite specific destination sets. From the destinations' standpoint this might well reflect their comparative advantages. However, it raises the question also of whether the intermediaries' destination sets are more closely matched with objective sets rather than the subjective ones promoted by the destinations. In other words, the intermediaries could have a clearer (more objective) understanding of the destinations' comparative advantages than they do themselves. What evidence exists suggests that this is not the case. Intermediaries in origin areas pursue their own aims which may be contrary to the interests of the inhabitants of destination areas.

THE DEVELOPMENT OF INDUSTRY OPPORTUNITY SETS

The concept of opportunity sets as it relates to the industry has not been detailed apart from identification of two possible lines of investigation. Goodall et al. (1988) have emphasised the organisational dimension of different categories of holidays in their preliminary investigation of inclusive tours by charter (ITCs) marketed in the United Kingdom. Research into the hierarchy of industry opportunity sets can be undertaken on a 'bottom up' basis, i.e. moving from the local to the national level, or the converse, a 'top down' one. This distinction is important because the empirical work conducted so far has been on a 'bottom up' basis, an approach which is likely to continue. However, there is a danger in projecting the results obtained as representing national characteristics. It might emerge that homogeneous national industry opportunity sets exist only along certain dimensions of holiday. For example, in the UK summer sun ITCs, as promoted through the national media by the major tour operators, do not appear to vary markedly in different geographical areas, whereas holidays offered by regionally based operators or travel agents are, prima facie, likely to give rise to distinct local industry opportunity sets. Though noted, this spatial disaggregation of industry sets will not be pursued further here.

An important area of research in developing the concept of industry opportunity sets lies in demonstrating the pivotal position occupied by intermediaries in generating areas. Though the holidays marketed must reflect consumer preferences and tastes, the supply side does not play a purely passive role. It endeavours not only to anticipate changes in consumer demand but generates it by policies of aggressive marketing in the face of fierce competition, particularly in the IT sector. Therefore, the industry will select types of holidays and destinations which while meeting consumers' requirements, also assist it to achieve its own objectives such as maximising profits, sales, growth or market share. In the UK there is some evidence to suggest that in the mass IT market tour operators largely dictate not only the nature of holidays but also the destinations at which they are taken (Goodall et al., 1988). Thus, industry opportunity sets comprise holidays, a significant proportion of which are devised by the industry itself, over which it can exercise considerable control (see Chp. 9). There are two consequences of this supply-led demand.

The first is that tourists receive specific place images from the industry which narrow holiday choices contained in opportunity sets. Thus, at a local level there are likely to be quite wide variations in the destinations promoted within the holiday packages on offer, i.e. the local industry opportunity set might reflect the preference of travel agents based on the tour operator's commission, their own experience and what they consider local inhabitants want. Similarly, as mentioned above, at a national level the industry markets holidays which it perceives as being in accord with the requirements of the population.

The second consequence is the impact which the industry's actions have on the destinations themselves. Official organisations and commercial enterprises in tourist destinations attempt to convey what they regard as favourable images to potential tourists in origin areas in order to induce them to take holidays in their country. However, quite apart from the possibility of misconceived advertising by those organisations and enterprises in destination areas, the origin area tourism intermediaries often present a contrasting image of that area, perhaps promoting different resources, attributes and places as alluded to earlier (see also Chp. 9).

These interrelationships in the generating area between the industry and consumers and their impact on destinations are now examined in more detail in considering the spatial context of opportunity sets.

The consumer, industry, destination linkage

Tourists may be classified according to the importance they ascribe to various place characteristics and the industry needs to be sensitive to the tastes and preferences of consumers for whom the holiday destination is important and also be alert to changes in fashion. Notwithstanding the influence the industry can exert through its promotion of particular forms of holiday, consumers ultimately determine at which destinations they wish to take them.

Clearly, the other main constraint under which the industry operates is that determined by the characteristics of destinations themselves, though this is not entirely separate from constraints concerning its objectives. The industry has two elementary considerations in marketing holidays. First, destinations must possess suitable access points such as ports and airports and adequate rail, road or river transport networks. Second, there must be accommodation of sufficient capacity to cater for quite large numbers of visitors. The resources and attributes of destinations, although important, are of little value if these other two requirements are not met.

It is an expensive operation for tour operators to seek out and promote new destinations. If they anticipate that sufficient potential demand exists for an extremely attractive but undeveloped area, large tour operators may consider, in conjunction with agencies in the destination, providing the necessary accommodation and facilities, perhaps even contributing to or improving the required infrastructure. Clearly, however, especially if opening up a new niche in the market, tour operators would expect these basic resources to exist already.

If the destinations are those attracting mass tourism, the capacity of their transport and accommodation must match the industry's capacity. This is essential in a market where economies of scale must be fully exploited for profits to be earned. According to Fitch (1987) tour operators need to work at over 90 per cent transport and accommodation occupancy rates in order to make profits. However, he argues, so tight are the margins that changes in such factors as exchange rates, fuel costs and prices in destination areas will eliminate any profits so that operating at almost full capacity is essential.

Given the intense competition in the tourism industry arising from its economic structure, which allows entry at relatively low costs (Sheldon, 1986) and that tourism is still rapidly expanding, the likelihood of earning high profits for the foreseeable future is remote. Consequently, tour operators, certainly in the IT market, will endeavour to control costs as far as is possible by standardising the product offered to consumers and by exercising any monopoly power they have in destination areas by forcing down the prices of local transport, accommodation, facilities and excursions that might be included in particular holiday packages. Alternatively, if vertical integration is likely to yield substantial cost-savings and control over their operations, then tour operators will acquire ownership of resources in destinations areas.

In short, therefore, commercial considerations determine the destinations which tour operators select and promote. The process of marketing holidays starts with the destination areas so that consumers tend to be at the end of the decision chain. The outcome is, as already stated, that holiday opportunities offered tend to reflect the industry's objectives rather than fully meeting tourists' preferences. Whether this action can be sustained is uncertain as tourists are likely to become more discriminating as they travel more widely and gain both confidence and knowledge. However, one point to be emphasised here, as has been shown in the economic analysis of competitive structures, is that large tour operators dominate the market. They not only dictate the terms on which smaller firms trade but also the business activities and economies of destination areas as well as influencing consumer behaviour.

What emerges from this brief discussion of links between consumer, industry and destination is that tour operators are attempting to strike an acceptable balance between their objectives and the constraints under which they operate. There are three main variables with which they are concerned in determining profits; these are the costs of providing and promoting a holiday, the price at which it is offered and the number of holidays sold. However, the problem is more complex than this because there is no unique balance. This will be determined by each firm's current business strategy and the actions of competitors. For example, attempting to increase market share will tend to put the emphasis on the number of holidays sold whereas maximising profits will necessitate more attention being paid to price and costs. Moreover, the strategy may need to be modified in the light of changing conditions as the season progresses. These matters are now examined within the spatial context of opportunity sets in a matrix approach before considering the implications for the marketing of destination areas.

A matrix approach to industry opportunity sets

Attention continues to be focused on tour operators in this section which presents an analytical framework for considering the nature of industry opportunity sets. There are two aspects of tour operators' operations which are relevant to the construction of this framework. The first is their external environment which includes some discussion of the constraints which have already been identified. The second is the internal structure and management of each which embraces questions of company objectives, also referred to earlier. This latter aspect is essentially concerned with decision-making.

There is a need for a new perspective because of the shortcomings of current methods of analysis of business activity. Economic theory has concentrated mostly on the external environment, particularly the competitive structure of the markets in which firms operate. It has been argued that the tourism industry, especially with respect to the marketing of inclusive tours, is an example of an oligopolistic market structure (Sheldon, 1986; Goodall et al., 1988) in which a few large firms predominate. However, for two reasons there is no clear theory of oligopoly. First, the actions of one company will affect the trading conditions of other, rival companies, thus most likely precipitating a reaction. Second, because the form of the reaction, if any, cannot be ascertained a priori, the outcome of a specific action is uncertain. Furthermore, lack of knowledge of consumer behaviour and the response to changes in, say, market price or the nature and quality of the product, adds to the uncertainty. Thus, in essence, notwithstanding Cyert's (1988) development of the behavioural theory of the firm, it is not unfair to state that although economic theory can, to an extent, explain oligopolistic behaviour, given certain assumptions about market conditions, its predictive power is weak. Currently, the state of the art in economics is that a number of illustrative cases exist reflecting the assumptions made. Indeed, in situations of uncertainty recourse has to be made to game theory in which a range of outcomes is predicted from given circumstances.

Economics has not concerned itself centrally with internal decision-making in either an organisational or a technical sense. It has tended to consider this as lying within the province of management or accountancy. Also, given the principal variables cited in the previous section - costs, price, and number of holidays (output) - though economic theory can offer prescriptions on the necessary and sufficient conditions for maximising profits, it is less certain where other objectives are pursued, particularly when the level and pattern of demand cannot be clearly estimated. Therefore, since in the analysis of tourism its temporal, spatial and oligopolistic market structure characteristics need to be taken into account, a new approach with the emphasis on the external environment is justified.

Pred's (1967) behavioural matrix approach, also adapted by Kent (Chp. 3) to consider the consumer's holiday decision-making process, appears to be an appropriate method of analysing tour operators' behaviour concerning their objectives and the constraints acting on them. Moreover, applying the approach to the tourism industry has two further benefits. First, it enables the selection sequence to be traced of the holidays that the industry, or firms in it, would most wish to sell. Second, it suggests the range and content of the industry opportunity sets, thus complementing the consumer opportunity sets decision framework.

As Kent (Chp. 3) quite correctly points out the consumer three-dimensional matrix approach is a heuristic device and it remains so as applied to the tourism industry. It is essentially a way of conceptualising business behaviour in a rather more holistic manner than hitherto. Nevertheless, it remains a simplification for it is possible to consider a matrix of many dimensions. Echoing Kent's analysis, in which the most preferred holiday is that located at the bottom of and in the extreme left-hand corner of the 'matrix block', it can be shown that, suitably redesignated, the industry's or individual tour operator's preferred choice is likewise based at that point if profit maximisation is the main objective. This of course does not mean that the respective consumer- and industry-preferred holidays are synonymous. Consumers' choice is governed by their attainable and perceived sets in which price is but one factor to be assessed. In general consumers will seek to maximise their satisfaction while endeavouring to minimise the price they pay, notwithstanding that in certain instances they will judge quality by price. In contrast, tour operators, while meeting the requisite economic conditions of profit maximisers, will seek to sell holidays at the highest price possible consistent with an acceptable level of costs and selling a sufficient number of holidays in order to attain their objectives. What is certain, however, is that the preferences of both consumers and the industry will be contained within the realised opportunity sets, otherwise no holiday will ever be sold through the industry. The adaptation of Kent's matrix model to industry opportunity sets is shown in Fig. 2.2. In the horizontal plane cost is plotted from zero along AD/EH to some maximum at BC/FG on the x axis. A discontinuity is shown to the left of this axis as clearly no holiday can be supplied at zero cost. Similarly, price is shown as zero along AB/EF rising as it moves diagonally and downward from left to right along the y axis towards DC/HG; a discontinuity is also shown for this as again no holiday will be offered by the industry at zero price. Finally, profit is shown on the vertical, z axis, being zero on the 'base line' along AB/DC of the matrix (along the x axis) and rising towards the bottom of the matrix block at EF/HG. The number of holiday choices is shown as a square or rectangle in a two-dimensional matrix or cube or cuboid in three dimensions.

Figure 2.2 is certainly not meant to reproduce the analysis found in economic textbooks but it is consistent with economic theory. Moving along the x (cost) axis suggests that as more holidays are supplied or marketed costs will rise. This axis does not need to be calibrated in equal increments of cost; both increasing and decreasing returns to scale can be shown according to the cost structures likely to prevail in the industry and the degree of specialisation or diversification. Likewise, moving along the y (price) and z (profits) axes will give the industry an incentive to supply more.

The matrix could be used to consider industry opportunity sets for a single firm, a specific type or dimension of holiday or for all types of holiday. For example, at a disaggregated level it could illustrate a particular type of IT in which case the complete 'block' would constitute the total number of holidays. At a rather more aggregated level it could embody every type of holiday on a particular dimension, say, for the 18-30 age group. At the highest level of aggregation it would include every type of holiday offered by the industry. The author considers that the concept is best suited, if it is to complement consumer opportunity sets, to show holiday choices or types rather than number of holidays. Consideration of three illustrative cases will indicate the constraints imposed on tour operators in attempting to achieve their objectives.

Profit maximisation.   Referring to Fig. 2.2, clearly tour operators pursuing profit maximisation wish to be on plane EFGH. At E they will be selling the minimum range of choices at low prices and low cost whereas at F the choice of holidays will be wider at high cost but low prices. At H cost will be low but price high, the number of choices being the same as at F, assuming that the matrix is a cube. The highest number of choices will be sold at G but at high cost and at high prices. Which will be the preferred strategy will depend on such factors as the cost structure of the company, its capacity, the extent of the market for each holiday choice and the actions of rivals. These factors can be incorporated into a multidimensional model.

In general it could be argued that high cost strategies, perhaps reflecting an expensive promotional campaign, are riskier than low cost ones. Thus, positions E and H would be preferred to F and G. In like fashion it might be suggested that H is preferred to E because a greater range of holidays is marketed, so appealing to more segments of the market than a strategy of concentrating on a specific type. Other locations in the matrix could

Figure 2.2: A three-dimensional matrix approach to industry opportunity sets

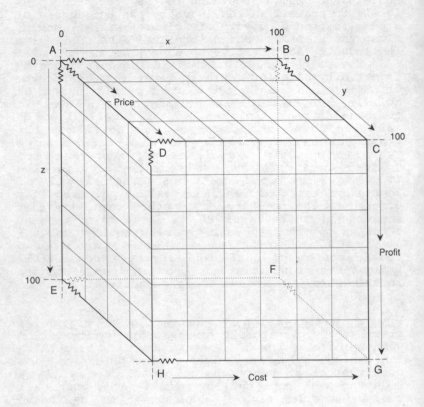

of course be assessed, for example, lower levels of profit on planes above EFGH.

What the matrix cannot show, as presented, is the profit maximising position in an economic sense as there is no way of establishing output (number of holidays sold) and marginal revenue and cost.

Sales maximisation. A strategy of selling as many holidays as possible without regard for profit would suggest that a tour operator would be located on plane ABCD at C. Here costs would be high but so would price, profits being low. However, the range of holidays sold would be higher than at A, B or D. It would depend on the extent to which a company specialised as to how many holiday choices it would offer and also on economies of scale.

Market share maximisation. The best position for a tour operator wishing to increase its market share, i.e. maximise the size of its company opportunity set, would be to move as near G as possible. In breaking into a specific segment of the market it is conceivable that a firm could be at B where it has incurred high promotional costs, selling holidays at low prices and making zero or low profits. Location at B could be stated to represent the 'loss leader' case.

Other objectives or a combination of those illustrated could be considered within the matrix. Also, the matrix could be modified to accord more closely with economic notions that at high costs profits are likely to be lower. It is possible to conceive of a 'wedge-shaped' matrix as shown in Fig. 2.3(a) rather than a cuboid one. This would suggest that at higher costs profits would be lower. To accommodate the likelihood that holidays supplied at high prices and at high cost will yield higher 'profits' the matrix could be shaped as shown in Fig. 2.3(b). Naturally as more dimensions are added the model has to be given in mathematical terms. Nevertheless, these simplified diagrammatic approaches do illustrate the basis for deriving industry opportunity sets.

The temporal dimension of industry sets can be embodied in the matrix approach. One aspect of this is that as the season for, say, summer sun or skiing ITs progresses, a tour operator's strategy may well change. If, for example, holidays are not selling fast enough to fill the company's capacity it may well cut prices at the expense of profits. In terms of location in the matrix this would mean moving to a position such as B, particularly if the price cut is accompanied by a vigorous and expensive advertising campaign. Another temporal feature of the industrial opportunity set matrix is that it is likely to 'degenerate' as certain types of holidays are sold out or withdrawn because of lack of demand. In effect the total industry opportunity set contracts but not in a uniform way; it is possible for it to become 'perforated' depending on the cost, price and profit levels of the holidays no longer available.

Figure 2.3: Variants of the industry opportunity sets

a. Assumption of low profits at high costs

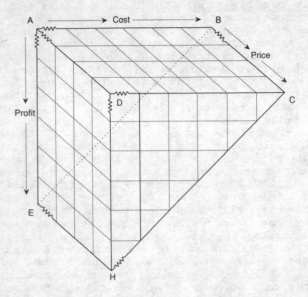

b. Assumption of higher profits at high price/high cost than at low prices/high cost

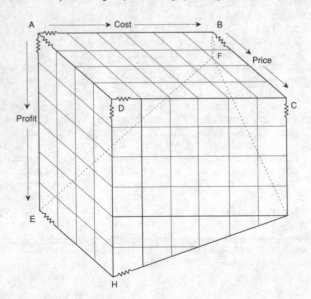

THE INTERRELATIONSHIP OF CONSUMER AND INDUSTRY OPPORTUNITY SETS

The consumer matrix as explained by Kent (Chp. 3) can be related to the industry one in the same way as the original concept posited by Goodall et al. (1988). Obviously, the two sets can be conceived as 'intermeshing' rather than overlapping as in the two-dimensional approach. However, whereas Kent suggests a structured sequence of elimination as the consumer moves from a perceived set to the final choice, for the industry, though it has holidays it most wishes to sell, the process is much more haphazard in the face of uncertainty over the total level of demand, the actions of rivals, etc. as discussed above. The 'intermeshing' of the two matrices is the realised opportunity matrix. It is in the industry's and individual tour operator's interests to attempt to create as large a realised set as possible, because, in doing so, consumers will purchase more holidays through the industry rather than non-commercial holidays outside it.

PLACE AND THE INDUSTRY OPPORTUNITY SET MATRIX

To this point the industry matrix has been examined in a general way. It is, however, easily related to some aspects of place by considering either matrices containing choices specifically concerned with place or by suggesting where such holidays are positioned in a more general choice matrix. An example of the former approach might be to consider all holidays to a particular country or region, such as Austria or Florida. With respect to the latter, some observations can be made on the likely positions of holidays to different destinations. Radburn (1988) has investigated the price of holidays of different qualities for the low and high season in the Spanish Costas and the Balearic Islands. In his industry opportunity sets for a specific country, quality holidays at three-star hotels at attractive resorts would tend to be positioned towards C while one-star hotels at popular resorts would be located towards A.

How this conception of industry opportunity sets can be of assistance to place marketing clearly depends as much on the destination areas themselves as initiatives by the industry in origin areas, who have their own priorities as outlined above. Destination areas need to lobby not only agents, carriers and tour operators in origin areas but also to appeal direct to consumers. Their objective should be to ensure that holiday choices to them should figure as prominently as possible in the realised set.

CONCLUSIONS

As stated at the outset, this chapter has largely concentrated on the conceptual issues concerning the development of tourism industry opportunity sets. An attempt has been made to indicate, in a three- or multi-dimensional matrix model, what the composition and pattern of industry sets is likely to be, given the objectives and constraints under which the industry operates. The intermediaries play a central role in the origin (consumer)-destination (product) link. The model derived reflects the structure of a similar approach for consumers so that the tourist-intermediary interrelationship can be established. The same development has yet to be done for destination area sets to complete the linkage and thus facilitate the analysis of choices, such as place marketing, in a complete model.

It is apparent that the model requires further refinement, as outlined in the text, and one aspect of this might be to consider other dimensions in the matrix. Furthermore, little empirical work has been done. Of particular importance is the categorisation of different types of holiday which are offered and taken so that appropriate aggregated and disaggregated opportunity sets can be derived. Though the matrix approach to opportunity sets is a useful heuristic device, if it is to be made operational it needs to be tested from both the industrial and other viewpoints.

REFERENCES

Cyert, R.M. (1988) _The Economic Theory of Organisation and the Firm_, Harvester-Wheatsheaf, Hemel Hempstead

Fitch, A. (1987) Tour operators in the UK, _Travel and Tourism Analyst_, March, The Economist Publications Ltd, London

Goodall, B., Radburn, M.W., & Stabler, M.J. (1988) Market opportunity sets for tourism, <u>Geographical Papers No 100: Tourism Series</u>, 1, Department of Geography, University of Reading, Reading

Marble, D. & Bowlby, S. (1968) Shopping alternatives and recurrent travel patterns, <u>Studies in Geography</u> No 16, Department of Geography, Northwestern University, Evanston

Pred, A. (1967) <u>Behaviour and Location: Foundations for a Geographic and Dynamic Location Theory</u>, Vol.1, C.W.K. Gleerup, Lund

Radburn, M.W. (1988) Market opportunity sets and the price structure of ITC products, paper presented at Leisure Studies Association 2nd International Conference, University of Sussex, Brighton

Sheldon, P.J. (1986) The tour operator industry: An analysis, <u>Annals of Tourism Research</u>, 13, 349-363.

Stabler, M.J. (1988) Modelling the tourist industry: the concept of opportunity sets, paper presented at Leisure Studies Association 2nd International Conference, University of Sussex, Brighton

Ulm, S. & Crompton, J.L. (1987) A cognitive model of pleasure travel destination choice, unpublished manuscript, Department of Recreation and Parks, Texas A & M University, Houston

Woodside, A.G. & Ronkainen, I.A., Reid, D.M. (1977) Measurement and utilisation of the evoked sets as a travel marketing variable, in <u>Proceedings of Eighth Annual Conference, Travel Research Association</u>, 123-130

Woodside, A.G. & Sherrell, D. (1977) Traveller evoked set, inept set and inert sets of vacation destinations, <u>Journal of Travel Research</u>, 16, 14-18

Chapter 3

PEOPLE, PLACES AND PRIORITIES: OPPORTUNITY SETS AND CONSUMERS' HOLIDAY CHOICE

Peter Kent

INTRODUCTION

In order to 'sell places' it is important to understand how consumers reach their final purchase decisions. The processes behind choice, the outcome of which is the discrimination and selection of a single product or place from a large initial range, is central to an understanding of buying behaviour and therefore a fundamental consideration in sales strategies.

Various researchers have attempted to model this choice process for individuals and provide an insight into which factors are important when alternatives have to be considered (e.g. Goodrich, 1978; Scott et al., 1978; Gyte, 1988). These approaches, however, have generally failed to provide wholly accurate or acceptable explanations and predictions of tourist choice behaviour. This is because such studies usually ignore the social and cultural context within which individuals make choices (Desberats, 1983). They also recognise only the main attributes during selection and ignore the relationships which may exist between such factors and the overall process.

Consider the analogy of a doctor who wishes to cure an illness. To do so he/she must recognise the symptoms, formulate a diagnosis and implement a remedy. To be successful, however, that doctor must have an intimate knowledge of the complex interactive system of the human body. It would not be sufficient for the doctor simply to acknowledge that organs, such as the liver, heart or kidneys are important, without realising that their interaction (with others) is essential for the healthy functioning of the body as a whole. To prescribe treatment on limited knowledge has obvious drawbacks.

In the same way, when choice is modelled it is insufficient to identify 'a good beach', 'a wide variety of sites' and 'attractive scenery' as key attributes and consider them to be accurate bases for developing marketing strategies. Understanding **how** choices are made and **how** attributes are related in the choice process are central considerations in addition to identifying **which** attributes are important during selection. This chapter therefore develops a conceptual framework which addresses the relationships between holiday attributes and the choice process.

UNDERSTANDING HOLIDAY CHOICE

Initial analyses of holiday choice, viewed as basic statements of demand, tend to confuse person-specific motivations with resort-specific attributes; tourists are classified as 'sunlust' and/or 'wanderlust' or considered to seek 'sun, sea, sand and sex' experiences (Mathieson & Wall, 1982). Recent studies, however, distinguish the influence of motivations - which 'push' holiday-makers into a decision - from the attractive draw of holiday images (including images of both holiday destinations and types) - which 'pull' holiday-makers to certain holiday experiences.

'The push' - motivations

Motivations provide definite and positive inclinations to do something and are related to an individual's needs and desires. Various analyses have examined the role of motivations in holiday choice (for a review see Dann, 1981). Crompton (1979) suggests that push factors can be reduced to a few deep-rooted motivations, which reflect the socio-psychological condition of the individual. He argues that individuals live in a socio-psychological equilibrium which may become unbalanced over time (i.e. over a period of routinised and repetitive action, such as at work or in the home environment). The only way to correct this disequilibrium is by taking a break from routine. This break, however, should address itself to that aspect of the socio-psychological continuum which is in imbalance, thus returning it to equilibrium. Crompton recognised seven areas which suffer imbalance and can therefore be considered as central motivations for holiday-making.

Dann (1976), suggests that 'holidays are essentially experiences in fantasy' and identifies two types of fantasy: 'ego-enhancement' (the psychological boosts through real or imagined activities which enhance an individual's self-image and appreciation) and the escape from 'anomie' (the monotony of everyday life). The latter was also alluded to by Cohen in his classification of tourists:

> based on the place and significance of tourist experience in the total world-view of tourists, their relationship to a perceived 'spiritual' 'centre' and the location of that centre in relation to the society in which the tourist lives (Cohen, 1979: 179).

Therefore, at one extreme tourists perceive their spiritual centre to exist in their home society and regard tourist experiences as opportunities to reaffirm meaning and orientation to this 'centre' **(the recreation mode).** At the other extreme tourists consider their home environments to be inadequate and perceive their spiritual centre to exist in another more authentic and genuine environment **(the existentialist mode).**

'The pull' - images

The 'pull' component of choice represents the images individuals possess of the real world. Images form the foundation for behaviour as '... the image is what I believe to be true, my subjective knowledge' (Boulding, 1956). Such 'truths' are especially important for potential tourists because the holiday product is a service and accordingly options cannot be sampled before purchasing as with material consumer products. Tourists must therefore base their decision on their mental images of the alternatives.

Holiday images are often thought to consist of only place images but they can also encompass other aspects of the tourism product and the holiday experience. For example, images related to the type of holiday, such as seaside holidays, activity or adventure holidays. The type of holiday can implicitly suggest the activities, such as sunbathing or rock climbing, and therefore facilities, like a nice beach or good climbing faces, that the tourist may prefer.

Other factors in holiday choice

Other factors are important in holiday choice (Moutinho, 1987). **Holiday preferences** are important because, although motivations provide a definite inclination to undertake a certain course of action, a number of actions may correct the socio-psychological imbalances. Which course is selected and which rejected, depends on the individual's preferences. This in turn suggests that holidaymakers generate a number of **holiday goals** - explicit targets for achievement. **Experience** of past holidays and hearsay of the experiences of others, help the tourist recognise important goals to be achieved and preferred methods of achieving them. Failure to satisfy holiday goals, and therefore meet expectations, means that the overall experience is unsatisfactory: this is noted for reference in future holiday choice.

One of the most important factors in holiday choice, however, is the range of opportunities open to the consumer at any given time. If tourists seek a certain holiday, yet limited availability denies an opportunity, choice is clearly directed elsewhere. If holidaymakers are still determined to visit that place they will have to make independent arrangements. Even so, the ability to holiday at that or any other destination is conditional on there being adequate facilities to satisfy their needs.

OPPORTUNITIES AND THE HOLIDAYMAKER

The opportunities open to a consumer at a given point in time can be analysed using the opportunity set approach. An opportunity set is a collection of products, here holiday opportunities, which possess similarities in terms of some pre-defined classificatory characteristics. Suitable criteria for generating these sets include the product characteristics, such as location or price, as well as the characteristics of potential consumers. A tourist may be aware of only a portion of the range of available holidays thus limiting choice to a **'perceived opportunity set'**, i.e. those holidays of which the tourist is aware.

45

Similarly, holidays which the tourist can afford to purchase lie within an **attainable opportunity set.** Those opportunities of which the holidaymaker is both aware and able to afford (i.e. exist within the overlap of the perceived and attainable opportunity sets) are potential selections and lie within a **realisable opportunity set.**

Differences in the nature and economic status of potential tourists lead to variations in the size of these opportunity subsets. For example, holidaymakers who base their choice on large stocks of holiday information will have larger perceived sets than holidaymakers who do not. Holidaymakers able and willing to spend more on their holidays will possess a wider attainable set. The combination of the quality and quantity of information and the ability to use such information therefore determines the number of holiday opportunities open to a consumer at any given time.

Pred (1967) used these same two variables in his **behavioural matrix,** a heuristic device which represents decision-making ability as a function of two vectors - the quantity and quality of perceived information available at a specific point in time and the ability to use that information. Individuals can be located on the matrix according to their decision-making abilities and processes. This matrix approach may be applied to tourists choosing holidays: tourists may be located on a behavioural matrix according to the quality and quantity of information each possesses about holiday opportunities and their ability to interpret that information in order to select the holiday which best satisfies their needs. The possession of, and ability to use, holiday information are analogous to an awareness of holiday opportunities (that is the individual's **perceived opportunity set**) and attainment ability (their **attainable set**), respectively. Moreover, if each opportunity within the **realisable set** can be classified in terms of its relative attainability (i.e. graded according to the price of competing holidays) and awareness (i.e. graded by differences in tourist awareness of opportunities - themselves functions of marketing and promotional strategies of tour operators) each cell in the matrix will represent a single holiday opportunity. The tourist's position on the matrix will therefore represent not only the decision-making ability of that tourist but also the types of holidays that he/she can choose from.

Figure 3.1: The holidaymaker's behavioural matrix

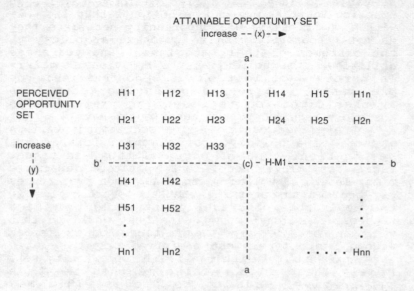

In Fig. 3.1 holidaymaker H-M1 is assumed to have a level of attainment (vertical line a'a) and level of awareness (horizontal line b'b). H-M1's **attainable opportunity set** is all holidays to the left of line a'a. Similarly, all holidays above line b'b represent H-M1's **perceived set.** The **realisable set** is therefore the area bounded within b'Ca' (where C is the point of intersection between a'a and b'b) and the x and y axes. H-M1 is therefore aware of opportunities H14, H15, H24 and H25 but, falling outside the attainable set, they are not realisable. In the same way opportunities H41, H42, H51 and H52 can be attained but as H-M1 is unaware of them they too cannot be realised. The behavioural matrix is therefore a consumer's opportunity set matrix.

A THREE-DIMENSIONAL MATRIX

Analysis of holidaymaker's opportunity sets on a two-dimensional behavioural matrix, does not allow identification of the opportunity chosen from the realisable set. Optimality implies tourists purchase the most expensive and best known opportunity they are aware of and can afford. The most able decison-makers exist at the bottom right-hand corner of the matrix, and accordingly the most suitable holiday should also be found there. In practice tourists may choose holidays that lie well within their realisable opportunity set since they do not necessarily wish to purchase a holiday at the extremes of their attainment and awareness abilities. The holidaymaker's behavioural matrix is merely a collection of opportunities; no preference is expressed or can be deduced. A further dimension representing preference is therefore required to the behavioural matrix.

Preference can be expressed towards various aspects of a holiday: for example, towards the destination, type of accommodation, services, facilities, travel mode, tour operator, departure time, length of holiday, etc. All such preferences may be used to determine whether opportunities in the realisable opportunity set would provide a successful holiday or not. The best would be that with the most preferred destination, most preferred accommodation type, most preferred services, etc. which exists within the realisable opportunity set. If all these do not coincide then the best alternative needs to be chosen. This may necessitate the prioritisation of preferences so that the most important attributes are sought in order to achieve maximum satisfaction.

As a consequence the realisable set is reduced, first, to a **consideration opportunity set** (which consists of those holidays with suitable and satisfactory attributes), then a **choice opportunity set** (which consists of a number of possible holidays with the most preferred attributes), and latterly a **decision opportunity set** (a smaller set of probable holidays from which the final choice is made) (see Chp. 2).

The simultaneous evaluation of opportunities over a number of attributes means, however, that there is a multi-dimensional evaluative matrix (of N dimensions, where N = the number of attributes which the holidaymaker considers to be important in evaluating holiday opportunities). The use of a three-dimensional matrix below is a simplification for the purposes of illustration: the preference aspect is explored with special reference to spatial preference as the third dimension.

PLACE PREFERENCE AND EVALUATION

Preference and evaluation are intimately

related in holiday choice. As noted above, motivations represent a predisposition to undertake a certain course of action, but preferences, based on experiences and influential information, suggest which course of action, out of the possibilities that exist, will fulfil needs in the most satisfactory manner. The interaction of motivations and preferences generate holiday goals which are then used to evaluate opportunities (Kent, 1989).

There are a number of methods of evaluating products and opportunities (see MacInnes & Price, 1987). The evaluation of several destination attributes over a range of alternatives, as in multi-attribute models (Scott et al., 1978), is termed **discursive processing**. In this form of evaluation potential consumers identify the attributes they consider to be important for a successful product and then evaluate product range according to the perceived presence or absence of these features. A second form of evaluation compares alternatives through **imagery processing**: here an image of the product is formed (based on available information) and is pictured 'in action' in a number of situations. The prospective purchaser may even put him/herself 'into the picture' to test the compatibility between product image and self-image.

MacInnes and Price (1987) acknowledged that these forms of evaluation may be used independently or together. In the latter situation, individuals assess the range of alternatives using key attributes (discursive processing) and then use imagery processing to evaluate the few that remain. In holiday choice, destinations or holiday packages may be evaluated in terms of their basic destination attributes (e.g. whether seaside or in the mountains) and then through imagery processing the alternatives that remain are evaluated for compatiblity with self-image (Kent, 1988).

Studies of place preference and evaluation

Discursive and imagery evaluation of destination images correspond to the evaluation of physical (i.e. objective attributes) and sentimental (i.e. subjective values) components of place. Discursive evaluation assesses the 'identity and structure' components of place image, whilst imagery evaluation assesses the 'meaning' component of place image (Lynch, 1960).

A number of studies have recognised key attributes which holidaymakers consider to be important in destination evaluation (e.g. Fridgen, 1987; Goodrich, 1978; Gyte, 1988). However, in examining the contents of destination images they used discursive methods which are insensitive to the role of imagery in evaluation. Gyte (1988), for example, identified 28 attributes considered to be important in the evaluation of the tourists' chosen holiday destination, Majorca. Many of the attributes he elicited relate well to those Goodrich (1978) used to evaluate destinations: they include 'a good beach and sun holiday', 'a wide variety of sites', 'friendly inhabitants', and 'a peaceful holiday location'.

Other studies have related personal meanings, values and emotions to places (thus focusing on imagery processing, e.g. Pocock, 1981; Relph, 1981; Tuan, 1974, 1976). Tuan (1974), coined the term **topophilia** to relate sentiment to place. This is similar to Wright's (1947) concept of **geosophy** which also focuses on places as either carriers of emotionally charged feelings or as perceived symbols. A more intensely personal use of **topophilia** was developed by Relph (1976) in his sense of place concept which extended **topophilia** to include the existential qualities related to spaces and places. These sentiments reflect 'a social or psychological interaction, a reciprocal relationship between place and person' (Pocock & Hudson, 1978). Place is therefore:

> a characteristic bounding with internal structure and identity such that insideness is distinguished from outsideness. At its most obvious and familiar, it is wherever an individual feels 'at home', where things 'fall into place', beyond which we feel 'out of place', intruders into someone else's domain (Pocock, 1981).

Thus places, and the ways they are evaluated, extend well beyond their physical and structural composition to include attributed meanings and emotions.

Measuring place preference and evaluation

The technique for measuring place preference developed by Gould and White (1974) was used

Figure 3.2: Place preference for holidays in Great Britain

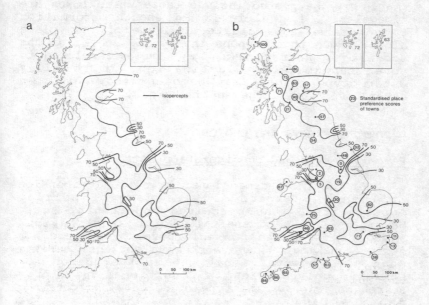

experimentally to produce a map of place preference for holidays in Great Britain. Twenty geography undergraduates studying tourism were asked to score the counties of Great Britain on a seven-point scale in terms of how they perceived these places as possible locations for a main summer holiday. From mean scores, a standardised score was generated for each place and mapped in Fig. 3.2a. It can be seen that place preference generally correlates with topography: the areas of Highland Britain all score highly. The lowest scores, are associated with highly industrialised areas.

The relationship, however, is more complex. The same students also scored a number of towns and cities around the country in a similar fashion. The results are shown in Fig. 3.2b. It is clear that town scores vary considerably from the county scores (i.e. image scores are not necessarily 'nested' one inside another - towns in a high scoring county do not necessarily score as highly, and vice versa). This is because each respondent reacts to different name stimulii: the name 'Avon' generates a different image and response from that of 'Bath', which is in Avon. Situations where images may be nested include those where towns are 'imageless', i.e. there is not enough information to generate and evaluate an image of that place alone. When this happens the county score, or the score of a nearby town, may be extrapolated to cover the imageless destination. In this way 'stereotype images' may be generated, which can extend over very large spatial areas.

OPPORTUNITY SETS AND CHOICE

Perceived sets and consideration sets

In the three-dimensional matrix one dimension influencing choice is awareness of holiday opportunities (the **perceived opportunity set**). Normative models of spatial choice and behaviour assume individuals possess perfect knowledge for decision-making. Recent work with package tourists suggests, however, that the active search for holiday opportunities is conditioned by a pre-search decision on the type of holiday and possible destinations that would provide the most satisfactory experience (Kent, 1989). The active search process is an attempt to find opportunities which fit these requirements; search is limited to brochures of these places or services. The extent and nature of tourists' **perceived opportunity sets** becomes quite selective. A **consideration set** is formed as the perceived set is condensed into a number of preferred holiday options worthy of detailed consideration.

If opportunity searches are largely confined by type of holiday, for example, then the **consideration opportunity set** becomes a function of destination images and the perceived presence or absence of certain services or facilities at given places (i.e. evaluative images of these places). Place preference (as measured above by the students) represents evaluated place images in terms of their perceived potential for satisfying holiday goals: places with higher scores suggest a greater potential than those with lower scores. The implication is that if these students were seeking a place to holiday their search would be immediately limited to those places perceived as being most able to satisfy their holiday goals;

i.e. the **perceived set** of all known opportunities is reduced to a **consideration set** of preferred options. For example, a search for a holiday in England may be automatically directed to counties such as Cornwall, Devon and Somerset as they are perceived as having the potential for satisfying holiday goals to the greatest extent.

The size of the **consideration set**, however, can vary considerably between individuals depending on the degree to which they are concerned about the specific location of their holiday. If individuals are unconcerned about destination their **consideration set** will equal their **perceived set**. If, however, individuals are more discerning, limits on the perceived set will be applied to reduce the number of destinations for active consideration and search.

Inadvertent exposure to other opportunities may occur although the outcome depends on existing predispositions towards the exposed places (i.e. the degree to which they are already preferred). The holidaymaker may therefore be more inclined to widen the scope of the search in the **consideration set** if exposed to information about Durham (71) or North Yorkshire (78) than if exposed to information about Essex (24) or Northamptonshire (26). However, holidaymakers unconcerned with the location of their holiday may search for opportunities in another manner.

The attainable set

Selection from the **realisable opportunity set** is also conditional on an individual's attainment ability. Operational models of spatial behaviour, e.g. gravity models, use approximate cost functions, such as time or distance between places, as indicators of distance decay. Table 3.1 lists counties in terms of their distance from an origin (Reading). If the cost of opportunities at each destination is a function of distance from Reading then Table 3.1 represents variations in an individual's **attainable opportunity set.**

Place preferences

Place preferences can be grouped into simple preference sets. If opportunities, such as those in Fig. 3.2 exist at each place then these sets become

Table 3.1: Standardised distances from Reading

Standardised Distance Scores	Counties
0-24.9	Berks (0) Surrey (4) Bucks (4.5) Hants (4.6) Oxon (4.7) Gt. London (6.2) W. Sussex (6.6) Herts (6.7) Wilts (7.4) Glos (9.3) E. Sussex (10) Northants (10.8) Warwicks (10.8) Avon (11.7) Dorset (12) Cambs (12.7) Hereford & Worcs (13) Kent (13) Leics (14) W. Mids (14.6) Somerset (15) Gwent (15.8) Suffolk (16.9) S. Glam (18.3) Salop (18.8) Staffs (19) M. Glam (19.5) Norfolk (19.5) Derby (20) Notts (20) Lincs (20.4) Powys (20.8) Devon (21.7) W. Glam (22.5) S. Yorks (23) Cheshire (23.5)
25-49.9	Dyfed (25.3) Gwynedd (25.3) Gt. Manchester (25.4) Clwyd (26.1) Merseyside (27) S. Yorks (27) Humberside (27.5) Lancs (30.8) W. Yorks (32.9) Cleveland (36.7) Durham (38.7) Cumbria (39.5) Tyne & Wear (32.9) Northumberland (44.6)
50-74.9	Borders (50) Dumfries & Galloway (50) Lothian (54.6) Strathclyde (60) Central (61.6) Grampian (71) Highland (73)
75-100	W.Isles (85) Orkney (90) Shetland (100)

destination area opportunity sets stratified by preference. If a holidaymaker expresses no preference as to where to holiday all the destinations (and their opportunities) will be located within the opportunity set. However, if the holidaymaker expresses some preference (for example, a county must score more than ten on the preference scale) then the opportunity set diminishes (viz. Humberside, W. Midlands and Gt. Manchester are rejected). Destinations are rejected from the total opportunity set according to the level of preference holidaymakers exercise in choosing a destination; the greater the desire to visit a more preferred place, the smaller the opportunity set of possible destinations becomes.

UNDERSTANDING A HOLIDAY CHOICE USING THE MATRIX

The **attainable, perceived** and **preferred destination opportunity sets** may now be incorporated into a single matrix (Fig. 3.3). To illustrate use of the matrix in the holiday choice process the students' place preference data will be used in conjunction with other data to form a series of constraint maps which are shown in Fig. 3.4. For the purposes of this example it will be assumed that a single opportunity exists at each destination (as represented by the county name) so responses to county scores are reflected as responses to opportunities. Other factors which may influence choice (e.g. standards of accommodation) are assumed to be constant.

The first stage of holiday choice is the pre-search evaluation of possible destinations and holiday types to decide how and where to find the best form of holiday experience. At this stage motivations and preferences set goals for the nature and location of the holiday. These goals are then used to evaluate the holidaymaker's internal information and image store. Preferred locations and holiday types are recognised and this focuses the next (active) stage of the opportunity search (i.e. the **consideration set** is formed from the **perceived set**).

In Fig. 3.4a the consumer(s) are assumed to be quite discerning about the specific location of their holiday and thus only destinations with a 70 score or over will be considered. The **consideration set** therefore includes counties such as Cornwall (100), Avon (81), Powys (71), Durham (71) and Strathclyde (73) but ignores counties such as Buckinghamshire (36) and South Glamorgan (20).

The **consideration set** can be further differentiated by the distance (and therefore the cost) of the remaining counties from Reading. If individuals are unconcerned with expense then all the opportunities within the **consideration set** are realisable. In that case final choice will reflect the relative desirability of place images and the holidaymakers will visit the most desirable county, Cornwall. In Fig. 3.4b, individuals are assumed to be able to afford travel only within the 50 cost/distance zone: the **consideration set** north of this line (i.e. the remaining opportunities in Scotland) is now excluded.

The opportunities that remain are both considered and attainable, i.e. within the

Figure 3.3: A three-dimensional approach to consumer's holiday choice

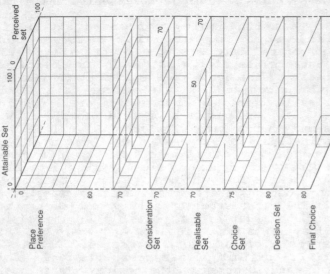

TOTAL OPPORTUNITY SET
All Counties of England, Scotland and Wales

CONSIDERATION SET
Cornwall, Devon, Somerset, Avon, Dorset, Hereford & Worcester, N. Yorks,
Cumbria, Durham, Powys, Gwynedd, Clwyd, Dyfed, Dumfries & Galloway,
Strathclyde, Fife, Highlands, Grampian, W. Isles, Orkneys, Shetlands

REALISABLE SET
Cornwall, Devon, Somerset, Avon, Dorset, Dyfed, N. Yorks, Cumbria, Durham,
Powys, Gwynedd, Hereford & Worcester, Clwyd, Dumfries & Galloway

CHOICE SET
Cornwall, Devon, Somerset, Avon, Dorset, N. Yorks, Cumbria, Gwynedd, Clwyd

DECISION SET
Cornwall, Devon, Somerset, Avon, Dorset

Figure 3.4: Preference and cost constraints on choice

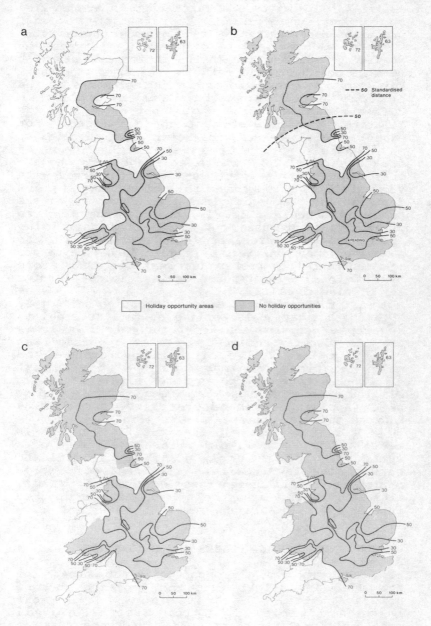

a

b

--- **50** Standardised distance

□ Holiday opportunity areas   ▨ No holiday opportunities

c

d

realisable opportunity set. The reduction of these options to a **choice set,** depends on other suitability parameters. Further goals are applied to the realisable set to differentiate the most preferred opportunities which form the **choice set.**

The factors used to discriminate between the remaining opportunities in the **choice set** vary with personal circumstances and the relative importance holidaymakers attach to individual elements of the holiday experience. In this example the differentiation of the **choice set** depends on the relative importance of cost against image. For example, holidaymakers who prefer cheaper holidays, may ignore opportunities beyond the 30 or 40 distance/cost score while holidaymakers who are less concerned with costs and more concerned with visiting a desirable location, may ignore destinations that score less than 75 or 80 on the preference scale. Clearly, combinations of these strategies can be used. A range of constraining criteria may therefore be introduced to limit the number of opportunities. In Fig. 3.4c holidaymakers are considered to prefer destinations that score over 75 on the preference scale, giving a **choice set** of nine counties.

All the opportunities in the **choice set** comply with the holiday goals applied so far. In order to develop a **decision set** a further set of goals is used to identify the most suitable opportunities (again in line with individual preferences and prioritisations for image/cost). Only slight differences between opportunities may be needed to eliminate some of those remaining from the **choice set.** Applying an image preference score of 80 reduces the **decision set** to five (Fig. 3.4d).

It is from this set that the final choice is made, which again involves the development of a further set of preferred goals to discriminate between the few remaining alternatives. Which option is finally chosen rests on which of the many alternative strategies the holidaymaker employs to further differentiate the remaining alternatives.

CONCLUSIONS: PEOPLE, PLACES AND PRIORITIES

Application of the opportunity set concept has provided an insight into the processes behind holiday choice. The differences between the subsets identified, which rise in overall acceptability, suitability and preference rest on the evaluation of each holiday via more refined goals and preferences at each stage. Using two variables, as in the example above, suggests that the decision stages between the sets can be trite; it is therefore possible to envisage a choice process combining these steps (thus making intermediate stages redundant). When other factors and attributes are re-introduced to the matrix, (returning it to a matrix of n dimensions) the relative importance of each dimension, that is each attribute that is perceived as being necessary by the tourist, becomes important. It appears likely that a hierarchy of goals, or attributes exists whenever choice has to be exercised.

The nature of this hierarchy is such that the first set of goals has to be satisfied before the next set of goals is applied. Holiday destination and type attributes may therefore not only be differentiated by their significance in holiday choice (Goodrich, 1978; Gyte, 1988) but also temporally, in terms of the point in the process at which they assume that significance. In this way some factors are important at the outset of the choice process and other factors more important towards the end of the process.

The composition of each individual's hierarchy of goals, and thus of each set at each stage, is a function of personal decisions, preferences and goals at that time. How attributes are placed towards the top of the hierarchy is related to the perceived importance of the role each plays in the overall satisfaction of the experience. So, for example, if 'attractive scenery' or 'a good hotel' are very important for a satsifactory holiday experience these might be expected to exist at the top of the 'goals' hierarchy, and be crucial in the formulation of a **consideration set.** When these goals are perceived to have been satisfied the next level of significant attributes is applied. This process continues until a final choice becomes apparent. The final stages of choice may therefore rest on the some of the least significant destination attributes. This hierarchy may be related to the perceived risk and uncertainty individuals attach to each factor and the impact on the overall holiday experience that would be felt if each factor were not satisfied (Kent, 1989).

Does an understanding of this choice process help in selling places? The nature of marketing strategies may need to be reassessed. Logically the order in which attributes are evaluated in the choice process should not matter as the final choice should possess all the preferred attributes and that choice should be reached whichever attributes are applied first or last. In reality, however, the order in which attributes are applied can assume a greater importance. This is because the recognition of major attributes at the pre-search decision stage may condition patterns of information collection. If, for example, an individual wants self-catering accommodation foremost, and would then like that accommodation to be in an attractive town, information collection may concentrate on brochures which are primarly concerned with the promotion of the first attribute. Each suitable alternative may then be evaluated by the second goal, location in an attractive town. If, however, these goals are reversed, information collection may concentrate first on brochures of attractive towns and when a suitable alternative has been found, it is evaluated by the second goal. As different opportunities may be marketed in different ways the individual may be exposed to different ranges of opportunities, so the final choice may in fact be different although the same attributes are applied.

Those concerned with marketing destinations as holiday bases need to be aware of the priorities and goals of the segment(s) of the market they are targeting. This form of 'functional' market segmentation could therefore be used to recognise not only which attributes need to be promoted to attract tourists but also how important these factors are in tourist choice. This may also suggest the form, type and relative expenditure on alternative forms of promotional activity which will be most successful. The implications of understanding the importance of attributes to holiday choice apply equally to destination region tourism agencies and to tour operators.

REFERENCES

Boulding, K.E. (1956) The Image: Knowledge in Life and Society, Univ. of Michigan Press, Ann Arbor

Cohen, E. (1979) Rethinking the sociology of tourism, Annals of Tourism Research 6, 18-35

Crompton, J.L. (1979) Motivations for pleasure vacation, <u>Annals of Tourism Research</u> 6, 408-424

Dann, G.M.S. (1976) The holiday was simply fantastic, <u>Tourism Review</u> 31(3), 19-23

Dann, G.M.S. (1981) Tourist motivation: an appraisal, <u>Annals of Tourism Research</u> 8, 187-219

Desberats, J. (1983) Spatial choice and constraints on behaviour, <u>Annals, Association of American Geographers</u> 73, 340-357

Fridgen, J.D. (1987) Use of cognitive maps to determine perceived tourism regions, <u>Leisure Sciences</u> 9, 101-118

Goodrich, J.N. (1978) The relationship between preferences for and perceptions of vacation destinations: application of a choice model, <u>Journal of Travel Research</u> 16, 8-13

Gould, P.R. & White, R.R. (1974) <u>Mental Maps</u>, Penguin, Harmondsworth, Middlesex

Gyte, D.M. (1988) Repertory grid analysis of images of destinations: British tourists in Mallorca, <u>Trent Working Papers in Geography</u>, Trent Polytechnic, Nottingham

Kent, P.J. (1988) The desire to conform: another role of image in the destination choice of potential tourists, paper presented at the Leisure Studies Association 2nd International Conference, University of Sussex, Brighton

Kent, P.J. (1989) An examination of the spatial choice processes of package holidaymakers, <u>Geographical Papers: Tourism Series No. 3</u>, Dept. of Geography, University of Reading, Reading

Lynch, K. (1960) <u>The Image of the City</u>, MIT Press, Cambridge, Massachusetts

MacInnes, D.J. & Price, L.L. (1987) The role of imagery in information processing: Review and extensions, <u>Journal of Consumer Research</u> 13, 473-491

Mathieson, A. & Wall, G. (1982) <u>Tourism: Economic, Physical and Social Impacts</u>, Longman, London

Moutinho, L. (1987) Consumer behaviour in tourism, <u>European Journal of Marketing</u> 21, 2-44

Pocock, D.C.D. (Ed)(1981) <u>Humanistic Geography and Literature: Essays on the Experience of Place</u>, Croom Helm, London

Pocock, D. & Hudson, R. (1978) <u>Images of the Urban Environment</u>, Macmillan, London

Pred, A. (1967) <u>Behaviour and Location: Foundations for a Geographic and Dynamic Location Theory</u>, Vol. 1, C.W.K. Gleerup, Lund

Relph, E. (1976) <u>Place and Placelessness</u>, Pion, London

Relph, E. (1981) <u>Rational Landscapes and Humanistic Geography</u>, Croom Helm, London

Scott, D.R., Schewe, C.D. & Fredrick, D.G. (1978) A multibrand, multiattribute model of tourist state choice, <u>Journal of Travel Research</u> 17, 23-29

Tuan, Yi-Fu (1974) <u>Topophilia; A Study of Environmental Perception, Attitudes and Values,</u> Prentice-Hall Inc., Englewood Cliffs, New Jersey

Tuan, Yi-Fu (1976) Geopiety: a theme in Man's attachment to nature and to place, pp 11-40 in D. Lowenthal & M.J. Bowden, (Eds) <u>Geographies of the Mind</u>, Oxford Univ. Press, New York

Wright, J.K. (1947) Terrae incognitae: the place of imagination in geography, <u>Annals, Association of American Geographers</u> 37, 1-15

Chapter 4

OPPORTUNITY SETS AS ANALYTICAL MARKETING INSTRUMENTS: A DESTINATION AREA VIEW

Brian Goodall

THE OPPORTUNITY SET CONCEPT – AN APPLICATION TO TOURIST DESTINATION AREAS

The concept of opportunity sets can be used to aid an understanding of the structure and processes underlying the marketing of tourism products. So far application of the concept has focused on holiday opportunity sets from (i) the consumer's viewpoint, i.e. within the range of holidays available at any given time individual consumers will have sub-sets conditioned by their preferences, awareness and socio-economic circumstances, and (ii) the industry's viewpoint, especially that of the tour operator, i.e. the range of holidays offered by the industry in any given tourist-generating market can be subdivided into various holiday travel and accommodation packages. The supply-oriented approach has emphasised tourism products as holiday types, especially inclusive tours. The destination viewpoint has been neglected even though industry opportunity sub-sets acknowledge that destination is a basis for market segmentation and product differentiation within and between tour operators. Destination is an inescapable component of every tourism product and can be analysed using opportunity sets. Two approaches are possible: destinations as viewed from outside, e.g. by tour operators based in tourist-generating countries, and from inside, e.g. the view projected outwards by destination area tourism agencies. This chapter emphasises the former approach (whilst Chp. 9 illustrates the latter for a particular destination).

Previous analyses also concentrated upon markets in individual tourist-origin areas. However, holidays in a particular destination will be available to tourists from many origin areas,

63

Figure 4.1: Relationship between tourist-origin area and destination area opportunity sets

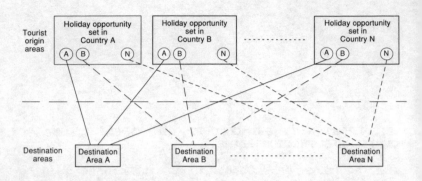

i.e. a given destination area appears in the total holiday opportunity set of several tourist-origin countries as Fig. 4.1 illustrates. The total holiday opportunity set available at a given time in any particular tourist-origin area could be disaggregated spatially into **destination area opportunity sub-sets**, e.g. in Fig. 4.1 for country A the non-overlapping sub-sets A, B .... N, and explained in terms of market segmentation and product differentiation practiced by tour operators based in country A. But tourist-origin country A's destination area sub-set A represents only part of the holiday supply available in destination area A, which must be aggregated with the corresponding sub-set for country B, and so on, in order to give the full **destination area opportunity set** (DAOS) for destination area A. A DAOS is therefore a supply-based opportunity set which includes all the holiday possibilities available in a particular destination area during a given period, ranging from a single night's bed and breakfast on a touring holiday through longer stay hotel and self-catering packages to timeshare and second home arrangements as well as holidays visiting friends and relatives (VFR).

Characteristics of destination area opportunity sets

It is important to understand the spatial extent and form of the destination area(s) represented in such opportunity sets. DAOSs should be interpreted not as single locations (in which case each location would be a unique, point-form DAOS) but as **resort sets**, i.e. locations characterised by the same sought-after tourist attraction(s). Viewed as resort sets DAOSs may be interpreted in one of two ways, distinguished by spatial form. On the one hand, DAOSs may be viewed as **environments**, i.e. classified according to their physical attributes, e.g. mountains and lakes, capital cities, tropical islands, sun-sea-sand, sailing centres. On the other hand, they may be **place-specific**, i.e. a particular country - France or Spain - or region - French Riviera, Costa del Sol. In the latter case the resorts comprising any DAOS will be contiguous, i.e. nearest neighbours, and experience similar access conditions to potential markets in tourist-origin countries. In both cases there is considerable variation in the number and size of resorts within any DAOS.

Given that the definition of a DAOS includes all holiday possibilities in an area **an industry or commercial DAOS** can be distinguished from a **non-commercial DAOS** (the latter covering the VFR arrangements). This chapter concentrates on commerical DAOSs.

Interdependence of destination area opportunity sets

Resorts within any environmentally-based DAOS compete for a share of the tourists seeking that particular type of holiday environment. Different environmental DAOSs are complementary in the sense that they seek to meet different holiday demands and may be viewed as interdependent in the case of two-centre or touring holidays which combine two or more environments in a single holiday package, e.g. a two-centre summer holiday contrasting a week at the beach with a week in the mountains or a coach tour of Great Britain designed to introduce Americans to both Highland and Lowland landscapes as well as cultural and historic features.

Resorts within place-specific DAOSs enjoy both an interdependent and a competitive relationship with each other within their particular DAOS: they have a common interest in attracting tourists to their destination area but compete for a share of actual visitors. A competitive relationship generally exists, however, between one place-specific DAOS and other DAOSs with similar physical attributes, e.g. Portugal's Algarve, the Spanish Costas and the French Mediterranean coast.

The competitive position of each resort in an environmental DAOS, of each resort within a place-specific DAOS, and of each place-specific DAOS reflects the comparative advantage of that resort's/area's resource base, i.e. in the first instance opportunity sets applied to destination areas have, when viewed in marketing terms, a product orientation. With the growth of destination area tourism organisations, however, selling and marketing orientations have been introduced in order to improve a destination's competitive position. Place-specific DAOSs nest in both spatial and environmental terms as Fig. 4.2 demonstrates for sun-sea-sand holidays. The opportunity set approach therefore allows the identification and grouping of resorts/resort areas with common interests and provides a crude measure for gauging the nature and extent of the competition.

Figure 4.2: Nesting of destination area opportunity sets

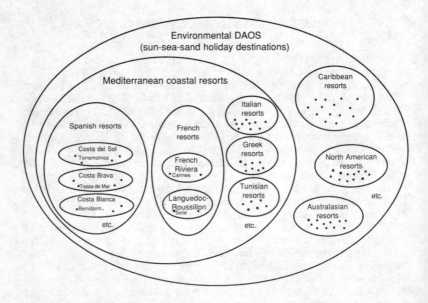

Segmentation of destination area opportunity sets

As an alternative to the nesting of place-specific DAOSs discussed above any place-specific DAOS at the first or higher levels of nesting can be disaggregated spatially. Such spatial disaggregation is but one possible form of market segmentation and any DAOS may be subdivided into sub-sets on a variety of criteria, many of which are associated with some underlying spatial variable. Firstly, resorts in a DAOS may be grouped into sub-sets according to their accessibility via different transport modes. With increased use of private and hire cars and of coaches most resorts are accessible by these means, albeit with degrees of variation in the time/distance factor between individual resorts in the set, but major differences can occur within a destination set in terms of access via scheduled rail and bus services and especially transfer times with respect to regional airports. If connections between the destination arrival airport(s) and tourist-origin area departure airports are considered, whether scheduled or charter flights are involved, the resort set in the destination area can be further subdivided: certain regional departure airports give access to a wider range of DAOSs and resorts within a given DAOS than other departure airports in that country. Such modal opportunity sub-sets obviously overlap since certain resorts are accessible via several transport modes.

Secondly, resorts in a DAOS may be subdivided according to the type of accommodation provided, with the basic distinction being between serviced and self-catering categories. Further subdivision is possible where differing qualities of accommodation are recognised within a category by means of a generally accepted grading scheme for hotels or campsites, etc. Destination area accommodation sub-sets obviously overlap because many resorts offer both serviced and self-catering accommodation, as well as hotels or campsites of a variety of qualities. The accommodation base also permits resort classification in a destination area by size, in terms of bednight capacity.

Thirdly, a DAOS's resorts exhibit varying degrees of commercialisation and may be divided into two sub-sets: **mass tourist resorts** which cater for the package holidaymakers brought in by tour operators and **select resorts** which rely largely on independent holidaymakers. Such a distinction is seen clearly in many Mediterranean countries: for example, Spain - on the Costa del Sol the major coastal resorts of Marbella, Torremolinos, and Fuengirola cater for mass tourists and deal with northern European tour operators whereas the **urbanizaciones** have extensive developments of private holiday homes (Pearce, 1987a); or on Mallorca where resorts such as Palma Nova cater for the mass tourists whereas exclusive 'village' developments such as Benindat cater for up-market independent tourists.

Fourthly, the differing characteristics of tourists infered above suggests a more detailed segmentation of resorts is possible on the basis of visitor characteristics. Two types of segmentation may be attempted, i.e. on the basis of nationality and of socio-economic characteristics of the tourists. One resort in a DAOS may target tourists from a particular country as its major market whilst another resort in that DAOS targets tourists from a different country. For example, considering Greece as a DAOS, Corfu is a destination with a high concentration of British visitors whilst Crete is the most favoured destination of Germans and Kos of the Swedes (Pearce, 1987b). Spill (1981) suggests this is the result of the activities of particular tour operators although no explanation is given of tour operator destination selection procedures. Likewise, resorts can develop their accommodation and facilities to attract particular types of tourist - funfairs and similar entertainments alongside lower grade accommodation if catering for the lower socio-economic groups and golf courses, marinas, leisure centres and high-class accommodation for the up-market tourists. In the case of winter sports destinations it is not only the tourist's socio-economic characteristics which are significant but also the expertise of the skier: thus skiing resorts in a DAOS may specialise in meeting the needs of beginners, intermediates, powder hounds or other expert skiers as well as for 'fun lovers', 'chalet groupies' or 'slush yuppies' (for whom après-ski is especially important).

PENETRATION OF DESTINATION AREA OPPORTUNITY SETS

So far emphasis has been placed on the total potential supply of holidays available in a destination area to would-be tourists from outside that area. To what extent are these holiday opportunities taken up by tourists? If tourists are to select one of the holidays available in a given DAOS then that holiday has first to appear in a tourist's perceived opportunity set and then survive filtering through their consideration, attainable and choice opportunity sets before emerging as the final selection from the tourist's decision opportunity set (see Chp. 3). For a given destination this can happen in a variety of ways.

In the case of a non-commercial DAOS the tourist's perception of the opportunity and their decision to select that holiday may be the result of direct (and repeated) invitations from friends/relatives resident in the destination area to visit and stay. The availability of such non-commercial holiday opportunities is an imponderable, although it can be an important component of tourism in certain destination areas, e.g. Eire.

For most destination areas it is the commercial opportunity sub-set which is most significant and the attraction of tourists depends on the ability of the destination area to sell itself in the face of substitute opportunities in competing destinations. Personal recommendations to friends by tourists who have enjoyed a holiday in that destination can help but much more depends on the steps taken by destination area tourism entrepreneurs and agencies to promote and market their holidays in tourist-origin areas.

Destination area tourism organisations face considerable problems in promoting their holiday opportunities to final consumers in distant tourist-origin markets. Dissemination of information direct to potential tourists scattered in many distant markets will not be economic because the proportion of those tourists who actually holiday in that particular destination area will be very restricted. At best some informative advertising in general media outlets could be undertaken by organisations such as destination area tourist boards: this would identify the existence of the destination area as a potential holiday location. Such tourist boards do not, however, have an actual holiday product to retail but merely represent the interests of the range of enterprises involved in the tourism industry in the destination area. It would be even more unrealistic to expect a single hotel or other tourist attraction to market holidays at such a distance, especially if language and cultural differences intervene.

It is to other tourism organisations such as tour operators that a destination area must turn. Tour operators are normally based in tourist-origin areas since there are organisational and scale economies to be gained when supplying tourists from a market location and transporting them to a variety of holiday locations compared to a single destination drawing tourists from a variety of origins. Place-specific, destination area tour operators are therefore uncommon although they do exist, mainly in the form of **incoming tour operators**, e.g. in the United Kingdom to provide circuit tours for visiting Americans. Destination area tourism agencies therefore need to persuade origin area tour operators to include their resorts in the operators' current and future programmes (and brochures). Persuasive advertising and selling by destination area tourism organisations therefore needs to be directed at tour operators. To what extent have destination areas succeeded in selling themselves to tour operators? Or, recognising that tour operators continuously re-evaluate their resort profiles and actively seek new locations, to what extent have tour operators penetrated DAOSs?

The interface between supply-side opportunity sets, i.e. for destination areas and tour operators, is therefore a critical one, but the basis of the approach by destination area tourism agencies to tour operators and of the selection of resorts by tour operators have not been fully researched. Mass tour operators seek to include in their company opportunity sets the widest possible range of locations, within and between destination areas, consistent with appealing to as wide a range of customers, incuding repeat business, yet maintaining economies of operation, especially in travel and bargaining for accommodation. Specialist tour operators seek resorts which cater for their particular market niches (activity holidays, particular socio-economic groups, etc.) and such resorts may be a limited proportion of any DAOS - although the area specialist tour operator will have a company opportunity set which parallels the DAOS. Resorts of varying size are usually included in a company opportunity set because mass tour operators in particular need to be represented in all of the most popular/fashionable resorts: but they also include one or two resorts in a destination area which are unique to that tour operator.

Except where tourists use their own cars or scheduled rail or air services the tour operator seeks to 'bundle' tourists into economic-sized units for coach travel or charter flights. Generally the holiday bases are within 24 hours travel time (door-to-door) of the tourist's home. With air travel the tour operator has a fine balance to maintain between flying time and transfer time from arrival airports to resort destinations: short transfer journeys are favoured where flight durations are normally two to four hours, as in Europe. Thus a wider spatial choice within any DAOS is usually available where overland transport is the prime means of tourist movement whereas air travel tends to restrict choice within any DAOS but may give access to more distant DAOSs.

Penetration of a given DAOS by tour operators is, therefore, a question of profit expectations on the part of tour operators and resorts (even destination areas) may be added or dropped from one season to the next.

DEPENDENCY OF DESTINATION AREA OPPORTUNITY SETS

Penetration of DAOSs by tour operators has a corollary - **dependency.** For destination areas, dependency is a form of export concentration within the tourism sector of an area's economy. The destination area receives visitors only or mainly from a single tourist-generating country (in the case of the individual resort dependency may imply, in the extreme case, that only one tour operator offers package holidays to that resort). Dependency is a conditional relationship resulting not only from the interaction of destination area and tour operator opportunity sets but also from factors external to the tourism industry such as a destination area's historical connections with a particular tourist-generating country. For example, Malta's tourism industry has been especially reliant upon British visitors and Oglethorpe (1984) writes of 'a crisis of dependence' on British tour operators.

Size of destination area, and especially of resort, has a bearing on dependency: the smaller the area or resort (in terms of bednight capacity) the more likely is dependency upon a few tour operators. Even where visitors are drawn from several tourist-generating countries, destination areas/resorts are still dependent upon the activities of tour operators based in tourist-origin countries. As pointed out above, the tour operator section of the industry is one where scale economies are enjoyed in serving many destination areas where knowledge of tastes in origin markets is required, and where connections with origin-based airlines give rise to substantial barriers to entry for destination area-based tour operators attempting to market a single destination in many tourist-generating countries. The highly concentrated international tour operator market places tourism enterprises, including hotels, based in destination areas at a bargaining disadvantage.

FRENCH SKI RESORTS - A CASE STUDY

Little development had taken place in France to cater for the European skiing market prior to 1945 (Megève was the principal exception). With the post-war expansion of skiing France emerged as a major European skiing destination and today rivals Austria in terms of the number of skiers attracted from overseas. This has been achieved by developing the so-called third generation ski resorts - purpose-built, high ski stations, with ultra-modern lift systems, on virgin sites where the 'village' is no more than a service station for skiers. Courcheval, Alpe d'Huez, La Plagne, Les Arcs, Les Deux Alpes and Val'd'Isère in the French Alps were in the vanguard of this development.

The pattern of French skiing DAOSs

Suitable skiing terrain and climatic conditions exist not only in the Alps but also in other parts of France - the Pyrénées, Massif Central, Jura and Vosges. The French skiing DAOS must include resorts in all of these regions as well as the Alps. There are 131 resorts identified by L'Association des Maires des Stations Francaises de Sports d'Hiver (1986), of which 89 are members of L'Association. These 131 resorts can be considered as the French skiing DAOS. As Table 4.1 shows, over two-thirds of the resorts are located in the French Alps. Bednight capacities are only available for Association members and their regional distribution suggests an even greater

Table 4.1: The French skiing opportunity set: regional distribution of resorts and bednight capacity

Location	Member No	%	Beds	%	Other No	Total No	%
Alpes du Nord							
Savoie/Haute Savoie	41	46	509,630	53	6	47	36
Isère	11	12	116,540	12	7	18	14
Alpes du Sud	16	18	161,510	17	9	25	19
Pyrénées	11	12	115,880	12	14	25	19
Massif Central	3	3	27,000	3	1	4	3
Jura	2	2	18,000	2	2	4	3
Vosges	5	6	21,435	2	3	8	6
Totals	89	100	969,995	100	42	131	100

Note: Percentages do not add up to 100 due to 'rounding'.

concentration (+80 per cent) of French skiing supply in the Alps. This is confirmed by Table 4.2 which classifies Association member resorts by region and size and demonstrates that resorts with +20,000 bednight capacities are only to be found in the Alps (indeed, with the exception of one resort - Serre Chevalier - they are located in the northern Alps).

Consider the penetration of the French skiing DAOS by UK tour operators. For Association resorts Table 4.3 shows that less than two-thirds (60 per cent) appear in the skiing holiday programme of all UK tour operators for the 1986/87 season. It also suggests that the larger resorts are more likely to appear in tour operators' brochures than smaller ones: the largest resorts (over 15,000 bednight capacity) all appeared in at least one tour operator's programme - indeed over half of the 23 such resorts are listed in the brochures of at least 10 and up to 35 tour operators. Table 4.4 considers the full French skiing DAOS of 131 resorts and again examines penetration of that DAOS by UK tour operators in terms of the number of tour operators using each resort. Under half (45 per cent) of all resorts in the DAOS appeared at least once in UK tour operator programmes for 1986/87 and the popularity of resorts in the Alpes du Nord

Table 4.2: The French skiing DAOS: resort distribution by region and size (number of resorts)

Resort Size (Bed-capacity)	A	B	C	Regions D	E	F	G	All
< 5000	7	4	2	2	1	–	3	19
5000–9999	14	2	9	4	–	–	1	30
10000–14999	7	2	1	2	2	2	1	17
15000–19999	5	1	3	3	–	–	1	12
20000–24999	4	1	–	–	–	–	–	5
25000–29999	1	1	–	–	–	–	–	2
> 30000	3	–	1	–	–	–	–	4
All resorts	41	11	16	11	3	2	6	89

A = Savoie/Haute Savoie; B = Isère; C = Alpes du Sud; D = Pyrénées; E = Massif Central; F = Jura; G = Vosges

Table 4.3: French Skiing Association resorts: size (Bed-capacity) and use by UK tour operators

Size (Beds)	< 5000			5000–14999			> 15000		
Location	A	B	C	A	B	C	A	B	C
Alpes du Nord									
Savoie/Haute Savoie	7	2	29	21	17	81	13	13	100
Isère	4	1	25	4	2	50	3	3	100
Alpes du Sud	2	–	0	10	5	50	4	4	100
Pyrénées	2	1	50	6	1	17	3	3	100
Massif Central	1	–	0	2	1	50	–	–	0
Jura	–	–	0	2	–	0	–	–	0
Vosges	3	–	0	2	–	0	–	–	0
Total	19	4	21	47	26	55	23	23	100

Note: A = Number of resorts; B = Number of resorts used by UK tour operators; C = Percentage penetration of each size category by tour operators

(especially in the départements of Savoie and Haute-Savoie) is noted since some three-quarters of that area's resorts are included in UK tour operator brochures. Table 4.5 presents an alternative disaggregation of the overall DAOS, by region and by membership/non-membership of L'Association, and again demonstrates the strength of resorts located in the Alpes du Nord in UK tour operator programmes.

A summary of tour operator penetration of the French skiing DAOS based on L'Association membership shows that only 53 of the 89 member resorts are used by UK tour operators: 32 of these are used by UK mass tour operators (compared to just 14 by Dutch mass tour operators). Figure 4.3 shows 13 of the resorts are common to Dutch and UK mass tour operators, a further 19 are used by both UK mass and other tour operators, one by both Dutch mass tour operators and UK other tour operators, and 20 just by other UK tour operators. Thirty-six resorts do not appear in any UK or Dutch tour operator programmes: these 36 resorts represent a crude measure of the extent to which further innovation of destinations would be possible in tour operator or company opportunity sets. In terms of dependency nearly a quarter of the resorts available in UK tour operator programmes are used by just a single UK tour operator (although the data available did not allow identification of tour operators from other countries, except The Netherlands).

Figure 4.3: The French ski resort opportunity set and its representation by British and Dutch tour operators

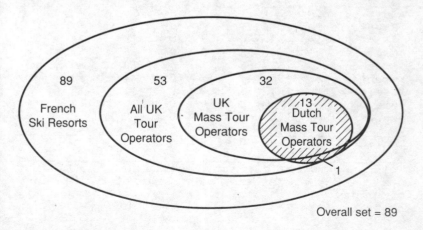

Overall set = 89

Table 4.4: The French skiing DAOS: penetration by and dependence on UK tour operators

Resort Location	0	1	2-5	6-9	10-19	20-29	>30	% Used by TOs
Alpes du Nord								
Savoie/Haute Savoie	12	5	10	4	11	3	2	74
Isère	12	2	2	–	1	–	1	33
Alpes du Sud	15	3	2	2	3	–	–	40
Pyrénées	18	3	4	–	–	–	–	28
Massif Central	3	1	–	–	–	–	–	25
Jura	4	–	–	–	–	–	–	0
Vosges	8	–	–	–	–	–	–	0
Totals	72	14	18	6	15	3	3	45
% of All Resorts	55	11	14	5	12	2	2	N/A

N/A = not applicable

Table 4.5: The French skiing DAOS: penetration by resort sets

Resort Location	A		B		Total Resorts Used by UK TOs	
	No	%	No	%	No	%
Alpes du Nord						
Savoie/Haute Savoie	32	78	3	20	35	74
Isère	6	55	0	0	6	33
Alpes du Sud	9	56	1	11	10	40
Pyrénées	5	45	2	15	7	28
Massif Central	1	33	0	0	1	25
Jura	0	0	0	0	0	0
Vosges	0	0	0	0	0	0
Total	53	60	6	14	59	45

Note: A = L'Association resorts used by UK tour operators; B = other resorts used by UK tour operators

Table 4.6: The French Pyrenean skiing DAOS: distribution of resorts and bed-capacity

Département	Resorts In P. Fed No	%	In N. Fed No	%	Bed-capacity No	%
Pyrénées Atlantiques	4	11	1	25	10,500	8
Hautes-Pyrénées	11	30	4	36	64,447	51
Haute-Garonne	4	11	2	50	4,860	4
Ariège	5	14	1	20	9,650	8
Aude	1	3	-	0	450	0.5
Pyrénées-Roussillon	12	32	3	25	35,800	28
Total	37	100	11	30	125,707	100

Notes: (1) Percentages do not add up to 100 due to rounding. (2) P. Fed = La Fédération Pyrénéenne des Stations et Centres de Sports d'Hiver; N. Fed = L'Association des Maires des Stations Francaises de Sports d'Hiver

On a regional scale, it is possible to demonstrate that the DAOS may be even wider. For example, only 11 ski resorts are listed by the French National Association in the case of the Pyrénées but a further 26 ski resorts exist in that region (La Fédération Pyrénéenne des Stations et Centres de Sport d'Hiver, 1986). Table 4.6 disaggregates the French Pyrenean DAOS by département in terms of resorts and bednight capacity: Hautes-Pyrénées and Pyrénées-Roussillon stand out as areas of resort concentration but, although they each have a similar number of resorts, Hautes-Pyrénées has double the bednight-capacity of Pyrénées-Roussillon. Table 4.7 disaggregates resorts by size and demonstrates how small many of the resorts are: 26 resorts supply only 22 per cent of bednight-capacity (and four resorts supply nearly half the capacity).

To what extent do Pyrenean ski resorts figure in tour operator programmes? Table 4.8 illustrates the low penetration of the French Pyrenean DAOS by UK ski tour operators with less than one in five resorts (19 per cent) being included in their overall 1986/87 programme. Of the seven resorts used, all are located in the Haute-Pyrénées and Pyrénées-Roussillon départements and all but one

Table 4.7: The French Pyrenean skiing DAOS: size distribution (number of resorts)

Bed-capacity	A	B	C	D	E	F	Total No	%
< 1000	2	2	1	2	1	4	12	5
1000-2499	1	3	3	2	-	5	14	17
2500-4999	-	2(2)	-	-	-	1	3(2)	10
5000-7499	-	1	-	1	-	-	2	8
7500-9999	1	-	-	-	-	1(1)	2(1)	13
10000-12499	-	1(1)	-	-	-	-	1(1)	8
12500-15000	-	-	-	-	-	1(1)	1(1)	11
15000-19999	-	1(1)	-	-	-	-	1(1)	12
> 20000	-	1(1)	-	-	-	-	1(1)	17
Total	4	11(5)	4	5	1	12(2)	37(7)	100

Notes: (1) Percentages do not add up to 100 due to rounding; (2) Figures in brackets refer to number of resorts used by UK tour operators
A = Pyrénées Atlantiques; B = Hautes-Pyrénées; C = Haute-Garonne; D = Ariège; E = Aude; F = Pyrénées-Roussillon

Table 4.8: The French Pyrenean skiing DAOS: penetration by UK tour operators

Département	P. Fed. only No	% Used by TOs	Resorts N. & P. Fed. No	% Used by TOs	% All Resorts Used by TOs
Pyrénées Atlantiques	3	0	1	0	0
Haute-Pyrénées	7	14	4	100	45
Haute-Garonne	2	0	2	0	0
Ariège	4	0	1	0	0
Aude	1	0	-	0	0
Pyrénées-Roussillon	9	0	3	67	17
Total	26	4	11	55	19

Note: P. Fed and N. Fed as defined in Table 4.6.

are members of both the national and Pyrenean associations. Of particular note is the fact that UK mass tour operators have penetrated the French Pyrenean skiing DAOS to a greater extent than other UK tour operators, the former being responsible for over 60 per cent of occurrences of Pyrenean ski resorts in company opportunity sets. Again, about a quarter of the resorts are dependent upon a single tour operator. No Dutch mass tour operators included Pyrenean resorts in their programmes. Therefore the French Pyrenean skiing DAOS has been penetrated to a lesser extent than the French national DAOS, implying a high penetration for the French Alps.

The pattern explained

How can the varying penetration of DAOSs by tour operators be explained? Differences in penetration between DAOSs offering essentially the same type of holiday rest on the resource base, which reflects in the differing comparative advantages of DAOSs in meeting tourist demands. The differences may also reflect initial advantage and varying promotional and marketing inputs of destination areas. The same reasoning applies to resorts comprising any one DAOS. Therefore, DAOSs with the greatest comparative advantages are most likely to be actively involved in receiving tourists and to show the highest degree of penetration by tour operators. That comparative advantage is a function of both general and local accessibility and of the range and quality of the physical environment and facilities available.

Both marketing and general access factors are operative in the French case. L'Association des Maires des Stations Francaises de Sports d'Hiver is a more significant organisation than La Fédération Pyrénéenne des Stations et Centres de Sport d'Hiver: the former's promotional activites are both more extensive and effective in reaching tour operators in tourist-generating countries. Thus, as noted above, all Pyrenean resorts which were members of the national association appear in the UK tour operator (industry) opportunity set. The other factor, general accessibility, influences the relative penetration of the French skiing DAOS by, for example, British and Dutch mass tour operators. Penetration by the former is highest because French ski resorts, Alpine or Pyrenean, are as accessible by air for British skiers as Austrian or Swiss ones but for Dutch skiers, travelling overland, the French resorts, especially the Pyrenean ones, are at an access disadvantage compared to Austrian and Swiss ones. The corollary is that Dutch mass tour operators have penetrated the Austrian skiing DAOS to a greater extent than their UK counterparts.

Which resorts from a DAOS will be included by tour operators in their company opportunity sets? Resorts with superior physical conditions and facilities and/or a local accessibility advantage will be favoured. Facilities, including accommodation and in the skiing case, lift systems, are usually a function of resort size: the larger a ski resort the more likely it will be used by tour operators, particularly mass tour operators. The Pyrenean skiing resorts demonstrate this well since the many small resorts, with limited accommodation and lift capacities, are ignored by UK tour operators.

Moreover, the skiing market is heterogeneous. Even where skiers are of the same ability they differ in terms of other personal characteristics. Mass tour operators include some smaller (but not the smallest) resorts in their company opportunity sets. This allows them to tap all segments of the market as well as including some resorts where competition from other tour operators is less severe. Allowing for skiers of different standards may also help explain variation in resort take-up within a DAOS: some resorts may be most suitable for beginners, others for advanced skiers, yet others for intermediates and a few for all combinations. Penetration will be highest where the resort DAOS can cater for all skiers and involve both mass and specialist tour operators in providing holiday packages. French Pyrenean resorts are considered particularly suited to beginners compared to the high Alpine stations. This results in both a lower penetration of the Pyrenean DAOS by UK tour operators in general and in a larger representation of mass tour operators (who cater for the majority of first-time skiers).

A major factor in resort selection is local accessibility. This is particularly important where the journey from tourist-origin country to destination region is made by air travel: transfer time from arrival airport to resort is a prime consideration relative to flight time. The use of charter flights may be a further factor restricting the number of resorts from a DAOS offered by a

Table 4.9: Accessibility of French skiing resorts used by UK tour operators

Transfer time	Pyrenean resorts No	%	Alpine resorts No	%
< 1 hr	5	71	1	2
1-2 hrs	2	29	11	22
2-3 hrs	-	-	15	30
3-4 hrs	-	-	10	20
> 4 hrs	-	-	13	26

Note: Based on shortest transfer time from nearest airport where a resort can be reached via alternative airports

particular tour operator (or group of tour operators where aircraft seats are subcontracted). The transfer time is critical in the case of skiing since roads need to be driven with extra care in winter and delays due to severe weather are more common. Pyrenean skiing resorts do not enjoy the same popular image as their Alpine rivals and British skiers will be prepared to tolerate longer overall journey times to reach Alpine resorts. Since flight times from Gatwick/Heathrow to Lourdes and Toulouse (for the Pyrénées) and Chambéry, Geneva, Grenoble, Lyons, Nice and Turin (for the Alps) are similar, differences in overall journey times are largely due to differences in transfer times. Transfer times do not exceed two and a half hours in the case of the Pyrénées (and are usually about an hour from Lourdes) whereas transfer times of up to four and a half hours are not uncommon for French Alpine resorts accessed via Geneva, Grenoble and Lyons. Table 4.9 summarises the differential access to French skiing resorts for British skiers.

DAOSs: AN EVALUATION

The above discussion has demonstrated the application of the opportunity set concept to destination areas as a research tool in understanding one aspect of the structure of the tourism industry - the participation of destination areas in the supply of holiday opportunities. In both its environmental and place-specific guises the concept gives an indication of the extent and strength of the competition but it is still essentially a research or information tool rather than an explicit marketing aid. In its place-specific form, particularly where the interaction of DAOSs with the actions of tour operators is considered, application of the concept can have more practical value (as well as raising additional questions for the researcher).

From the destination viewpoint, comparison of one resort with other resorts within a DAOS or with resorts in other destination areas offering similar types of holiday allows that resort not only to gauge the nature of the competition but also to identify new market opportunities. These may be in the form of additional tour operators who might bring more tourists from traditional origin areas or tour operators based in potential tourist-generating areas. The extreme position would be the creation of a destination-based tour operator as in the case of Tourarc, the specialist, place-specific tour operator marketing holidays to the French ski resort of Les Arcs.

For the tour operator the DAOS concept is also of value because tour operators are continually seeking ways to improve and extend their holiday programmes. Tour operator strategies for resort selection aim to find resorts which contribute to the overall successful marketing of their holiday programmes. Company opportunity sets are not static in terms of the resorts contained therein. Whilst, for any tour operator, currently successful resorts may be sufficient to attract new tourists and a certain proportion of repeat holidaymakers, new resorts need to be added to offer different destinations to the remainder of the 'repeat business' and so maintain market share. Moreover, resorts which prove unpopular are quickly dropped from a tour operator's company opportunity set.

Tour operator resort selection procedures are worthy of further research and, in particular, an analysis of changes in resort participation from any DAOS and of tour operator penetration of DAOSs could be rewarding. Penetration of DAOSs by tour operators is a dynamic process. For example, using information for UK tour operators who are ABTA members (ABC International, 1986 and 1988), the French skiing DAOS appears at first sight to be relatively stable, comprising 51 resorts used by UK tour operators in 1986/87 and 52 in 1988/89. However, only 38 resorts are common to both winter seasons and 65 different resorts have been used in total, implying an exit ratio of 26 per cent and an entry ratio of 27 per cent. (High rates of change are also characteristic of company opportunity sets, e.g. for the 1986/87 skiing season entry ratios for new resorts in UK mass tour operator holiday programmes exceeded 20 per cent - Enterprise 31 per cent, Horizon 32 per cent, Intasun (ILG) 21 per cent, Thomson 22 per cent.) An analysis of the 'survivors' could be instructive for destination areas!

The interface between DAOSs and company opportunity sets is therefore to be emphasised since the inclusion of a resort from a given DAOS in a particular tour operator's opportunity set is no guarantee that a destination area has a firm foothold on the ladder of successful tourism development as the exit ratio above warns. The destination area's tourism organisations must be aware that company opportunity sets will usually include resorts offering similar holiday opportunities from several competing DAOSs. Does a particular destination area or resort receive distinctive treatment in a tour operator's brochure which covers several DAOSs? How the resorts are presented in the brochures can influence potential tourists' choice of destination. Analysis of brochure contents and resort profiles within and between brochures is another line of investigation that would repay further study (see Chp. 10). In the skiing context, the regular publication of 'independent' guides to resorts, such as The Good Skiing Guide (Gill, 1986) suggests brochure descriptions of resorts are incomplete and even misleading. Brochures, however, are intended to persuade holidaymakers to buy a particular tour operator's product, rather than that of a rival operator. For destination areas the implication is that tour operators should be made clearly aware of the destination's comparative advantage and that there is a role for destination area promotional activity in tourist-generating countries to ensure an appropriate image is transmitted to potential tourists.

REFERENCES

ABC International (1986) ABC Holiday Guide, Winter 1986/87, ABC International, London

Opportunity Sets - Destination Areas

ABC International (1988) ABC Holiday Guide, Winter 1988/89, ABC International, London

Gill, C. (Ed)(1986) The Good Skiing Guide, Consumers' Association and Hodder & Stoughton, London

L'Association des Maires des Stations Francaises de Sports d'Hiver (1986) Ski France, Edition 86/87, L'Association, Paris

La Fédération Pyrénéenne des Stations et Centres de Sports d'Hiver (1986) Les Pyrénées A La Carte, La Fédération, Toulouse

Oglethorpe, M. (1984) Tourism in Malta: a crisis of dependence, Leisure Studies 3(2) 147-162

Pearce, D. (1987a) Tourism Today: A Geographical Analysis, Longman, London

Pearce, D. (1987b) Mediterranean charters - a comparative geographic perspective, Tourism Management 8(4) 291-305

Spill, J.M. (1981) L'avion et les iles: le cas de Grèce, Iles de la Méditerranée, Cahier No 4, Editions du CNRS, Marseille

Chapter 5

HEDONIC PRICES AND THE MARKETING OF PACKAGE HOLIDAYS: THE CASE OF TOURISM RESORTS IN MALAGA

M. Thea Sinclair, Ann Clewer and Alan Pack

INTRODUCTION

Pricing policy is a key component of an effective strategy for marketing tourism destinations, as has been stressed in Chp. 1. The relative cost of the holidays sold in different resorts has evident implications for the commercial viability of the resorts. At first sight it would appear that the price competitiveness of package holidays in different resorts could be determined simply by comparing the prices of the holidays advertised in brochures, but this is not the case. Most package holidays consist of different combinations of characteristics such as accommodation in hotels of different star ratings, with different facilities, at varying distances from key locations such as the beach or local shopping centre. Since it is rarely possible to compare identical packages the determination of the price competitiveness of package holidays in different resorts is not straightforward. For similar reasons, identification of the price competitiveness of the holidays supplied by different tour operators is difficult.

Unlike goods and services which are sold individually and for which market prices are readily available, package holidays consist of a bundle of goods and services - transport, accommodation, facilities such as sports activities, discos, etc. - and individual components of the package are not assigned market prices. Therefore the problem of estimating the price competitiveness of different holidays in different destinations cannot be overcome by comparing the market prices of the components of the package. This problem has been recognised in studies of the pricing of other products which consist of a bundle of characteristics, for example houses (Clewer & Pack, 1986; Witte, et al., 1979) and consumer durables such as cars (Griliches, 1961). It has been tackled by the use of a hedonic price model which permits the estimation of the price differentials which are due to the variations in the mixes of characteristics (for example, in the case of houses, the number of rooms, availability of a garage, size of garden, etc.). The model can thus provide useful information about commercial pricing policy and consumer preferences.

In this study the hedonic price model will be applied to the prices of package holidays in resorts in the province of Malaga on the Costa del Sol. This will provide estimates of the price variations which are due to differences in the characteristics of the holiday. It will also quantify the variations which result from factors other than the mix of characteristics, such as differences between tour operators and between resorts. By standardising holiday prices for the characteristics of the holiday, it is possible to identify those resorts and tour operators which are most expensive; i.e. to estimate the relative price differences which are due to factors other than the previously identified characteristics of the holiday. Since holidays are consumed in their entirety and have no asset value, many of the complications which have been present in past applications of the technique to the housing market, in particular, are not relevant.

THE TOURISM RESORTS

Spain is clearly the major destination for UK residents who purchase package holidays; during the 1980s one-third of package holidays were spent in Spain and approximately 70 per cent of UK tourists visiting Spain arrived via an inclusive tour (Fitch, 1987). Between 1985 and 1986 the number of UK package holidays in Spain rose by 38 per cent (Department of Employment, 1987). The southern province of Malaga, which includes resorts such as Torremolinos and Marbella, shown in Fig. 5.1, has been a popular destination for British tourists (Board et al., 1987). In 1986, for example, 921,422 UK nationals arrived at Malaga's airport and UK residents spent 3.7 million nights in hotels and hostals in the province, constituting 39 per cent of the total bed-nights for all nationalities (MTTC, 1986).

Figure 5.1: UK package holidays to resorts in Malaga

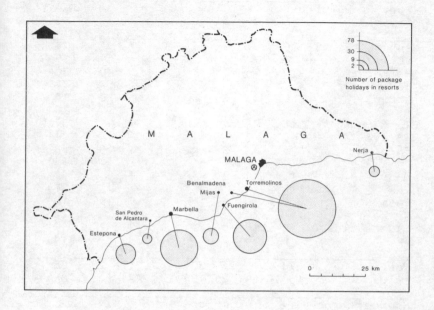

How are the package holidays offered by UK tour operators distributed between the province's resorts? Table 5.1 shows the holidays which were supplied in August 1988, the data having been obtained from the brochures which were available in travel agencies. Although a marginal number of additional holidays may have been supplied by relatively small tour operators whose brochures were not obtained, these are unlikely to make a significant difference to the ensuing results. Thus, by far the largest number of holidays (50 per cent of the total) are supplied in the Torremolinos/Benalmadena resorts, nearest to the airport (Torremolinos and Benalmadena have been considered together owing to their proximate locations). The next highest concentration is in Marbella which has 19 per cent of the total, followed by Fuengirola with 17 per cent, each of the other resorts having less than 10 per cent.

Table 5.1 also shows that Thomson, with 31.5 per cent of the total UK market in 1987 (Bote et al., 1988), provided the greatest number of

Table 5.1: The distribution of package holidays by tour operators and resorts

Tour Operator Group	A	B	C	D	E	F	G	Total (%)
International Leisure Group	16	0	6	6	0	0	1	29 (19)
BA/Redwing	10	1	2	6	1	0	0	20 (13)
Arrow	0	3	0	5	2	0	0	10 (6)
Thomson Travel	25	2	5	4	1	0	0	37 (24)
Falcon	6	0	2	0	0	0	0	8 (5)
Bass	15	1	7	4	1	4	0	32 (21)
Cosmos	6	1	4	1	0	0	0	12 (8)
Cadogan Travel	0	1	0	4	1	0	1	7 (4)
Total (%)	78 (50)	9 (6)	26 (17)	30 (19)	6 (4)	4 (2)	2 (2)	155 (100)

Source: brochures of tour operators cited above.
Resorts: A = Torremolinos/Benalmadena, B = Estepona, C = Fuengirola, D = Marbella, E = Mijas, F = Nerja, G = San Pedro Alcantara

holidays - 24 per cent of the total offered in the province, as shown by the figures in brackets in the table. Thomson was followed closely by Bass (including Horizon and Wings) and the International Leisure Group (ILG; including Intasun, Lancaster, Select Holidays) with 21 per cent and 19 per cent, respectively. British Airways (BA)/Redwing (including Enterprise, Flair, Martin Rooks and Sovereign) offered 13 per cent, Cosmos 8 per cent and the remainder were supplied by the smaller tour operators Arrow, Cadogan Travel and Falcon. The tour operator groups which have the largest shares of the UK market (Bote et al., 1988) thus dominate the supply of package holidays in the resorts.

Table 5.2 shows the mean prices of the holidays supplied by different tour operators, together with the mean star ratings of the hotels used (given in brackets). The prices related to a seven night holiday, with air transport, for one

Table 5.2: Mean unstandardised prices (and hotel star ratings) of package holidays by tour operator and resort (rounded to nearest pound)

Tour Operator Group	Resorts							Overall Mean
---	A	B	C	D	E	F	G	
Inter-national Leisure Group	282 (3.1)	–	273 (3.2)	456 (3.7)	–	–	269 (3.0)	315 (3.2)
BA/ Redwing	268 (3.4)	432 (4.0)	279 (3.5)	436 (3.7)	482 (4.0)	–	–	339 (3.6)
Arrow	–	459 (4.0)	–	596 (4.2)	869 (5.0)	–	–	609 (4.3)
Thomson Travel	283 (3.2)	411 (4.0)	263 (3.0)	547 (4.25)	451 (4.0)	–	–	320 (3.4)
Falcon	251 (2.8)	–	262 (3.5)	–	–	–	–	254 (3.0)
Bass	296 (3.2)	400 (4.0)	291 (3.0)	515 (4.5)	500 (4.0)	303 (2.0)	–	333 (3.0)
Cosmos	270 (3.3)	349 (4.0)	266 (3.3)	239 (2.0)	–	–	–	273 (3.3)
Cadogan Travel	–	419 (4.0)	–	589 (4.0)	419 (4.0)	–	467 (4.0)	523 (4.0)
Overall Mean	279 (3.2)	422 (4.0)	274 (3.2)	506 (3.9)	598 (4.3)	303 (2.0)	368 (3.5)	345 (3.4)

Source: Brochures of tour operators cited above.
Resorts: Key for A-G as in Table 5.1

adult in a resort hotel in Malaga in the first full week in August 1988 and were obtained from tour operators' brochures. Since the main interest is in the comparison of the prices of the holidays supplied in different resorts, and not in the effective demand for the holidays, the prices are not weighted by the number of holidays purchased. It can be seen that the smallest tour operators, supplying the lowest number of holidays, charge both the highest (Arrow, Cadogan) and the lowest mean prices (Falcon). Cosmos consistently charges relatively low prices. However, although the mean price ordering of the largest tour operators, from high to low, is BA/Redwing, Bass, Thomson, ILG, the ordering varies between the different resorts. In Marbella, for example, the ordering is Thomson, Bass, ILG, BA/Redwing. In general, the mean prices for the holidays tend to be highest in Mijas, Marbella and Estepona, and lowest in Torremolinos/ Benalmadena and Fuengirola. Although the mean prices charged broadly correspond to the hotel star ratings, there are, for any given mean star rating, large variations in the prices charged, both within and between resorts.

The previous tables showed the total number of holidays provided by the different tour operators. However, it has been argued (Barke & France, 1986; Goodall et al., 1988) that one marketing strategy pursued by tour operators is that of segmenting the market, supplying holidays of different prices in different brochures. This strategy is likely to have spatial implications, as more expensive holidays are offered in some resorts and cheaper holidays, targeted towards 'mass' tourism, are offered in others. Tables 5.3 and 5.4 provide the numbers, unweighted mean prices and hotel star ratings of the holidays supplied in the different brochures of the three major tour operators. It can be seen that considerable variations occur. Thomson's A la Carte, ILG's Select and Bass' Wings brochures target the more expensive segment of the market and higher proportions of the holidays are offered in the resorts of Mijas, Marbella and Estepona. Thomson's Small and Friendly and Bass' Horizon Small Hotels brochures, though targeting the same segment of the market, are offered in different resorts. Their prices are similar to those of the holidays offered in the remainder of the brochures, with the exception of Thomson's Portland holidays which are significantly cheaper in Torremolinos, and Bass' Horizon holidays, which are more expensive.

Although comparison of the mean prices charged by the different tour operators is of interest, it is only able to provide limited information since the holidays which are supplied by the tour operators are not identical. The package holidays consist of different bundles of characteristics (availability of different combinations of facilities such as entertainments, sports activities, etc.) and are supplied in different resorts. More meaningful estimates of the price competitiveness of the different holidays offered by the different tour operators in different resorts must therefore be based on a comparison of holiday prices which have been standardised to take account of the variations in the characteristics of the holidays. This is undertaken below.

Table 5.3: The distribution of package holidays in tour operators' brochures and resorts

Tour Operators' Brochures	A	B	Resorts C	D	E	F	G	Total
Thomson Travel								
A la Carte	2	2	0	3	1	0	0	8
Portland	2	0	1	0	0	0	0	3
Skytours	5	0	0	0	0	0	0	5
Small & Friendly	1	0	0	0	0	0	0	1
Summer Sun	15	0	4	1	0	0	0	20
Bass								
Horizon	11	0	5	1	0	2	0	19
Small Hotels	0	0	1	0	0	2	0	3
Wings	1	1	1	3	1	0	0	7
International Leisure Group								
Intasun	3	0	2	1	0	0	1	7
Intasun Sol	10	0	4	0	0	0	0	14
Select	0	0	0	4	0	0	0	4

Source: Brochures of tour operators cited.
Resorts: Key for A-G as in Table 5.1

THE HEDONIC PRICE MODEL

The hypothesis underlying hedonic price models is that goods can be viewed as 'bundles' of characteristics and are valued for these characteristics. Hedonic prices are the implicit prices of the characteristics and they can be determined from the relationship between the prices of the goods and the characteristics associated with them. The application of the model thus requires the identification of the characteristics of which the good is thought to consist and the appropriate relationship between the good's price and the previously selected characteristics. Past studies have usually estimated the relationship between the price of the good and its characteristics by means of regression analysis but, as is often the case, the theory provides little guidance as to the appropriate functional form to use in the analysis. The choice of function in any application may be determined on

Table 5.4: Mean unstandardised prices (and hotel star ratings) of package holidays in tour operators' brochures and resorts (rounded to nearest pound)

Tour Operators' Brochures	Resorts							Overall Mean
	A	B	C	D	E	F	G	
Thomson Travel								
A la Carte	454	411	–	641	451	–	–	513
	(4.5)	(4.0)	–	(5.0)	(4.0)			(4.5)
Portland	235	–	260	–	–	–	–	243
	(3.0)		(4.0)					(3.3)
Skytours	260	–	–	–	–	–	–	260
	(3.0)							(3.0)
Small & Friendly	280	–	–	–	–	–	–	280
	(3.0)							(3.0)
Summer Sun	275	–	264	263	–	–	–	272
	(3.2)		(2.8)	(2.0)				(3.1)
Bass								
Horizon	302	–	293	409	–	334	–	309
	(3.3)		(3.0)	(4.0)		(3.0)		(3.2)
Small Hotels	–	–	268	–	–	272	–	270
			(2.0)			(1.0)		(1.3)
Wings	284	400	302	550	500	–	–	448
	(3.0)	(4.0)	(4.0)	(4.7)	(4.0)			(4.1)
International Leisure Group								
Intasun	254	–	264	259	–	–	269	260
	(3.0)		(2.5)	(3.0)			(3.0)	(2.9)
Intasun Sol	292	–	277	–	–	–	–	288
	(3.2)		(3.5)					(3.3)
Select	–	–	–	537	–	–	–	537
				(4.0)				(4.0)

Source: Brochures of tour operators cited.
Resorts: Key for A-G as in Table 5.1

empirical grounds although there has been some controversy concerning the method of doing so (Halvorsen & Pollakowski, 1981; Cassel & Mendelsohn, 1985).

A related issue concerns the interpretation of the results obtained from the estimated equation. Rosen (1974) discusses the interpretation of hedonic prices determined under pure competition. The good, **Z**, is represented by the bundle of associated characteristics:

$$Z = (Z_1, Z_2, \ldots\ldots, Z_n)$$

where Z_i represents the amount of characteristic i present. The price of the good is a function of the characteristics so that the hedonic price function is given by:

$$P(Z) = P(Z_1, Z_2, \ldots\ldots, Z_n)$$

The prices that consumers are willing to pay (the consumer bid prices) are functions of the characteristics, Z, income, y, and tastes, α:

$$D(Z) = D(Z_1, Z_2, \ldots\ldots, Z_n, y, \alpha)$$

The prices for which producers are willing to supply the good (the producer offer prices) are functions of the characteristics Z, the profit level p, and the cost conditions for each producer, β:

$$Q(Z) = Q(Z_1, Z_2, \ldots\ldots, Z_n, p, \beta)$$

D_i, the first partial derivative of D with respect to Z_i, represents how much the consumer would be prepared to bid for an extra unit of the ith characteristic. Q_i, the first partial derivative of Q with respect to Z_i, represents how much extra the firm would be prepared to charge for producing a good with an extra unit of the ith characteristic. Consumers maximise their utility subject to a budget constraint and firms maximise profits. The coefficients of the hedonic price equation are interpreted as the equilibrium values of the implicit prices of the characteristics, given the demand and supply conditions.

The equilibrium price for which the good is sold is determined such that sellers and buyers are matched for all characteristics. At equilibrium:

$$Q^d(Z_i) = Q^s(Z_i) \text{ for all i}$$

and $D_i = Q_i$ for all i

An equilibrium price is determined for each of the different combinations of characteristics of which the good consists. The hedonic price function gives the relationship between the range of equilibrium prices and the range of different combinations of characteristics. Although it depends upon the underlying range of consumption and production functions corresponding to the different combinations of characteristics, the hedonic function does not itself provide information about the relative importance of demand and supply in the determination of prices.

The hedonic price model was used to estimate the relationship between the prices of package holidays in Malaga and the characteristics of the holidays supplied. Since the data consist of information provided by the producers, they relate to the supply rather than the demand for holidays. The prices quoted in the brochures may not be the prices paid by all consumers if some of the holidays which are offered are not taken up and are sold at last minute 'bargain' prices. However, unless this happens to a great extent it is appropriate to assume that the implicit prices derived from the hedonic equation approximate market clearing prices.

The characteristics of the holiday were obtained from brochures and from the Spanish Hotel Guide (MTTC, 1988), and included the star ratings of the hotels and the supply of facilities such as swimming pools, discos, air conditioning, televisions and shops. Clearly hotel star ratings are correlated with hotel characteristics, and the estimation of a price equation which included both star ratings and all the facilities as explanatory variables would suffer from the problem of multicollinearity. However, the relationship between the star rating and the presence of different hotel facilities is not clearcut. For example, all the five star hotels in the brochures had air conditioned bedrooms, but so did 78 per cent of the four star and 35 per cent of the three star hotels. The same applied to other facilities. This means that resort prices cannot be compared simply by comparing hotels with similar star ratings; within any star rating category hotels have different 'mixes' of facilities.

The problem of multicollinearity was addressed by considering the correlations between the group of variables representing the hotel facilities and the group of hotels included in the different star ratings. Since there was no guarantee that the relationship between the star ratings and the hotels would be linear, the star ratings were treated as a set of dummy variables S1, S2, S3, S4 and S5 where, for example, S5 = 1 if the hotel had five stars and S5 = 0 otherwise. Because only a small number of holidays were offered in one star hotels, one and two star hotels were grouped together and this group was used as the base; thus the dummy variables which were actually included in the regression equation were S3, S4 and S5.

A suitable technique for examining the correlations between groups of variables is canonical correlation analysis (Johnston, 1978). This technique identifies the maximum correlation that exists between linear functions of two groups of variables; by examining the coefficients of the linear functions it is possible to see which variables are contributing most to the correlation. Using this technique it was found that there was a linear combination of hotel facilities which were highly related to a linear function of the star ratings of the hotels (the correlation coefficient, $R = 0.97$). Clearly severe multicollinearity problems would occur if all the hotel facility variables were included in the equation with the star rating dummies.

Simply omitting the star rating dummies is not the answer to the problem. High star ratings imply that standards of hotel furnishing, food and service are likely to be better and other variables to measure these factors were not available. The star rating variables are therefore partly proxies for these unmeasured characteristics and should not be excluded from the hedonic function. Moreover, there are high intercorrelations between the hotel facility variables. For example, the squared multiple correlation between the variable representing air conditioned bedrooms and all the other hotel facilities is 0.87, and the same order of magnitude exists for many of the other variables. Since the aim of this study was not to estimate implicit prices for the hotel facilities, the use of a small number of star rating dummies which 'capture' the effect of some hotel facilities is preferable to the use of a large number of facility variables.

Examination of the weights associated with the hotel facility variables in the canonical analysis suggested that the dominant influences on star rating were, not surprisingly, availability of sitting rooms, air conditioning, radios, televisions, telephones, barbers, beauty parlours, saunas, gymnasiums, gardens and terraces. When all these variables were removed from the analysis, the maximum correlation between the star rating dummies and the remaining hotel facilities fell to 0.59, still statistically significant but less likely to give rise to severe problems of multicollinearity.

Using regression analysis, the prices of the package holidays were then related to the following explanatory variables: tour operator dummies, resort dummies, star rating dummies and the remaining hotel facilities. Rosen (1974) has argued that if consumers cannot purchase different combinations of characteristics from those on offer (by repackaging characteristics) or if producers supply characteristics jointly, the functional form for the hedonic price equation is non-linear. Since consumers cannot create their own package holidays by purchasing and combining selections of characteristics from holidays offered by different tour operators, the appropriate functional form is non-linear. Popular non-linear specifications for hedonic price studies are the semi-logarithmic and log-linear functional forms. Given that most of the explanatory variables in this study were dummy variables, the semi-logarithmic specification was used on the grounds of goodness of fit and ease of interpretation. The interpretation of the coefficients is very straightforward. Where a dummy variable has coefficient β, the effect on the price of the presence of the characteristic is a change of $(e^{\beta} - 1) \times 100$ per cent (Halvorsen & Palmquist, 1980). Thomson was chosen as the base for comparison of tour operator prices; Torremolinos/Benalmadena was chosen as the base for resort prices. The explanatory variables provided an excellent explanation of the package holiday prices; the coefficient of determination for the fitted equation was $R^2 = 0.95$.

Further tests were used to ensure that not all of the variation in holiday prices was due to differences in the hotel star ratings and facilities. The use of F tests for the joint significance of groups of variables showed that the tour operators and resorts had separate, significant effects on the package holiday prices. An examination of the price competitiveness of both tour operators and resorts is therefore important.

RESULTS

The effects of the different explanatory variables - star ratings, tour operators, resorts and hotel facilities - on the prices of package holidays are given in Table 5.5. The implied percentages included in the table show how, other things being equal, the price of the holiday is affected by the presence of the associated variable. Since the set of variables used in this study was obtained from tour operators' brochures and the Spanish Hotel Guide, the percentages should be interpreted with a degree of caution as some may include the effects of other unmeasured variables. The point estimates of the percentage differences between the standardised prices of holidays in one or two star hotels and holidays in three, four and five star hotels were 11, 28 and 110 per cent, respectively.

Considering the tour operators, the estimated equations showed that three tour operators supplied holidays which were (at the 10 per cent confidence level) significantly more expensive than those supplied by Thomson. The point estimates of the price differentials for Arrow, Bass and Cadogan were 29, 6 and 7 per cent, respectively. The figures referred to differentials over and above any price differences resulting from variations in the resorts and hotel facilities. The holidays offered by Arrow and Bass were more expensive at the 5 per cent confidence level. The results thus indicate that these tour operators are less price competitive, since they supplied identical holiday packages for higher prices, although the application of the model to data for other months of the year or to other tourist destinations could lead to different conclusions. The smaller tour operators may charge higher prices owing to an inability to take advantage of the economies of scale which are available to the larger tour operators, but there may also be differences in quality of service during the package holidays which have not been taken into account in the data.

Five resorts, Mijas, Estepona, San Pedro Alcantara, Marbella and Nerja, appeared to be more expensive (at the 5 per cent level of significance) than the base resorts, Torremolinos and Benalmadena, after allowing for the effects of differences between the tour operators and the hotel facilities. The point estimates of the price differences were 47, 33, 22, 20 and 13 per cent, respectively. Although the signs were invariably positive, the sizes of the resort coefficients were rather sensitive to the specification of the rest of the equation. Thus, the magnitudes of the resort price differences were less precise than those relating to the tour operators, which were

Table 5.5: The determinants of the prices of UK package holidays in Malaga

Independent Variables	Estimated Coefficient		Implied % Effect Relative to Thomson
Constant	5.799	(63.22)	
Tour Operators			
Arrow	0.253	(6.43)	28.8
BA/Redwing	-0.02	(-0.77)	-2.0
Bass	0.06	(2.60)	6.2
Cadogan Travel	0.069	(1.65)	7.1
Cosmos	-0.048	(-1.57)	-4.7
Falcon	0.05	(1.23)	5.1
ILG	0.025	(1.03)	2.5

Resorts			Implied % Effect Relative to Torremolinos /Benalmadena
Estepona	0.284	(5.02)	32.8
Fuengirola	0.035	(1.30)	3.6
Marbella	0.182	(5.07)	20.0
Mijas	0.383	(5.72)	46.7
Nerja	0.117	(1.99)	12.4
San Pedro Alcantara	0.202	(2.04)	22.4

Star Rating			Implied % Effect Relative to 1 & 2 Star Hotels
Three Star Hotel	0.104	(3.05)	11.0
Four Star Hotel	0.245	(6.90)	27.8
Five Star Hotel	0.731	(14.11)	107.7

Hotel Facilities			Implied % Effect[1]
No of Rooms	-0.004	(-3.46)	-0.4
Half Board	-0.086	(-2.85)	-8.2
Landing Stage	0.199	(4.07)	22.0
Picturesque Spot	-0.065	(-2.64)	-6.3
Money Changing	0.178	(2.96)	19.5
'Freebies'	0.065	(3.31)	6.7
Children's Pool	0.116	(4.87)	12.3
Central Location	-0.038	(-1.70)	-1.7
Nursery	-0.057	(1.75)	-5.5
Lift[2]	-0.537	(-4.71)	
Nightclub	0.177	(3.26)	
Hairdresser	-0.035	(-0.66)	

Rooms x Lift	0.0043	(3.44)
Rooms x Nightclub	−0.0005	(−2.84)
Rooms x Hairdresser	−0.0001	(−0.47)
Children's Park	−0.015	(−0.61)
Doctor	0.028	(1.02)
Garage	−0.009	(−0.31)
Custody of Valuables	0.017	(0.64)
Facilities for Disabled	0.009	(0.36)
Reading Room	−0.024	(−1.09)
Cinema	−0.02	(−0.43)
No of Sports Activities	−0.013	(−0.97)
Shops	−0.011	(−0.37)
Bingo	−0.051	(−1.07)

Notes: (i) R^2 = 0.952; (ii) The t-values are given in brackets beside the values of the corresponding coefficients.
1. The implied percentage effect on the price is calculated for those variables which are significant at the 10 per cent level.
2. Implied percentage effects have not been calculated for variables with interaction terms since they are not readily interpretable.

considerably more stable. The price differentials are likely to be related to variations between the resorts' environments and images (see also Ashworth & Goodall, 1988), as well as to the limited supply of hotels in Mijas, Estepona, San Pedro and Nerja. Both Mijas and Estepona are very attractive small towns with few tall buildings, unlike Torremolinos and Benalmadena in which there are many blocks of flats and high rise hotels. Mijas differs from the other resorts in being located inland at a short bus or car ride from the Mediterranean. It is also smaller than the other resorts and, characterised by the whitewashed houses typical of the Andalusian region, is closer to the tourist's image of an Andalusian village than the other resorts.

Estepona and Nerja are somewhat larger towns and, though containing some three-storey blocks of flats, are generally characterised by low levels of urbanisation and a relatively attractive form of development. A number of hotels with high star ratings are located outside the town of Estepona and the beach in the whole area is less crowded than in most of the other resorts. The town of Marbella, though catering for less of a 'mass tourism' market and with fewer tower blocks than Torremolinos or Benalmadena, is larger than Estepona and Mijas and the density of development is greater. Like Estepona, a number of the hotels are located outside the town itself and the scenery is generally more attractive than that of the Torremolinos area. Moreover the municipality of Marbella, with its expensive Puerto Banus marina, and the publicity given to the visits to the area by stars such as Frank Sinatra, has cultivated an upper class image which may act as an additional attraction. Fuengirola, though lacking the 'luxury tourism' image of Marbella, has an attractive beach promenade and a good range of entertainments.

A number of the remaining hotel facilities and characteristics were significantly related to package holiday prices. The price was found to be negatively related to the size of the hotel, probably owing to economies of scale. It is possible that consumers interpret this variable as indicating a large, high-rise hotel which is less desirable than a smaller building - which may also be associated with additional, unquantified attractions such as a more pleasing design. This indicates that consideration of the form of hotel development in a resort is important for the future marketing of the resort. The effect on price of the presence of a lift varied for different sizes of hotel. The coefficient of the lift variable was negative but that of the lift x rooms interaction term was positive, indicating a positive price effect of the presence of a lift in large hotels (over 125 bedrooms).

The coefficient of the nightclub variable was positive and that of the nightclub x rooms interaction term was negative, suggesting that the price effect of the presence of a nightclub was smaller in larger hotels. The availability of 'Freebies' also affected the holiday price. 'Freebies' are the incentives which tour operators advertise in brochures, such as presents to clients celebrating birthdays, honeymoons, silver or golden wedding anniversaries, vouchers for a free drink or bottle of wine, nightly entertainments, etc. The 'Freebies' in fact added nearly 7 per cent to the price of a holiday! Additional variables having a significant positive effect upon the price included the presence of a special swimming/paddling pool for children and the availability of money-changing facilties. As expected, half board prices were significantly lower than full board prices.

An additional finding which reinforces the earlier results concerning the importance of location in marketing considerations is the negative effect of the central location of a hotel on the price of a holiday (significant at the 10 per cent level); prices of holidays in hotels which were 'centrally located' were, on average, 3.7 per cent lower. The implication is that hotels in central locations may be noisier and/or further from the beach, so that proximity to the beach results in higher prices. This conclusion is supported by the fact that a small number of hotels had landing stages and the presence of this facility was associated with higher prices. The negative coefficient of the picturesque location variable may also be explained by the location of the majority of such hotels at a considerable distance from the coast. It therefore appears that location is important not only in terms of the resort where the holiday takes place, but in terms of the location of the hotel within the resort; effective marketing of hotels located close to the beach can result in significant increases in price. Further work on the relationship between location and the pricing of tourist accommodation and facilities may therefore be worthwhile.

CONCLUSIONS

The application of the hedonic price model to package holidays in Malaga has demonstrated the effectiveness of the model as a method of estimating the price competitiveness of different tour operators and resorts, and of quantifying the effects of various facilities offered by the hotel or tour operator. The study showed that the star ratings and many of the hotel facilities had a significant effect on the price. The identification of those that were significantly associated with prices, together with the estimation of the extent to which the prices charged varied with their provision, provides tour operators and hoteliers with useful marketing information.

The model also enables the relative price competitiveness of different tour operators and resorts to be estimated. The study demonstrated that there are significant price differences between the tour operators and the resorts which are not related to the variations in the combinations of other characteristics offered in the package holiday. For example, the significant differences between the prices charged by some of the tour operators which supply holidays in the province may result from differences in the effectiveness of their advertising campaigns, or from the smaller operators' inability to take advantage of the economies of scale which are available to the larger tour operators. There may also be differences in the quality of service during the package holidays offered by these tour operators.

The study showed that the prices varied significantly between some of the resorts, probably owing to factors such as the resorts' environments. The importance of location as a marketing consideration was further indicated by the probable negative effects on prices of the size and central location of hotels. It thus appears that location is important not only in terms of the resort where the holiday takes place, but in terms of the location of the hotel within the resort and its proximity to the beach. Consideration of the form and spatial distribution of the hotel development in resorts, together with the resorts' environments, is therefore important for the future marketing of the resorts.

ACKNOWLEDGEMENTS

We would like to thank Betty Sinclair for her work on extracting the data. The support of the Research Committee of the University of Kent is gratefully acknowledged.

REFERENCES

Ashworth, G.J. & Goodall, B. (1988) Tourist images: marketing considerations, pp 213-238 in B. Goodall & G.J. Ashworth (Eds), Marketing in the Tourism Industry, Croom Helm, Beckenham

Barke, M. & France, L. (1986) The marketing of Spain as a holiday destination, Tourist Review, 41 (3), 27-30

Board, J., Sinclair, M.T. & Sutcliffe, C.M.S. (1987) A portfolio approach to regional tourism, Built Environment, 13 (2), 124-137

Bote Gomez, V., Sinclair, M.T., Sutcliffe, C.M.S. & Valenzuela, R.M. (1988) Vertical integration in the British-Spanish tourism industry, paper presented at the Leisure Studies Association, Second International Conference, University of Sussex, Brighton

Cassel, E. & Mendelsohn, R. (1985) The choice of functional form for hedonic price equations, Journal of Urban Economics, 18 (2), 135-142

Clewer, A. & Pack, A. (1986) A hedonic price function for housing in Canterbury, paper presented at the Annual Conference of the British Section, Regional Science Association, University of Bristol

Department of Employment (1987) Travel and tourism - latest statistics, Department of Employment Gazette, 95 (8), 380-392

Fitch, A. (1987) Tour operators in the UK. Survey of the industry, its markets and product diversification, Travel and Tourism Analyst, March, 29-43

Goodall, B., Radburn, M. & Stabler, M. (1988) Market opportunity sets for tourism, Geographical Papers 100: Tourism Series, 1, University of Reading, Reading

Griliches, Z. (1961) Hedonic price indexes for automobiles: an econometric analysis of quality change, in The Price Statistics of the Federal Government, NBER, No. 73, General Series

Halvorsen, R. & Palmquist, R. (1980) The interpretation of dummy variables in semilog equations, American Economic Review, 70, 474-475

Halvorsen, R. & Pollakowski, H.O. (1981) Choice of functional form for hedonic price equations, Journal of Urban Economics, 10 (1), 37-49

Johnston, R. J. (1978) Multivariate Statistical Analysis in Geography, Longman, London

Ministerio de Transportes, Turismo y Comunicaciones (1986) Anuario de Estadisticas de Turismo 1986, MTTC, Madrid

Ministerio de Transportes, Turismo y Comunicaciones (1988) Guia de Hoteles 1988, MTTC, Madrid

Rosen, S. (1974) Hedonic prices and implicit markets: product differentiation in pure competition, Journal of Political Economy, 82 (1), 34-55

Witte, A.D., Sumka, H.J. & Erekson, H. (1979) An estimate of a structural hedonic price model of the housing market: an application of Rosen's theory of implicit markets, Econometrica, 47(5), 1151-73

Chapter 6

STRATEGIES FOR TOURISM DESTINATION DEVELOPMENT: AN
INVESTIGATION OF THE ROLE OF SMALL BUSINESSES

Luiz Moutinho

OVERVIEW AND ROLE ASSESSMENT

The growth of a balanced and financially
healthy regional tourism industry is often viewed
as one major likely contributor to increased
employment and income amongst the region's resident
population. One of the main vehicles in realising
these economic goals is the role played by small
local entrepreneurs. The small business structure
with its self-employment characterisation is a
dominant component in the tourism destination area
product mix.

Small businesses, like large ones, are part of
the total product offered by destinations. Small
business units in tourism, here defined as, for
example, hotels with less than 50 rooms and
hotels/travel agencies with less than 10 employees,
project certain images which contribute to the
overall destination image. In this sense,
evaluation of these 'sub-images' is important to
the success of the tourism destination as a whole.
Few small businesses in the industry, however,
recognise how important they are to the expanding
business of tourism. Because their budgets are too
small to make a major impact on customer
perceptions, they have an even greater interest in
collaborative and cooperative marketing than their
larger competitors. The long-term interests of
smaller businesses therefore lie in finding more
imaginative, customer-relevant extensions to the
existing forms of collaboration.

The tourist's overall experience is composed
of numerous small encounters with a variety of
tourism service providers. Destination tourism
agencies could benefit from a coordinated effort to
assess tourists' perceptions of service quality in
their region and integrate the results into the
area's overall marketing plan. Promotion of

quality aspects may enhance a destination's image and increase tourist traffic to that area, benefiting local businesses.

In terms of environmental analysis in tourism, the practical response of the small business manager is twofold. Firstly, to recognise the collective desirability of both general planning requirements and the particular requirements in any specially designated areas. Secondly, and more fundamentally, to accept the need to consider the environmental impacts of both individual actions and the collective actions of developers. The small business manager should seek to develop environmentally sensitive tourism and, if possible, through the tourism product offered, to educate others in an appreciation of the environmental heritage (Prentice, 1989).

Severe changes in the market place may have a devastating effect on a small business whose resources are more limited than those of a large organisation. Effective management is therefore even more important in the small unit which should be able to adapt more easily to the changing environment. Also, by grouping around central tourism facilities, small business operators can overcome in part their size disadvantage.

Numerous factors contribute to the failure of small businesses, including inconsistent service, poor marketing execution and lack of market analysis. Small business operators must not become too concerned with day-to-day details, otherwise they fail to see the overall picture.

People managing small businesses in the tourism industry may presume that their day-to-day activities are unaffected by public sector policies. An active local authority tourism agency should maintain a close working relationship with all sectors of its tourism industry which is composed of a high proportion of small enterprises. The local businesses should be able to benefit from market information collected by the city department and area tourist boards. They may also be represented in promotional activities organised by these agencies and participate in their programme packages (see also Chp. 12). It is very much a case of knowing how to exploit opportunities resulting from policies emanating from all levels of the public domain. The availability of grant aid from tourist boards is an obvious example, but forms of assistance, from local authority tourism departments and from other government bodies, to train and recruit employees are becoming increasingly valuable (Brown & Essex, 1989). Local governments should review their policies on investment restrictions, seeing that many potential small developers may have equity in the form of land and buildings but not in cash.

Many small businesses in tourism are under-capitalised. Their ability to survive long periods of adverse economic conditions is often limited. Small businesses must seek to identify and occupy profitable niches in the market, although specialisation creates risks from competitive duplication and shifts in market demand. As the travelling public's tastes change, with increasing preference for customised vacations with special interest value, opportunities for smaller companies are created. A small business must identify its niche in the market, establish the requirements of that market and attempt to satisfy these needs.

The marketing function in small tourism businesses is often overlooked, because owners/managers are concerned with other functions, especially operations. Despite their modest investments and resources, marketing tools can be applied by small businesses when properly adjusted to their situational context in order to improve company performance. To be effective a small tourism business needs a sound marketing programme (Harris, 1986). Satisfied guests are a vital part of the marketing process. Certain aspects of marketing may be practised more effectively in a small unit, e.g. the individual needs of customers may be more easily served. Small firms stand to benefit where they service customers better because this leads to increased sales and customer loyalty.

The combined efforts of small businesses with respect to tourist behaviour are commonly seen both in travel market surveys (by analysing potential customers' needs and travel patterns) and in guest surveys (by identifying demographic profiles and level of satisfaction with the tourism product). In a multi-client study of the first type an individual hotel or travel agency can participate directly or through a trade association at a low cost. All businesses can also benefit from the research completed by national tourism agencies as a base for their own marketing strategies.

Small tourism businesses represent a crucial component which determines the domain open to local initiatives. Small entrepreneurs must come together to try to solve their problems and to gain expertise in the various areas of management, including project analysis and development. Small businesses should work together and with their regional tourist boards to ensure that their region is appealing to tourists.

RESEARCH DESIGN

Purpose of the study

This exploratory study attempts to quantify some of the factors which influence the growth strategy and role of small businesses in tourism destination development. Its objectives are:

(i) to establish the relative importance of pre-selected factors contributing to the growth of small businesses in the tourism sector;

(ii) to analyse the correlations among these factors in order to pinpoint action programmes to enhance the role of small tourism businesses in the development of a tourist destination.

Data collection

Data were gathered from a random sample of owners or managers of small hotels and small travel agencies located in the Scottish regions of Strathclyde, Central, and Argyll and Bute. The firms selected were independent businesses meeting the criterion of having the structural and behavioural characteristics dominant in established small businesses, i.e.:

structural   for hotels, not more than 50 rooms; for travel agencies, not more than 10 employees;

behavioural   seeking expansion-, growth- and profit-oriented involvement in destination development.

The data were collected through telephone interviews with the managers or owners of the sampled businesses. This method was selected because of time and cost savings due to the widespread geographical coverage of the sample and because the amount of information required was limited and well defined. Furthermore, it is usually easier to get the cooperation of managers over the telephone than in a face-to-face interview.

From each questionnaire, eight intervally-scaled variables could be extracted, representing eight factors contributing to the future growth of small businesses in tourism and to a more prominent role of the small business sector in tourism destination development. The comparison of intervals is legitimate with an interval scale because the relationships among the differences hold, regardless of the particular constants chosen. The study variables were measured through the use of itemised five-point rating scales, which had a set of distinct response categories associated with the eight main attitudes researched. The different itemised rating scales implied an attitude continuum underlying the response categories. The validity of these eight factors was tested by conducting ten preliminary in-depth interviews with small business managers, not included in the final sample, and preceding the data collection stage. Comments from the pilot study respondents were used in developing the final instrument which would provide the necessary information to conduct the study successfully. The eight most important factors contributing to the growth of small businesses in tourism, which emerged during interviews, were:

(i) <u>Staff training</u> - the need to improve staff technical and performance skills. The need for more knowledge about the 'total regional product' was also emphasised.

(ii) <u>Tax exemptions/incentives</u> - the need for suitable fiscal policies, including tax exemptions, incentives, and rates designed to facilitate new capital investment.

(iii) <u>Marketing support</u> - the need for assistance in marketing, including market research studies, cooperative advertising campaigns, new product development and availability of distribution channels.

(iv) <u>Financial support</u> - the need for making attractive investment loans and capital subsidies available to the small business sector.

(v) <u>Risk-sharing in capital investment</u> - the need to share certain financial risks involved in capital investment with the local tourism authorities according to the nature and strategic importance of each project.

(vi) <u>Better interaction with local tourism authorities</u> - the need to improve the flow of communication with the local authorities responsible for defining tourism policies, as well as to increase the scope of their advisory services.

(vii) <u>Human resources and staff subsidies</u> - the need to make special subsidies and schemes available to small businesses to help solve staff allocation problems: many of which relate to the seasonality factor.

(viii) <u>Management training</u> - the need for effective training programmes designed to provide updated managerial skills to owners and managers of small tourism businesses.

Besides the eight variables described above, two less important factors were mentioned by the small business managers: i) formation of local professional associations and ii) joint efforts in the area of public relations. These two additional factors were not explored in this investigation.

Hypotheses

The preliminary theoretical analysis has suggested the following hypotheses:

There exists a positive correlation between the need for more and better staff training and financial support,
- between marketing support and financial support,
- between the need for risk-sharing in capital investment and financial support,
- between the need for better interaction with local tourism authorities and the need for marketing support,
- between the need for better interaction with local tourism authorities and the need for financial support,
- between the need to obtain staff subsidies and financial support,
- between management training and staff training.

Data analysis

Data analysis involved several statistical

procedures and was conducted in three steps. Firstly, measures of the distributional characteristics of the data were obtained and analysed in terms of i) findings for the total sample and ii) results found for each sub-sample (small hotels and small travel agencies). Secondly, the data were subjected to a multiple regression analysis to determine the impact of seven predictor variables on the dependent variable representing the need for 'better interaction with local tourism authorities'. However, the explained variance was not conclusive in determining the hypothesised associations between the independent variables and the criterion variable. Instead, and thirdly, a correlation analysis was applied to measure the nature and degree of association or covariation between the research variables. The rationale for using correlation analysis was that if the relationships between the variables under study could be expected to persist, then the degree of future relationships could be forecasted.

DISCUSSION OF THE FINDINGS

Significant differences in the mean scores of the eight contributing factors are shown in Table 6.1. Staff training was considered to be the most important factor leading to future growth, followed by the needs for more and better management training and for more support related to the application of marketing techniques which would match the requirements of small businesses operating in the tourism industry. Results also show that a policy of better interaction and cooperation with the local tourism authorities, as well as the deployment of a programme designed to allow for some tax exemptions and incentives, are both perceived by the respondents as important factors contributing to the future growth of the sector. Less important considerations were attached to the remaining three factors which were predominantly related to financial requirements (i.e. financial support, staff and human resources/ subsidies and risk-sharing policies related to capital investment).

Figure 6.1 introduces the comparative rating profiles of small hotels and small travel agencies in relation to these eight factors contributing to future business growth. The comparative rating profiles indicate that, in general, managers of

Table 6.1: Preliminary statistical values

Variables	Mean Score	Std Dev. (σ)	C. of Var. $(\sigma/\bar{x})$	Median
Staff training	4.275	1.132	0.265	5.000
Tax exemptions/ Incentives	3.075	1.289	0.419	3.000
Marketing support	3.700	1.159	0.313	4.000
Financial support	2.375	1.514	0.637	2.000
Risk-sharing in capital investment	2.350	1.528	0.650	2.000
Better interaction with local authorities	3.325	1.328	0.399	3.000
Human resources and staff subsidies	2.525	1.339	0.530	3.000
Management training	3.775	1.387	0.367	4.000

small hotels are more concerned with the
implementation of policies related to all the
factors under investigation than their counterparts
in the travel agency sector. The exceptions are
the needs for 'human resources and staff subsidies'
and 'management training', the former being rated
slightly higher by the travel agents and the latter
being rated as equally important by both sub-
samples. Staff training was perceived as being the
most critical factor contributing to future growth
for both small hotels and small travel agencies.

Small hotel managers and owners regarded
marketing support, management training, better
interaction with local tourism authorities and tax
exemption and incentives as being important factors
contributing to their future growth. They have
considered factors such as, financial support,
risk-sharing in capital investment, and subsidies
related to the allocation of staff and human
resources as being less important areas for
cooperation with the tourism authorities.

Small travel agency managers and owners felt
that, besides the staff training factor, management
training and marketing support were the most
important areas for the future development of their
businesses. They have rated tax exemptions and
incentives, staff subsidies and the need for better
interaction with local tourism authorities as being
less important ways to boost their activities.

Figure 6.1: Comparative rating profiles of small hotels and small travel agencies for the factors contributing to future business growth

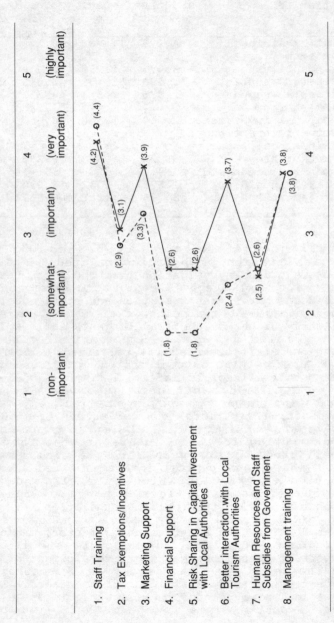

Hotels = solid line (x) ; Travel Agencies = dotted line (o)

Travel agencies were the only group of respondents to rate two factors, 'financial support' and 'risk-sharing in capital investment', as not being important for the development of their operations.

Table 6.2 presents the correlation coefficients between the factors contributing to future small business growth. It can be seen that a strong and statistically significant relationship ($p < 0.001$) exists between the need for financial support and risk-sharing in capital investment. The latter variable is also strongly correlated with the variable expressing the need to obtain staff and human resources subsidies ($p < 0.01$).

The contributing factors concerned with the need for both management and staff training have a positive and statistically significant relationship ($p < 0.02$). The need for better interaction with local tourism authorities is strongly correlated with the need for more support in the marketing area ($p < 0.05$).

The correlations reported in the table indicate that a positive and statistically significant association exists between 'risk-sharing in capital investment' and 'staff training' ($p < 0.05$) and between the needs for 'human resources and staff subsidies' and 'financial support' ($p < 0.05$).

The results reported in the table suggest that the need for more and better staff training is not dependent on the need for overall financial support, as well as that small business needs for both marketing support and financial support do not necessarily require to be associated. There is a very strong correlation between the need for risk-sharing in capital investment and the need for financial support.

The data suggest that there is a need for better interaction with local tourism authorities and the need for marketing support. However, there is no statistically significant correlation between the need for better interaction with local tourism authorities and the need for financial support. Thus, the results seem to indicate that the attainment of a better interaction with the local tourism authorities is more likely to occur through supportive policies in the marketing area than in the context of the financial assistance provided to small businesses.

The findings reveal a strong, positive and statistically significant correlation between the need for human resources and staff subsidies and

113

Table 6.2: Pearson product-moment correlation coefficients of the factors contributing to future growth of small tourism businesses

Variables	No	V1	V2	V3	V4	V5	V6	V7	V8
Staff training	V1								
Tax exemptions/incentives	V2	-.138							
Marketing support	V3	+.006	+.256						
Financial support	V4	+.148	+.143	+.226					
Risk-sharing in capital investment	V5	+.328*	-.183	-.041	+.518****				
Better interaction with local tourism authorities	V6	+.110	+.180	+.331*	+.104	+.220			
Human resources and staff subsidies	V7	+.207	+.021	-.094	+.318*	+.421***	+.089		
Management training	V8	+.367**	-.105	+.037	-.093	-.034	+.027	-.128	

*	$p < 0.05$
**	$p < 0.02$
***	$p < 0.01$
****	$p < 0.001$

N = 40; Source: Markstat

the need for financial support, and also between the need for staff subsidies and the need for risk-sharing policies in relation to capital investment. The need for staff training and management training in the small business sector are also strongly correlated and statistically significant.

The strong correlation representing the need for a risk-sharing policy in relation to the costs involved in staff training seems to indicate a promising strategy leading to the enhancement of the role of small businesses in tourism destination development.

Finally, a negative relationship exists between the need for 'risk-sharing in capital investment' and the need for 'tax exemptions and incentives', although not statistically significant. Further investigation is needed of the likelihood that the more a small tourism firm receives tax exemptions and incentives, the less prominent is its need for sharing capital investment risks.

Another interesting finding, which is also based on a negative correlation coefficient (although again not statistically significant), seems to indicate that an effective training policy for small business owners and managers would minimise the need for subsidies related to the allocation of staff and human resources. Other studies of small tourism business behaviour, such as the work developed by the Exeter Tourism Research Group (Shaw et al., 1987) on Cornwall (which examines marketing strategies of hotels among other factors) have produced results which confirm many of these findings.

CONCLUSION AND IMPLICATIONS

The study provides evidence that an effective training programme which is well-tailored to the needs of managers and staff of small businesses in the tourism field, could be a critical factor in the future growth of the sector. In view of this fact, it is important that additional training and management education (for example, in the field of how to implement the marketing concept in small business in tourism) should be undertaken. The provision of supportive services in the marketing area, such as those involving marketing research, the launching of advertising campaigns and new product development, would clearly help to increase the growth rate of small business in tourism.

The results also indicate that a revised policy of better interaction and communication between the small business sector and the local tourism authorities could greatly benefit the marketability of the region and increase the flow of tourists directed to small business operations. A good example of how this interactive policy can be achieved is the **Beautiful Berkshire** campaign developed by the Thames and Chilterns Tourist Board in conjunction with local authorities and tourism businesses (see Chp. 12). The strong correlation found between the need for better interaction with local authorities and the need for marketing support, clearly identifies the priority in setting up or improving the delivery of advisory services in this management area.

Finally, the application of tax exemptions, allowances and incentives in connection with certain types of investment projects and financial requirements could help to provide enough financial leverage and an increased cash flow which would enable small business managers to re-invest the outlays saved in order to upgrade the overall

115

quality of their tourism products. This policy would lead to improved profitability and might encourage further investments in the sector.

Financial implications

Fiscal incentives can have the dual role of removing obstacles to project profitability, where this would otherwise be marginal, and of accelerating the development process by making the investment climate more attractive than that in other destinations. Fiscal incentives are aimed at encouraging capital investment. They preserve or increase profits during operation. A careful assessment of small business projects will identify those developments of marginal profitability for which a fiscal incentive will actually realise a surplus. Tax incentives can include: income tax reduction, net operating loss carry-over, real estate tax exemption, preferential energy tariffs, tax credits on domestic capital equipment, tax exemption on re-invested profits and capital expenditure allowances. Whilst not geared specifically to provide assistance to tourism operations in the form of business planning and management services, enterprise agencies located in the destination area could play a major advisory role to local small tourism businesses.

A system of financial incentives which operates within the framework of a tourism policy is evidence of a commitment to tourism growth and will recognise and evaluate the opportunity cost of grant and loan financing (Bodlender & Ward, 1989). Small local businesses may be offered preferential rates of benefit, particularly as they form the dominant economic unit in the industry. The tourism authorities can play a key role: they may act as a catalyst by 'pump-priming' the project through cash grants, by expressing confidence in the project and in so doing stimulating the flow of commercial funds, and by giving or obtaining expert advice and training (Wanhill, 1989).

The quality issue

The establishment of service standards is a powerful means to guarantee a priori a level of excellence. Quality standard is, therefore, a reference value for the economic action of the small tourism firm. Quality control then becomes a regulating mechanism through which the elements of quality are maintained at an optimal value from the points of view of both the small company and the customer.

For example, the average hotel in the UK has approximately 25 rooms and is just as likely to offer a quality product as a hotel with 500 or more rooms. In fact, the small business is in some ways in a better position to supply a quality product than the large chains. The owner of a small hotel has more direct contact with the customers, as well as more direct control over and influence on the employees and their standards of performance. In addition, the small hotel is able to attract a very specific market segment and cater very closely to its needs (Lockwood, 1989).

Marketing implications

There is a tendency for small firms to add new services and broaden target markets in order to grow. The marketing planning process forces a systematic evaluation of strategies so that haphazard changes do not occur. For the small firm in the tourism industry, market penetration is probably the most important strategy available. Successful market penetration relies on more effective and efficient utilisation of available resources. Overall, the most critical element is to have a clearly defined business with a distinctive image serving the needs of a specific market segment.

Competent marketing research is needed, particularly as the range and number of tourist attractions, and thus competition, increases into the 1990s. Besides surveying one's own visitors, marketing research is properly a local authority or tourism association function, and the small business manager should seek to convince these agencies of this need. Marketing research may of necessity have to be undertaken at a less sophisticated level, however, this does not mean that the results are less effective.

Tourism management, especially on the local level, still lacks a proper understanding of how to evade competitive pressure by using the strategic tools of segmentation and positioning. Small companies in tourism can really afford to address only a 'known buyer' or a well-defined customer, and this is where psychographic segmentation can be of significant assistance (Crnkovic, 1989).

The application of positioning strategies for the development of small tourism businesses can be effective, efficient and profitable. New market opportunities can be defined and pursued; crucial segmentation and concentration strategies can be implemented; new tourism products can be developed; low-budget promotional campaigns can be defined and launched; after-sales service policies can be pursued in order to capture more repeat business; and an overall marketing plan can also be devised as well as marketing strategies designed to attain realistic goals and objectives.

Small businesses can use competitive analysis to their advantage. Large companies must through their size either have a cost advantage in delivering standardised tourism products or control a significant share of the market. The small firm has to avoid challenging the large firms directly on their own ground by developing new markets or redefining markets where large companies have no particular comparative advantage. Competitive analysis will help to determine the strengths and weaknesses of the current market and identify areas of potential growth, subject to the appropriate marketing strategies. Marketing control mechanisms such as cost analysis, sales analysis, profitability analysis and customer segment analysis should also be implemented.

Managing the promotion mix is just as important to small businesses as to large tourism organisations. Small businesses should work cooperatively to advertise their products. Personal relationships with the trade should be cultivated. Promotions via a local authority brochure or tourism association should be questioned for their effect. The entrepreneur should ask critically, 'how does the authority or association promote my product?' and 'can the authority or association better promote my attraction?' Individually, the small business is unlikely to be able to afford to target its promotion. However, local authorities and tourism associations do not need to be so unspecific in their marketing and promotion. Small businesses should press these bodies to justify or redirect their efforts. By pooling financial resources in a consortium, individual companies may be able to afford to advertise in expensive overseas markets.

Small businesses in tourism can manage their own promotion mix. Even on limited budgets, promotion can be accomplished through cooperative advertising. A small business company can find a powerful remedy to offset economies of scale and other competitive advantages of larger organisations by engaging in cooperative and joint promotional programmes. While advertising can be an effective medium of communication with the market, for some small businesses, such as hotels, personal selling may be more efficient. Publicity can be managed through news releases. Small businesses should work with regional tourist boards to keep informed, if possible, of travel writers who happen to be in the region.

The direct selling operation can be an effective form of distribution for a small tourism business. A major objective will be to ensure that an adequate level of awareness exists in the market. This can be achieved through the development of a suitable customer database or sufficient promotional effort. A benefit of the direct sell approach for small businesses is the ability to monitor and control all aspects of the selling process and simultaneously to establish and maintain contact with customers. This enables the business to obtain constant feedback on its marketing efforts and also to monitor changes in the market place. This information, gathered as part of the normal business routine, can help small businesses compete against the resources of larger companies (Parkinson, 1989).

A major problem facing small businesses which wish to undertake a marketing audit is how to obtain the required level of objectivity in assessment. Generally, it is difficult for small business managers to be objective about their operation, as they are invariably involved in all aspects of the business. The integration and assimilation of different perspectives may be a time-consuming task, but the results can be revealing. A regular review using checklists can build a database of the marketing performance of the small business which can be used to model outcomes of alternative actions (Parkinson, 1989).

Cooperative strategies

In the tourism industry, cooperative arrangements are almost inevitable. The diversity of firms, products and services in the industry increases the opportunities for cooperative agreements. Although, in most cases, the resulting impact of these cooperative strategies focuses on 'destination image', small tourism companies could implement action programmes specifically designed to enhance and strengthen their own 'business sub-image', either as a global sector of the economy or by total tourism product component (i.e. hospitality, tourism retailing, sports, leisure and amusement centres, shopping units, cultural organisations, etc.). For example, there are a number of hotels already offering entertainment as a focal point of visits and they could cooperate locally to promote the concept of 'entertainment-hotels'. As a tourist draw, the impact of many small entertainment enterprises can be considerable when concentrated, for instance, in a local festival. However, precise targeting of the market is required.

By combining resources, small firms can achieve greater economies of scale and lower unit costs than if they acted alone. Examples of cooperative strategies include horizontal and vertical arrangements in advertising, sales promotion, distribution and pricing. By joining forces, small firms can increase their negotiatory leverages with marketing intermediaries and institutions such as banks, wholesalers and retailers.

Through cooperation between the managers of small tourism businesses, much can be done in the area of destination development (e.g. collective, low- budget promotional and marketing campaigns, training programmes, etc.). Also relevant to smaller businesses is marketing cooperation between different sectors - especially accommodation and attractions - in which each can act as a promotional and distribution outlet for the other. Such cooperation may lead to the possibility of cooperative product formulation, advertising and promotion campaigns, joint representation at workshops and travel trade fairs, and so on.

Universities, polytechnics, colleges and consultancy companies can also be involved in these ventures. By providing executive development training programmes and consultancy services to small tourism businesses they can contribute to and facilitate the growth of the sector. Ultimately, small businesses in the tourism industry can influence all levels of government by playing an active role within the industry and trade associations.

FURTHER RESEARCH

The findings of this study are of an exploratory character. Further research on the role of small businesses in tourism destination development should be undertaken because the findings reported are limited by both the size of the sample and its nature. Future research analysis could also improve the reliability of the findings by adding several more factors contributing to the future growth of the small business sector in the tourism industry. Further research could also concentrate on the analysis of the degree of applicability of the eight contributing factors used in this study in the case of formation of new businesses, since new indigenous entrepreneurship is likely to be encouraged by regional tourism development. However, the results provide a benchmark and platform for future investigation and diagnosis.

REFERENCES

Bodlender, J. A. & Ward, T.J. (1989) A profile of investment incentive, in S.F. Witt & L.A. Moutinho (Eds) Tourism Marketing and Management Handbook, Prentice-Hall International, Hemel Hempstead

Brown, G.P. & Essex, S.J. (1989) The formulation and implementation of tourism policies in the public sector, in S.F. Witt & L.A. Moutinho (Eds) Tourism Marketing and Management Handbook, Prentice-Hall International, Hemel Hempstead

Crnkovic, S. (1989) Psychographic segmentation, in S.F. Witt & L.A. Moutinho (Eds) Tourism Marketing and Management Handbook, Prentice-Hall International, Hemel Hempstead

Harris, R. L. (1986) A six step marketing approach for the small business, pp 270-282 in B. Joseph, L.A. Moutinho & I. Vernon (Eds) Tourism Services Marketing: Advances in Theory and Practice, Special Conference Series, Vol. II, Academy of Marketing Science, Coral Gables, Miami, USA

Lockwood, A. (1989) Quality management in hotels, in S.F. Witt & L.A. Moutinho (Eds) <u>Tourism Marketing and Management Handbook</u>, Prentice-Hall International, Hemel Hempstead

Parkinson, L. (1989) Hotel marketing audit, in S.F. Witt & L.A. Moutinho (Eds) <u>Tourism Marketing and Management Handbook</u>, Prentice-Hall International, Hemel Hempstead

Prentice, R. (1989) Environmental analysis in tourism, in S.F. Witt & L.A. Moutinho (Eds) <u>Tourism Marketing and Management Handbook</u>, Prentice-Hall International, Hemel Hempstead

Shaw, G., Williams, A. & Greenwood, J. (1987) <u>Tourism and the Economy of Cornwall: A Firm Level Study of Operating Characteristics and Employment</u>, Tourism Research Group, University of Exeter, Exeter

Wanhill, S. (1989) Investment policy in tourism, in S.F. Witt & L.A. Moutinho (Eds) <u>Tourism Marketing and Management Handbook</u>, Prentice-Hall International, Hemel Hempstead

II

SHAPING THE PRODUCT

The main strength of opportunity sets as a descriptive and analytical instrument is that attention is concentrated upon the interaction between demand and supply - the customer and the product - the holidaymaker and the holiday. Unlike the more usual economic models, the opportunity set approach begins with this relationship and only subsequently develops an analysis of demand and supply as explanatory variables. It is therefore logical in the preceding chapters to focus upon the conjunction of the two main sets of 'opportunities', namely those offered by the industry (Stabler, Chp. 2) and those considered for purchase by the customer (Kent, Chp. 3). These applications of opportunity sets described in the above chapters have concentrated upon aspects of the marketing, or pricing in the Sinclair et al. case, of inclusive tour packages (Chp. 5). This focus has led inevitably to a series of implicit or explicit definitions about the tourism product, the producer, and the point and method of the marketing transaction. The product is defined in practice as the saleable package, the producer is the intermediary assembler, whether travel agent, tour operator or tourism association, and the point of transaction is in the places of residence of customers.

When the focus is shifted however onto the nature of the product being offered or consumed then a significantly different view is obtained which requires a re-evaluation of the nature of the 'sets' as defined so far, and of their conjunction. In particular the relationship between the tourism product and the tourism destination requires further attention. The next group of chapters all consider aspects of this relationship. In particular the most fundamental characteristic of tourism destinations is that they are places and this self-evident observation carries a number of consequences for the use of places as tourism products that are by no means so obvious. All four of the following chapters describe how places, at different spatial scales and offering different sets of holiday attractions can become tourism products, thereby incorporating the distinctly spatial qualities of destinations into the model as more than explanatory variables but as product sets in their own right. It should be stressed that in all four cases introduced below the process of 'becoming' such a product is emphasised. In other words places are not tourism products by virtue of their intrinsic qualities, but are made such by intervention of various sorts, that shapes the attributes of destinations into marketable tourism products.

There are a number of questions implicit in the descriptions of quite different tourism products in all the chapters in the following section. These are, 'who shapes the place product? and for which market?' and, 'what is the functional or spatial relationship between this tourism product and other place products?' In Jansen-Verbeke's example, tourism is one function among many that coexist in the particular spatial context of the 'festival market'. Ashworth's 'historic cities' are different products for different markets shaped from different aspects of the same place. De Haan et al. introduce the hierarchical characteristic of places by examining how different tourism products may be shaped at different spatial scales within the same region. In all three of these chapters public authorities of various sorts, operating at various scales for diverse motives, have initiated or coordinated the creation of the product, even where the private sector has had a major role in its marketing. In the Goodall and Bergsma chapter, however, the product has been shaped largely by commercial intermediaries and sold through the medium of brochures.

The character, attributes and components of destinations as tourism products differs according to the viewpoint adopted - that of the destination tourism agencies and businesses, that of the tour operators and that of the actual tourists. The destination tourism agency needs to ensure that its tourism place product(s) accurately reflects the destination's comparative advantage(s). However, as portrayed by different tour operators a particular destination or place product may be represented differently, even when sold within the same market segment. Place products are likely therefore to undergo some transformation, even

misrepresentation, when marketed via such
intermediaries, as Goodall and Bergsma demonstrate.
In the long run this is likely to be to the
disadvantage of the tourist destination in so far
as holidaymakers' satisfactions will not have been
maximised. Assuming tour operators' and
destination tourism agencies' product images of the
destination coincide, discrepancies may still
exist, as de Haan et al. show, between the local
place product promoted within the destination to
visitors by the destination tourism agency and the
visitors' image(s) of, more especially their
holiday behaviour within, that destination.

In all of these chapters the holiday
destination is the product. The holiday far from
being a mass produced identical experience sold by
intermediaries at the place of origin of visitors,
is an extremely varied set of individual
experiences offered by the equally varied
characteristics of places. But getting the product
right at the destination is only part of the
battle.

Chapter 7

LEISURE + SHOPPING = TOURISM PRODUCT MIX

Myriam Jansen-Verbeke

INTRODUCTION

Leisure shopping has become one of the buzz words in retail development planning and shopping is playing an increasingly important role in the tourism attraction of places. The combination of both trends explains why shopping areas in many inner cities in Western Europe are now being recognised as an element in the local tourism product. **Leisure shopping** has become an element in marketing in the tourism industry and in urban planning, despite the fact that the phenomenon as such has yet to be defined (Boudreau, 1983).

Shopping in the town centre has had a leisure dimension ever since people went to town to obtain goods and services. Our notions of attractive town centres are embedded in a long urban history; going into town for the weekly or yearly markets in medieval society is probably one of the origins of the urban leisure function (Brand, 1987). Why then is the concept of leisure shopping now being introduced as a new phenomenon? To some extent the present attention paid to leisure shopping can be explained as part of the increasing demand for leisure activities in general.

What turns a shopping area into a leisure environment, what makes shopping a leisure activity and how valid are the arguments which look upon shopping areas as a tourism resource? Some speculative reflections on this combination of leisure-shopping and tourism are discussed below. Four different aspects will be considered:

(i) the consumers' point of view which initiates a discussion on target groups;
(ii) the supply-side conditions or the characteristics of the product mix;
(iii) the role of urban planners;
(iv) the sense or nonsense of promoting shopping tourism.

LEISURE SHOPPING AND THE CONSUMER

Every attempt so far to define leisure shopping from the consumers' point of view has failed to give either precise indications of what it is or explanations of why, when, where, how and for whom shopping can become a leisure experience. Some indicators have proved to be useful in analysing shopping as a leisure activity and experience; such as personal characteristics, the company during the shopping visit or the motives for the visit. In addition a large number of external factors are assumed to play a role; such as the weather conditions, the time of the year (e.g. Christmas shopping is different from bargain shopping in the sales period) but no attention has been given to the environmental characteristics. These will be discussed in the context of defining the leisure product below.

Looking at the behaviour of the consumer can only give a partial indication of the leisure dimension of the visit. In the first place the motives for a visit are a direct indication; a visit with the intention of purchasing daily goods is clearly different from a visit with the explicit purpose of window shopping, meeting friends, looking around for interesting bargains, buying gifts, etc.

According to some surveys which dealt with visitors' behaviour there seems to be a relationship with the duration of the visit as well (Jansen-Verbeke, 1988). The more the leisure aspect is predominant, the longer a visitor tends to loiter in the shopping area or in town, possibly combining the visit with other activities such as having a drink in a pavement cafe, having a meal in a restaurant or even concluding the shopping visit with going to the cinema or some other kind of cultural activity. This raises the question, to what extent can leisure shopping be defined by analysing the visitors' pattern of activities? As a rule it proves to be very difficult to distinguish the actual behaviour pattern of visitors with leisure-inspired motives from that of other shopping customers. The leisure experience of shopping is dependent upon the state of the mind of the visitor.

In order to distinguish leisure shopping from regular shopping, the assumption was made that the kind of goods purchased and the amount of expenditure could be useful indicators. There is

129

cogency in this line of reasoning, but further research needs to be undertaken before generalisations can be drawn.

So far, the only valid indicator with respect to the leisure aspect of shopping lies in the information about the place of residence and the distance travelled to visit the shopping area. The hypothesis is that the further one travels from the home base (or the temporary place of residence if on holiday) to visit a shopping area, the more likely it is that this visit has a leisure-based motive and as a rule will lead to a leisure experience.

This line of interpretation focuses on the combination of leisure shopping and shopping tourism (Kent et al., 1983). The fact that shopping proves to be one of the most important activities of tourists leads to the conclusion that shopping facilities are playing an important role in the tourism attractiveness of a place. The simple statement 'shopping is what tourists do, so it's tourism' contains much truth and at the same time poses a major challenge for the researcher in this particular field of tourism. The first problem is to define as clearly as possible the characteristics of such a tourism product.

THE LEISURE-SHOPPING MIX

Not every urban shopping area has the same credentials for becoming an element in the local tourism product. Undeniably, the structure and symbolism of town centres play an important role. Strong symbolic values of historic centres assure their social significance as meeting places, places for shopping and eventually for fun and entertainment. Very little is known about the environmental conditions which foster the leisure experience of a shopping visit. In the context of the historic inner cities of Western Europe, there is the strong assumption that the historic setting is a major point of attraction which adds considerably to the appreciation of a leisure environment (Ashworth & de Haan, 1985). Empirical research in different historic inner cities confirms the hypothesis that the combination of an historic setting and a shopping area offers an inviting environment for leisure (Jansen-Verbeke, 1989).

Nevertheless, the growth of out-of-town

shopping since the 1970s, and the manner in which suburban shopping areas, and rebuilt inner urban shopping areas, are now developing, should also be taken into consideration. In general these shopping areas are easily accessible, have sufficient parking facilities, are designed as attractive pedestrian precincts and above all are offering a range of goods and facilities which is highly competitive with that of the traditional inner city shopping areas. Recently there is an even stronger tendency to add more recreational facilities to these modern shopping centres. Although Dutch physical planning has restrained this kind of development most other West European countries have developed suburban **mega-shopping centres** inducing a pattern of shopping behaviour which reflects in many ways the North American style.

The trend towards combined shopping and leisure centres, preferably indoors, is becoming very general nowadays. The shopping-leisure mix on the supply side seems to be a question of trial and error for both the developers and planners of shopping centres. As not much is known about the demand for leisure facilities in a shopping environment, there is a wide range of experiments now being carried out (Blomeyer, 1988).

In Dutch inner cities the idea of a shopping-leisure mix is usually handled in a small scale manner. The first step has been to create pedestrian precincts and find solutions for the parking problem. This procedure seems to be a primary requirement in planning for a leisure environment. Lately the interest in the conditions, potentials and effects of leisure shopping has increased. This has led to initiatives such as improving the image of the urban shopping areas, e.g. planning indoor shopping galleries, refurbishing the facades, improving the design, the pavement, the illumination, the sign boards, introducing new decorations, adding benches, flowers, water fountains, music, etc. So far these initiatives can be seen as an incentive for upgrading retailing in the town centre.

More fundamental intervention in the shopping-leisure mix, such as rearranging the spatial distribution of shops and other facilities or planning for new recreational elements to reinforce the attractiviness of the area, are still in a conceptual stage. In practice, the restrictions arising from the historic heritage of inner cities, the fact of dealing with small scale areas, the

131

traditional priorities in functional uses and the possible conflicts between different groups of users considerably complicate the attainment of an optimal shopping-leisure mix.

Why should there be leisure in the retail environment and, in addition, which kind of leisure facilities can function as a magnet in attracting more people to the shopping area? Traditional shopping areas usually include leisure elements such as eating and drinking places, gambling and entertainment. New trends have led to an enormous increase in fast food restaurants and take-aways and even in some places a new casino.

One major consequence of this trend towards a shopping-leisure mix in the urban centres is a growing emphasis on a particular type of retailing. The development of a more leisure-oriented shopping area implies a growing predominance of special shops, gift shops, souvenir shops and catering facilities. A good example of such changes in the range of shops is demonstrated in the well-known tourist streets such as the Kalverstraat in Amsterdam, Carnaby Street in London, or the small streets around the Grande Place in Brussels. These are examples of an unplanned growth in leisure shopping.

The problem posed by changing retail patterns and patterns of spatial behaviour in general is a fundamental one, for it affects a whole urban tradition (Brand, 1987). In many other places though, there are examples of a planned shopping-leisure mix. The quality of the environmental design is important as well as a system to control the combination of retail shops and different recreational facilities. Finding the optimal range of facilities in a particular situation seems to be the outcome of an experimental planning process. Undeniably some North American experiments are a source of inspiration. The Guinness Book of Records example, the West Edmonton Mall in Alberta, Canada obviously is the most debated experiment. This indoor shopping leisure mall is at the moment unique; offering more than 800 shops, parking space for 27,000 cars and including a wide range of varied leisure attractions so that leisure facilities account for approximately 10 per cent of the total floor space. The leisure 'ambiance' dominates throughout the entire mall, for instance in the way the catering facilities are integrated in the project, the theming of special shopping areas such as the European street and the Bourbon street. In addition to this shopping-leisure complex there is the Fantasyland hotel offering accommodation in 360 rooms, of which 120 are 'themed'.

Apparently all the ingredients are present to make this mega-shopping-leisure centre a major tourism attraction. The experiences with this largest shopping centre developed to date in the world will influence views in other countries. Long before the stage of evaluation of this project is reached, it will be copied, or at least the ideas, now unique, will become common.

A preliminary conclusion is that the shopping-leisure mix must be unique to be successful and attractive in the long run and to become a consistent element of the tourism product. This holds a major challenge for urban planners and tourism promoters.

LEISURE SHOPPING AS A PLANNING ASSET

Reshaping the traditional town centres into shopping-leisure areas has become the objective of many local planning policies. Why has it become so important to turn traditional urban retail areas into places for fun shopping and leisure and to promote these places as elements of the local tourism product? Concern about preservation of the historic heritage can be one reason, although it is more likely to be justified in economic revitalisation programmes. Spatial organisation and economic management of urban areas have become strongly interlinked in the views of urban planners. Slowly but surely the awareness has grown that preservation of the historic heritage could be an essential line in the tourism marketing of the place (Ashworth, 1988). The central function as such became threatened by an increasing trend towards decentralisation in retail supply and by a growing standardisation of products. In addition poor accessibility in many traditional shopping areas led to another point of weakness in the new competition with suburban shopping areas.

The development of modern shopping malls in the residential urban areas or at the urban fringe has increased the need to look for new impulses for the inner city shopping areas (Hadju, 1988). Speculation about the future role of town centres is one of the major issues (King, 1987). The search for planning instruments which could stop the current process of downgrading in many inner cities found a solid basis in the social changes towards a more leisure-oriented society in which urban recreation plays a role. The demand for leisure facilities is growing and the trick is to use this opportunity as an instrument for urban revitalisation. Adding a new function, or rather reinforcing an existing leisure function, fits in very well with the 'fourth wave society' in which the need for leisure plays a prime role (Robson, 1987). In order to turn leisure into a planning gain it needs sensible solutions in finding combinations between the traditional urban function and the new role as places for leisure.

The one solution of turning the historic centre into an open air museum with an increased value on the tourism market does not seem to be ideal for this purpose. Upgrading the central function of older towns needs more than the revenues of tourism. A second opportunity could be to integrate the existing leisure and tourism elements into a complete product. This often implies a face-lift of the retail shops and, not least, a careful planning of the shopping-leisure mix in terms of location and dispersion, branch assortment and quality of the environment. A third opportunity is more drastic and involves creating new leisure facilities within the existing urban network of shops, catering and entertainment facilities. Indoor facilities, such as theatres, cinema complexes, libraries, hobby centres, swimming pools and other cultural or sports facilities are strategically incorporated into the urban environment. In many cases public investment resources are insufficient to implement the third solution, so compromises have to be found.

Obviously the list of recreational facilities can be expanded, but it is clear that these are the ingredients for the 21st century town centre which corresponds with the fourth wave life-style. The anticipation of new forms of sociological and technological organisation of urban space needs to be expressed by a reformulation of planning views and planning instruments. The gap between the present well balanced and multifunctional town centre with a traditional shopping area, cultural, catering and entertainment facilities and the idea of a town centre as a social nub in a leisure society involves considerable rethinking about the quality of the urban environment and the range of facilities.

New retailing methods and inspired design of shopping areas are the tools not only for increasing the number of visitors and the invitation to spend more money, but also for producing an inviting leisure environment. The economic objective of planning thus becomes secondary to the leisure focus in the planning of shopping areas. Several empirical studies (Jansen-Verbeke, 1988) point out the risk that the more the leisure function takes over the shopping function, the more risky is the attraction of large groups of low spenders. Obviously this perspective does not fit in very well with the current economic views on urban planning and particularly on the planning and promotion of urban shopping areas.

SHOPPING TOURISM FILLS THE GAP

Can the development and the promotion of shopping tourism fill the gap, or take advantage of the investment in a shopping-leisure environment? An attractive urban shopping area, especially in historic centres, is considered to be a tourism resource, not merely by its supply of retail shops but mainly because of the historic setting. To some this is an additional value which needs to be exploited by strategic planning, to others the historic heritage needs to be preserved as intact as possible (see Chp. 8). Theoretically a combination of both objectives is possible, in practice it means a continous debate on how to manage the historic patrimony and finding new functions which can flourish in old forms (Fondersmith, 1988). A comprehensive programme of integrating historic buildings into the shopping-leisure mix is required as a starting point for the local tourism planning and promotion. Current planning policies are characterised by an emerging concern for tourism which risks producing a biased view of the future of urban centres.

Shopping tourism has become a marketing concept without realising fully the weaknesses of the present product mix or even the relevant trends in tourists' consumer behaviour. Given this perspective a number of concerns can be formulated as 'if' statements:

(i) If the glitter and the blitz of mega-shopping-leisure centres is a prime condition needed to attract large numbers of visitors

135

(Blomeyer, 1988), including tourists, then the competitive situation of traditional shopping centres is a very weak one.

(ii) If the process of standardisation of products and scale enlargement of retailing continues, then the pull capacity of one shopping place compared to another will gradually disappear.

(iii) If the trend towards equalisation of prices, at least within Western Europe, proceeds then a major incentive for shopping tourism will vanish.

(iv) If the trend towards imitative planning for tourism gains momentum then the risks of exchanging the uniqueness of a place for the benefit of an _ad hoc_ attractive tourism product are high.

(v) If there is no place for realism concerning the tourism potentials of urban shopping areas, even being part of an attractive tourism product, then disillusion will come quickly.

(vi) If the trend towards forms of low-budget tourism persists or becomes more general, the economic benefits of shopping tourism may be overestimated.

These speculative statements are a direct invitation to look more critically at the opportunities and threats of the 'shopping-leisure-tourism' product mix.

The current success of some shopping centres largely depends on their site and situation characteristics and on the uniqueness of the facilities and attractions they have to offer. Looking more closely into each of these particular success stories can accumulate experience in tourism planning and form the basis for new planning philosophies in which the uniqueness of the product is more highly valued than short-term success (Inskeep, 1988).

Nevertheless, there is a definite shift towards opportunistic planning, argued as an appropriate management style, to tackle urban problems. This trend may be criticised where it reflects only short-term objectives.

Continued research and experiments in this field of urban planning are needed, putting the challenges into a wider perspective of economic, cultural and social processes. Recognising the demands of a leisure society and responding to this demand by finding environmental and economic solutions within the existing framework of the West European urban heritage is not an easy task. Planning for the leisure environment of tomorrow means that today researchers in tourism planning need to work hard in their non-leisure time.

REFERENCES

Ashworth, G.J. (1988) Marketing the historic city for tourism, pp 162-175 in B. Goodall & G.J.Ashworth (Eds) Marketing in the Tourism Industry, Croom Helm, London

Ashworth, G.J. & de Haan, T.Z. (1985) The tourist historic city, Field Studies Series, 8, GIRUG, Groningen

Blomeyer, G. (1988) Myth of malls and men, The Architects' Journal, May, 38-45

Boudreau, G. (1983) Shopping for recreation, Canadian Parks, Recreation Association, September, 13-14

Brand, P. (1987) What are you doing? asked Milligan. Or the physics and metaphysics of town centres, The Planner, April, 23-26

Fondersmith, J. (1988) Downtown 2040; making cities fun, The Futurist, March-April, 9-17

Hadju, J. (1988) Pedestrian malls in West-Germany: perception of their role and stages in their development, Journal of the American Planning Association, 54(3), 325-335

Inskeep, E. (1988) Tourism planning: an emerging specialisation, Journal of the American Planning Association, 54(3), 360-372

Jansen-Verbeke, M. (1988) Leisure, Recreation and Tourism in Inner Cities. Explorative Case Studies, Netherlands Geographical Studies, 58, Amsterdam/Nijmegen

Jansen-Verbeke, M. (1989) Inner cities and urban tourism resources in the Netherlands; new challenges for local authorities, in I. Henry, et al. (Eds) Leisure and Urban Processes: Critical Studies of Leisure Policy in West European cities, Methuen, London

Kent, W.E., et al., (1983) Shopping: tourism's unsung hero(ine), Journal of Travel Research, 2, 2-4

King, W.(1987) The future role of town centres, The Planner, April, 18-22

Robson, B. (1987) The meeting of extremes in the inner city, The Planner, April, 13-15

Chapter 8

THE HISTORIC CITIES OF GRONINGEN: WHICH IS SOLD TO WHOM?

Gregory Ashworth

SELLING HISTORIC CITIES AS TOURISM PRODUCTS

The application of ideas and terminology drawn from marketing science has been particularly apparent in that sector of tourism which makes use of the past as a tourist attraction. Selling the past, in various forms, to the present has become one of the largest and most profitable parts of the tourism industry in many different contexts world-wide. Similarly, those concerned with the discovery and revelation of the past and the preservation and care of its surviving artefacts, whether in the form of buildings, museum exhibits or more broadly associations with historical events and personalities, have, for various reasons, become increasingly concerned with the economic potential of the information in their possession and the objects in their care. Thus, from two quite different origins a consensus has emerged that the past can be exploited as a resource, as part of a tourism product that can be marketed to particular groups of visitors.

As cities have in practice pursued this line of development most vigorously, the term **historic city** can be used to identify this product. The purpose of this chapter is not to pursue definitions of this term (which has been attempted from both the supply and demand sides by Ashworth & de Haan, 1986), nor to raise the practical difficulties of delimiting and regionalising such a concept (Ashworth, 1985). The more limited objective here is to identify and describe the **historic city** within a single urban area. To this end the main assumptions implicit in the concept of the **historic city** as a tourism product will be simply restated. On the basis of these assumptions and the corollaries that logically can be infered from them, the concept will be applied to the city of Groningen, The Netherlands. Such an application makes explicit many of the implications implicit in the initial assumptions and preconceptions contained in the concept. Finally this very clarification of what is implied in such a product-oriented approach will, it is hoped, actually increase its effectiveness in attaining its goals.

THE ASSUMPTIONS

Five main sets of assumptions are implicit in the concept of the **historic city** as a tourism product, as it is widely used. It is no part of this argument to claim that the following statements are either original, indisputable, let alone desirable; merely that they underpin the many practical expressions of tourism development and planning in the field of **historic tourism**, whether practictioners are aware of them or not, and are inescapable concomitants of the use of a marketing terminology and philosophy.

The **historic city** is a functional urban region. 'History' is being used in this context adjectivally to describe a set of activities, that in turn is being used as part of a regionalisation, categorising all or part of the city. The term is therefore used in precisely the same way as are such designations as 'industrial', 'shopping' or 'administrative' city. It is thus an identifiable, delimitable phenomenon within the contemporary city, interacting in various ways with other such functional regional designations. The **historic city** as a product is rarely in a monopolistic occupation of the city or its spatial sub-divisions. Although a distinguishable product it coexists in the same physical space with a range of other such 'cities'. The importance of this assumption will depend upon the nature of this coexistence within particular regional functional mixes, the problems that result and the local planning reactions to them. The **historic city** is shaped from relic survivals from the past. 'History', in the sense of that which has occurred in the past, is assumed to provide raw materials which are processed to create a contemporary product. To continue the manufacturing analogy, implicit in the use of marketing terminology, it is necessary to specifiy the nature of this process and describe its use of historic materials. The process can be labelled 'interpretation'. This is the selection from history of events, characters, relics, monuments or place associations, and the packaging and presentation of such a selection, by whatever means, to the consumer, in this case the tourist. Neither the individual elements selected nor the composition of the resulting packages and their communication to the market have any direct relationship to 'authenticity', in the sense of the accurate objective revelation of the past as an immutable truth. Mythology, literature, folk memory and popular fantasy can thus also be fed into the interpretation process. The product so manufactured can be labelled **heritage**. Heritage is thus a contemporary created saleable experience, produced by the interpretation of history. A critical assumption that must be stressed here is that, by logical and etymological derivation, heritage is defined by the consumer not by the raw materials that went into its construction. This in turn raises the potentially troublesome consequence that the link between the producers of the materials and the consumer market is incomplete. The market defines what is, or is not, heritage but those concerned with the discovery or care of the raw materials from which this product is constructed, such as for example the custodians of historic monuments or museums, define their tasks in terms of various values intrinsic to the materials themselves, and only subsequently, and often reluctantly, accept the existence of heritage markets. Finally it is implicit in the above assumption that the same historical raw materials can be processed through interpretation in different ways to produce a variety of different heritage products. Thus it is conceivable that many different **historic cities** can exist, or more accurately be created, from the history of the same city. Such variety will derive from the essential market orientation of the heritage concept. Different markets will produce different **historic cities** at the same time, and each time period will produce the **historic city** appropriate to the then existing market.

Thus we arrive at the composite assumption that the **historic city** is a recognisable urban functional regional designation composed of selected historic elements which have been processed by interpretation to produce a marketable heritage. The identification of such **historic cities** is not intended to be a test of the validity of such assumptions in general terms, as much as a means of examining their relevance to this important aspect of both tourism as an economic activity and cities as places.

THE CASE OF GRONINGEN

The necessity to examine a single case study in detail stems from the arguments above, as it is critical to a number of the stated assumptions that different **historic cities** be identified within the same urban entity.

The choice of Groningen in particular could have arisen purely from the coincidence that the international workshop whose deliberations promoted this book, was held in that city, and included an excursion examining in the field various aspects of the **historic city** as portrayed locally. However, a number of <u>post hoc</u> justifications can be convincingly made for the choice of example. The use of such cities as Bath, Florence, or Heidelberg immediately and decisively prejudices the objectivity of the defined **historic city**, as such cities have an established, and frequently monopolistic reputation as tourist-historic centres with a clearly defined heritage product. Multifunctionality is in any event a precondition of multiple **historic cities.** Similarly the large multifunctional world cities are generally multinodal, having developed a large number as well as a wide range of **historic cities.** Thus, a medium-sized (population 160,000), but multifunctional, self-standing, regional capital, which has accumulated the physical relics and associations of around 1000 years of historical experience, without self-consciously becoming any particular heritage product, is ideal for the purpose. In terms of the raw materials of history, it has a modest share, commensurate with its proportion of the national population. It is not a major centre of tourism or recreation, but nevertheless serves the recreational needs of its region, while attracting a small but regular stream of tourists including a substantial proportion of West German visitors. An expansion of the tourism industry through the development of the historic potential of the city would be welcomed as an additional support for the urban economy, but is not a major priority of the urban or provincial governments. This then is Groningen which, with cities like it throughout the continent, is in fact the home of most Europeans.

SOME HISTORIC CITIES IN GRONINGEN

The following list of identifiable **historic cities** is neither comprehensive in including all possible varieties nor complete in the sense of each such city being clearly demarcated.

The architect's/historian's historic city

This is the **historic city** that has long existed in the writings of local historians and architects. It is product-oriented and the nature of the product is defined by an appeal to 'authenticity', that is intrinsic qualities of aesthetic merit, age or association, graduated on the basis of the uniqueness of these attributes, and determined by an appeal to professional standards and norms prescibed by an expert elite selected for this purpose.

In fact of course the appeals to both objectivity and authenticity in the shaping of this city are in practice bogus, and at least two forms of selection of historic attributes for inclusion in such a **historic city** are undertaken. The first is the selection process of time itself, which destroys buildings and blunts and distorts contemporary visions of the past. Such selection produces a set of raw materials dependent upon such factors as the nature and robustness of building materials, the history of urban redevelopment, as well as the vicissitudes of war, fire and natural calamity. What survives is unlikely to represent any particular authenticity. An even more stringent selection process results from the subjectivity of those who select, who are necessarily a small and, by virtue of their expertise, untypical sample of society. If the word 'ideology' is used to describe the predispositions of such selection, then there is a danger that it is implied that there is a conscious manipulation of the selection procedures in accord with coherent political philosophies. There is no such implication, although particular examples of these have been documented (Bradbeer & Moon, 1987). Ideology here implies no more than that there are sets of prevailing conventions, norms, tastes and the like which determine what is selected, and this **historic city** has not emerged as a result of some entirely objective process beyond the influence of individuals or institutions. Notwithstanding these denials there is a widespread belief that not only is this the only genuine **historic city**, the others being less 'real' but also that it is an objective reflection of historical reality.

The answer to the question, 'how shall such a **historic city** be identified and delimited', poses no real problems to those who have selected its elements. The intrinsic qualities of age and beauty are regarded as obvious and visible in the morphology of the city itself. A map of building age would portray one element, although not of course its qualitative aspect. The main problem of treating this **historic city** as a functional region of the modern city is spatial. The areas of the contemporary city which are most 'historic' in this sense are those nearest the centre which have been under the most severe and continuous pressure over the centuries for redevelopment. The survival of physical relics is thus in inverse relationship to their importance if this is measured in terms of age. Even the relatively recent city of the mid-seventeenth century (see Fig. 8.1), a particularly favoured period of the historians, which occupied only about 10 per cent of the current area of the city, nevertheless coincides exactly with the present commercial centre. Only a fortunate spatial shift of the centre of commercial activity, or its effective stagnation, is likely to result in the survival of more than a few isolated relics, and this shift has not occurred in Groningen.

Quality is most easily represented in the designation 'monument', or its various equivalents and qualitative subdivisions. Groningen has 369 state designated monuments (Rijksmonumenten), and 1425 buildings designated as having a significance to the wider architectural ensemble (Beeldbepalendpand). The official criteria used for all such listings relate to intrinsic qualities; building age, artistic merit and historical association - the first is regarded as obvious, the second two a matter of expert consensus. There is currently in the city a conflict between 'experts' that is essentially a dispute between the 'age' and 'merit' criteria. The designation 'Rijksmonument' has a statutory requirement of 100 years, excluding architectural developments before and after the First World War which resulted in around 200 buildings of distinction, if not merit, in the city. This so-called 'young art', ineligible for national listing, is now being locally listed as 'Gemeentemonumenten' (Gemeente Groningen,1983).

Figure 8.1: The mid-seventeenth century historic city of Groningen

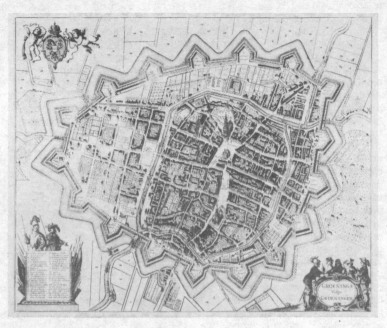

There are other means of identifying such intrinsic quality, such as reference to the opinions of experts other than those concerned with official monument designation. In Britain this may be possible using such a source as the 'Pevsner' county inventories, and some distinct differences can emerge (see the relevant maps of Norwich in Ashworth & de Haan, 1986) but unfortunately in The Netherlands the only comprehensive and authoritative city-by-city guides to monuments, the kunstreisboeken are actually compiled by the Rijksdienst voor de Monumentenzorg, the same department of state responsible for monument listing.

However identified, the resulting spatial patterns represent a splattering of such monuments throughout what is now the central area of the city (Fig. 8.2). Despite some clustering in particular areas there is insufficient contiguity to identify a particular functional region.

The answer to the question in the second part of the chapter title concerning the market, is that this **historic city** is not consciously sold to anyone, except perhaps as a purely abstract idea in academic architecture or urban history.

The legislative historic city

This could be regarded as logically a similar **historic city** to the one described above, and certainly is derived from it, but as a spatial entity it is significantly different. This is not the place to describe the hundred year long history of protective legislation for the built environment in The Netherlands (Nelissen, 1975), nor the changing attitudes towards the architectural and morphological survivals from the past that are revealed in such legislation and the practices it promotes (Ashworth, 1984). It is of interest here however that a series of parliamentary acts and executive orders have resulted in the imposition of a palimpset of overlapping protective designations of various sorts and strengths upon the fabric of the city and upon the functions that occupy it.

The inventorisation and subsequent listing of individual monuments has already been noted, but the Monument Act (Monumentenwet), 1961 decisively shifted the emphasis from the building to the ensemble and from the monument to the historic area. This implied that a much wider range of not only buildings but spaces, street patterns, water and 'green' areas were now included as 'historic'. Conservational status was now awarded to whole blocks of the city, on the basis of the 'historic' quality of the area as a whole and regardless of the inclusion within it of individual buildings of little or no individual merit. A major instrument for this was the 'protected urban facade' (Beschermde Stadsgezicht) which recognised the historic importance of whole streetscapes. Once this shift to block and area designation has been taken, the functioning of areas and the buildings within them becomes central to the criteria for designation and subsequent management. The local land-use functional plan (bestemmingsplan) becomes the most important instrument of conservation management, and the planner, with relevant planning norms and criteria, joins the historian and architect in deciding the selection of such areas.

The very spatial contiguity of such area designations makes them easier to delimit than the historic city of the historian. The difficulty that

Figure 8.2: Location of monuments in Groningen

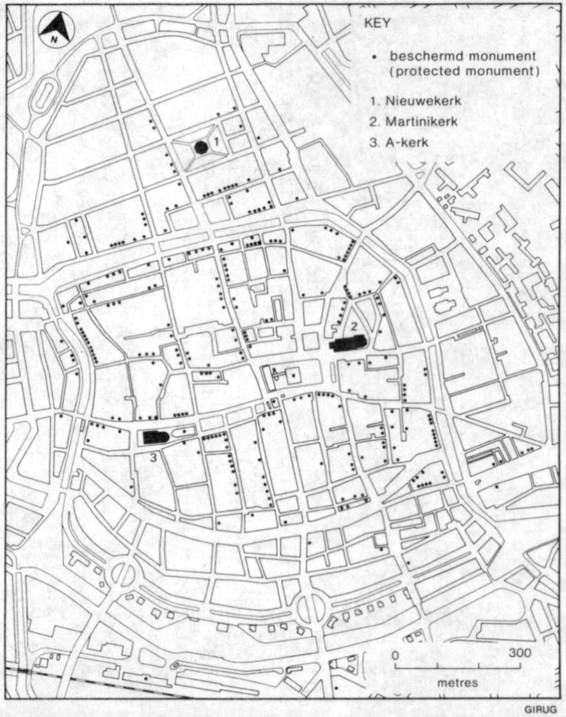

N
KEY
• beschermd monument
(protected monument)
1. Nieuwekerk
2. Martinikerk
3. A-kerk
1
2
3
0
300
metres
GIRUG

Figure 8.3: Protected areas in Groningen

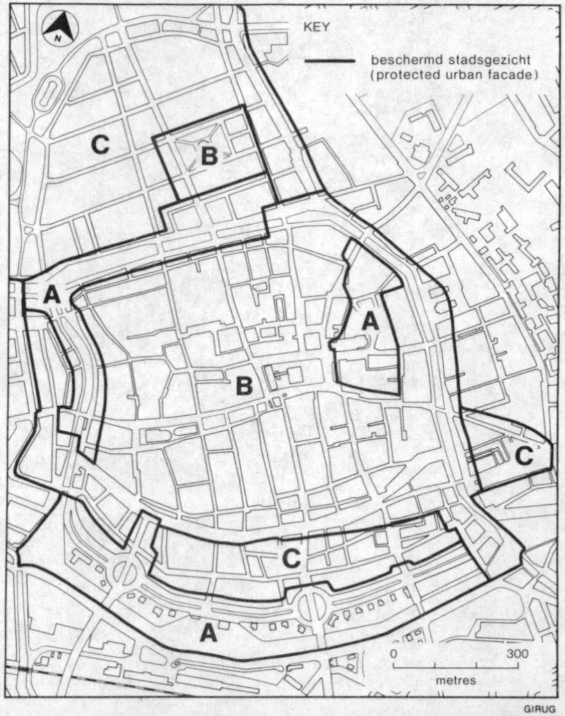

N
KEY
beschermd stadsgezicht
(protected urban facade)
A
B
C
0
300
metres
GIRUG

has arisen, however, is that the profligacy of the planners in the course of the 1960s and 1970s, when the designation of such areas was a prevailing fashion in local planning, has resulted in the whole of the inner city now being included under some such protection (see Fig. 8.3). Groningen is not exceptional in this respect in The Netherlands (NIROV, 1981), and such a situation is easily justified on the grounds, implicit in the legislation, that it is the whole patterning of inner city streets and spaces, within the circular canals (grachten) that is 'historic', regardless of the age of the individual buildings.

Thus, compared with the **historic city** of the historian and architect, that produced by the conservational legislation and its local implementation is all embracing of the inner city, is necessarily functional as well as formal, results from a combination of local practice and national criteria and is determined largely by public sector urban planners and managers. Like the historian's **historic city**, it is of course, selective but the criteria for such selection, and therefore its results, are significantly different. Isolated monuments outside the inner city are unlikely to receive such area designation, while buildings of lesser intrinsic value in the right location will.

In terms of the market this **legislative historic city** can be regarded as principally a statement by the city authorities that Groningen, and in particular its central area, is an **historic city**. Possession of an **historic city** centre, confirmed by the legislative designation, is in itself an important assertion, a piece of 'city marketing', intended for markets both internal and external to the city.

The urban planner's and manager's historic city

Although local authority planners were involved in the shaping of the **legislative historic city**, it is equally possible that within the broad protective designation of the inner city, they can select specific types of buildings or areas for attention. In Table 8.1 the types of buildings selected for protection in Groningen are compared with the national average and this demonstrates the local stress upon almshouses, a local phenomenon, and upon housing. In addition planners can choose

Table 8.1: Types of building on the Rijksmonument list in Groningen

	Groningen(%)	Netherlands (%)
Churches/Towers	7	7
Abbeys/Almshouses	5	1
Mills	1	2
Houses/Warehouses	84	80
Other	2	10
Absolute Total	369	500

Source: Gemeente Groningen, 1982

to shape what amounts to historic quarters. The criteria for the selection of such districts are partly morphological and partly functional. The presence of clusters of protected historic buildings and, even more important in practice, the existence of street and open space patterns that can be regarded as historic, is a useful basis. However, these quarters are fundamentally functional sub-regions of the city and are viewed by the planners in that light. They are selected on the basis of the urban functions, residential, cultural, commercial or symbolic, that they will perform and are located with regard to their interaction, positively or negatively, with other functional sub-regions of the city.

As a functional entity, the **historic city** of the planners depends principally upon sets of function management instruments, the most important of which is the local land use plan, which determines not only the use of sites, but also their building density, height, alignment and the like. The extent of local discretion in the granting of building permits allows quite minor details of new or altered fenestration, boundary walls, materials, etc. to be regulated. An important partner of the local authority in the creation of such districts is the City Rehabilitation Corporation (Stadsherstel). This is a non-profit-making, publically supported body that purchases, renovates and resells mainly residential property. Operating on the open market, this organisation plays an important stimulatory role in encouraging private renovation through example, and working closely with the local authority, it is an effective instrument of both building renovation and social change.

148

In Groningen a number of such **historic cities** can be identified in various stages of execution. The most obvious, complete and long-standing example is the Martinikerkhof created in 1974. It features not only three major monuments, but a cluster of protected buildings around a landscaped **'close'**. The most recent planning policy guidelines for the inner city (Gemeente Groningen, 1988) labels for the first time a 'Martinikwartier', being the Martinikerkhof and surrounding streets, as the 'historic core' of the city (Fig. 8.4). The extent to which this is a planning creation is underlined by the importance of the restructured vehicle circulation system (which previously allowed a road to bisect the 'close'), the creation of a set of pedestrian routes, the landscaping of the 'kerkhof' itself (previously used as a car park) and the expensive and detailed street furniture and paving, including the removal of all traffic and street signs and the installation of working gas lighting.

The other two 'kerkhofs' in the inner city have been less comprehensively treated. The Nieuwe Kerkhof which has a large open space around the church, similar to the Martinikerkhof, awaits the restructuring of its traffic circulation, and the architectural renovation in its surrounding housing stock. The A-Kerkhof is significantly different from the other, being dominated by the A-kerk, expensively restored in 1975. Its disadvantage lies in its location on the edge of a major commercial area (Vismarkt) and adjacent to one of the main entry routes to the inner city. It therefore lacks the potential for developing the same set of historic functions as the other two kerkhofs. The only other area of the inner city to receive substantial attention from the planners in this way is the western side of the circular canals (known as Hoge and Lage der Aa) where the existence of rows of warehouses, whose function has been lost, has fortuitously allowed conversion to residential apartments.

The market for this **historic city** was seen in terms of a range of possible residential and selective commercial functions. In practice in a locally democratically responsive administrative system, these customers played one of two critical roles. They have at times set limits upon the initiatives of the planners, by for example opposing conservation proposals and their associated pedestrianisation and vehicle circulation controls in shopping streets on the

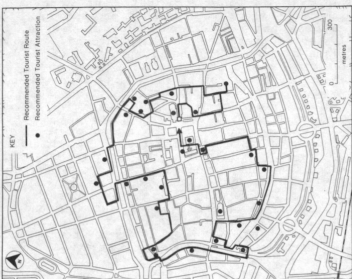

Figure 8.4: Groningen's historic core

N
KEY
GRONINGEN:
REGIONS OF THE INNER CITY
I. City centre
II. University Quarter
III. Martini Quarter
IV. Casino Quarter
V. The Singels
VI. Museum Quarter
I
II
III
IV
V
VI
0
300
metres

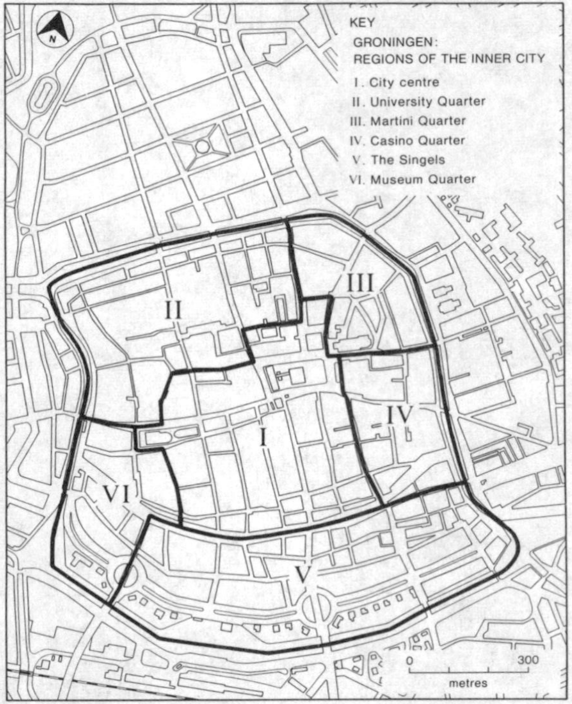

Figure 8.5: Groningen's town trail

N
KEY
Recommended Tourist Route
Recommended Tourist Attraction
0
300
metres

grounds of a potential loss of commercial revenues. Equally residential 'customers' have at other times proved to be both willing partners or even initiators of the authority's designation of conservation areas, in order to improve both perceived residential amenity and property values. Both local commercial and residential users of the city are thus important determinants of the ability of the planners to execute their plans. The possibility of a tourism market has only recently been added to this list, although these areas were always intended to have a collective symbolic and practical recreation function for residents from the city as a whole.

The tourist's historic city

The idea of consciously marketing the historic attributes of Groningen to tourists is relatively recent, if only because the city, in comparison with others in The Netherlands, has never developed a clearly defined tourism product nor targeted a particular tourism market. Consequently tourism has never been a major economic activity in this multifunctional city but has been regarded more recently as a useful windfall gain to be accommodated alongside other activities in the inner city.

In comparison with the other **historic cities**, that of the tourist is marked by selectivity and spatial concentration. The tourist visit is necessarily constrained by the visitor's limited time, mobility and knowledge. Only a small portion of the total available historic artefacts will be 'consumed'. The rigorous selection of resources for the creation of this **city** occurs as a result of a mutually reinforcing interaction between producers and consumers. Producers select on the basis of the intrinsic significance of the resource to the visitor which in turn is largely dependent upon expectations. These expectations are confirmed during the visit by recognition against a mental checklist that has been created by previous experience or by the 'marking' of attractions in various ways by official or private sources, before or during the visit. Thus a satisfyingly 'complete' tourist-historic product need be composed of only a very few 'highlights' of history but these must include the particular buildings, ensembles or 'historic atmosphere' that are expected.

Such 'highlights' need to be arranged in particular spatial patterns. The visitor will be on foot regardless of the mode of travel used to reach the city. (There is a daily city tour coach but this in practice merely rehearses or reiterates rather than substitutes for the pedestrian exploration.) The time spent on enjoying the **historic city** is unlikely to be more than one to two hours; although many visitors spend longer, the additional time is accounted for by shopping or refreshment rather than sightseeing. Lack of familiarity, together with a dependence upon visual information rather than either maps or memory, further limits the itinerary to those routes which appear obviously 'historic' and discourage penetration through the 'dead ground' of non-historic appearing areas. The locational patterns resulting from the operation of these sorts of factors is a **tourist's historic city** that is confined to the inner city, and composed of a few close clusters of obvious attractions, joined by short historic corridors.

This city can be delineated on the ground through the 'town trail' published and distributed by the local tourist information office (the 'VVV') (see Fig 8.5). This 'Walk through the city of Groningen' (VVV Groningen, 1987) is intended for tourists (and thus published in four different languages), is in practice concerned only with historic attractions, and is the most popular single piece of printed information distributed. It describes, with the aid of a route map, a two hour walk through the 'Hanse town of Groningen'. It circulates around the central and visually recognisable point of the city, the Tower of the 'Martini' church because this is both the location of the tourist office where the route is obtained and also because it provides a point of almost continuous visual reference allowing the walk to be prematurely terminated. The attractions chosen are the predictable highlights of the Martini tower (which can be climbed) and associated church, the princes gardens, (which are in that order the three most visited tourist atractions in the city), the four main city museums, and a selection of lesser attractions chosen more for their fortuitous location en route than their particular merit. Attactions outside the immediate inner city are ignored regardless of their architectural merit or importance in the **legislative city** described above. The routing problem is not only how to link the most important clusters by short attractive corridors but equally negatively how to avoid unattractive, or in tourist terms 'dead' areas, which in Groningen has included detours to avoid prostitution streets.

The local planning authority reinforces this pattern in the recently published guidelines for the inner city (Gemeente Groningen, 1988), where a number of 'tourist circulation routes' have been identified and deemed therefore worthy of special attention. In addition the creation by the planners of distinctive 'historic' districts, in particular the Martinikwartier, described earlier, has provided major tourist-historic resources, although that was not the original intention.

Tourists are of course a far from homogeneous market, and strictly speaking each segment of this market will select its own historic city based upon the different expectations of each group. Thus domestic visitors on short breaks and day trips, shopping visitors from neighbouring West Germany, intercontinental tourists on European tours and many more will each require a different tourism product and thus **historic city**. In practice the numbers of visitors are too small for such segmented promotion, and although produced in different languages the promotional literature for each language group contains identical information.

IMPLICATIONS FOR MARKETING THE TOURIST-HISTORIC CITY

The intention of this brief description of a number of the possible **historic cities** is not to suggest that Groningen is in this respect unique, still less is it to imply that there is anything dishonest in this plurality. None of the cities described are more authentic than the others. The purpose is simply to assert that distinctive sets of attributes, or different interpretations of such attributes are selected for different purposes, and that this selection results in distinct although often overlapping, spatial patterns.

Such a conceptual assertion has serious implications for the management of many cities, including those, such as Groningen, which do not self-consciously conceive of themselves as being major 'heritage' cities. If the concept **historic city** is defined by the particular market for which it is created, then it needs much closer definition in relation to these markets than it generally receives. In practice the term **historic city** is being widely, but loosely, used by a range of urban planning, management, and marketing agencies, as the basis of policies which are intended to serve local residential, commercial, or social functions as well as attracting external economic activities and various sorts of tourism. Each distinctive usage, intended for each particular market, fails to consider how the same term is being used by others, despite the utilisation of the same set of resources and frequently the same physical spaces.

An obvious implication of this for the selling of the **tourist-historic city** is that this may be supported or hindered by the simultaneous marketing of other **historic cities**, in so far as their markets cannot be kept completely separate from each other. In Groningen, as in most European cities, the tourism market developed subsequent to, and substantially on the basis of, other previously created historic cities. As a consequence of this, and of the lack of major differences in cultural or historical background between residents and visitors, there is little direct conflict between the promotional images so long as these remain at a highly generalised level. However, effective marketing in any of these markets, and especially the development of the nascent tourism industry which has been now adopted as municipal policy, will depend upon increasingly specific targeting on segmented markets. Once that occurs then the distinct differences between the historic city of the potential commercial investor, conservation area resident, and 'heritage' visitor, whether local, near-neighbour or intercontinental, will all require distinctly different promotion. As each of these markets is currently the responsibility of different 'producers', each with its own marketing strategy, then the possibility of image interference will be compounded by the lost opportunities of mutual reinforcement.

The historic factor, however it is defined, has a major role to play in the functioning of cities including medium-sized, provincial towns with a relatively undistinguished historic heritage, such as Groningen. The effective management of this factor for tourism needs to take into account its significance for many other urban markets. The recognition of this diversity, and the description of its character, are the necessary preliminaries to such management.

REFERENCES

Ashworth, G.J. (1984) The management of change: conservation policy in Groningen, The Netherlands, _Cities_, November, 605-16

Ashworth, G.J. (1985) The evaluation of urban tourist resources, pp 37-44 in G.J. Ashworth & B. Goodall (Eds) _The Impact of Tourist Development on Disadvantaged Regions_, Socio-Geografisch Reeks No. 35, GIRUG, Groningen

Ashworth, G.J. & de Haan, T.Z. (1986) Uses and users of the tourist-historic city, _Field Studies_, No. 10, GIRUG, Groningen

Bradbeer, J.B. & Moon, G. (1987) The Defence town in crisis: the paradox of the tourism strategy, pp 82-99 in M. Bateman & R.C. Riley (Eds) _A Geography of Defence_, Croom Helm, London

Gemeente Groningen (1982) _Nerken aan Monumenten_, Groningen

Gemeente Groningen (1983) _Jongere Bouwkunst en Monumentenzorg in Groningen_, Werkgroep Jongere Bouwkunst, Groningen

Gemeente Groningen (1988) _Plan voor Aanpak voor de Binnenstad: een ontwikkelingsstrategie_, Groningen

Nederlands Instituut voor Ruimtelijke Ordening en Volkshuisvesting (1981) _Zorgen om Monument_, Werkgroep Monumentenzorg, The Hague

Nelissen, N.J.M. (1975) _Monument en Samenleving_, Council of European Communities, Maastricht

VVV Groningen (1987) _A walk through the town of Groningen_, Groningen

Chapter 9

THE TOURIST DESTINATION AS PRODUCT: THE CASE OF LANGUEDOC

Theo de Haan, Gregory Ashworth and Mike Stabler

THE PRODUCT 'LANGUEDOC': THE PRODUCT, THE PACKAGE AND THE PLACE

As shown by Stabler (Chp. 2), Kent (Chp. 3) and Goodall (Chp. 4), the development of opportunity sets has concentrated on the tourist origin area perspective. Consequently the emphasis has been on the holiday opportunity as perceived by consumers or as assembled and marketed by the industry or as projected (perhaps more correctly as interpreted) in the origin area by destination area agencies. In effect it is, the 'package' aspects of the holiday which have been studied, i.e. travel and accommodation.

A very different perspective is obtained if the actual consumption of the holiday at a destination is considered, i.e. if attention is focused on the chosen 'product'. To an extent in adopting such a perspective, two important features of tourism are taken into account. Firstly, it enables an essential characteristic to be identified, namely, that it is the interaction between the consumer and the resources in a destination area at a particular point in time which actually creates the tourism product. Secondly, it allows for the dynamic nature of tourism in so far as tourists may well modify their perceptions of and attitude on a destination as a consequence of their experiences, thus very likely changing their behaviour and future holiday decisions. This is of especial interest where a visit is being made for the first time.

Each tourism product is necessarily unique to each tourist. However it can be posited that the extent of the interaction between the tourist and the destination and the impact which the latter has on the former will almost certainly be related to the nature of the holiday packages and personal characteristics of the purchasers. Allocentric tourists, for whom place is probably important, assemble the greater proportion of the package themselves and therefore the product is largely of their own creation. In essence they, not the tourism industry, are the holiday producers. Psychocentric tourists, even though they may assemble their own holiday packages, are not so likely to create their own product because they possibly have less sense of place (Stabler, 1988b). The contribution made by the destination to any holiday experience is therefore determined by three principal factors - the consumer, the package and the product created by the consumer. Ascertaining the importance of the destination as a component of the tourism product is an empirical question, notwithstanding suppositions arising from the categorisation of tourists made above. Indeed these categorisations, which tend to suggest that tourists are predominant in creating the product, are misleading because the destination does not necessarily play a passive role as merely a location in which holidays are 'consumed'.

The destination as part of the tourism product cannot be delimited solely in terms of an inventory of the physical and functional content of places, nor even, one stage removed, as an arbitrary selection of place characteristics. The destination yields three major holiday elements: the range of facilities on offer; the perception of these facilities held either by actual or potential holidaymakers, or promoted by tourism enterprises; and the use made of them during the holiday experience. Facilities include not only the goods and services consciously provided for holidaymakers, such as accommodation and catering, but also those supportive services of places whether consciously so provided or not, such as public utilities, and, more widely, all those aspects of the built or natural environments which form part of the holidaymaking experience. Similarly the perception of these place attributes includes those expectations and preconceptions described by Kent (Chp. 3) as influencing consumer choice, but in this case extended to influence holiday behaviour in general. The third element, the use of facilities, is clearly the resultant of the interaction of the first two, being what holidaymakers do in, and with, the destination.

The central importance of place image, in its various forms, within this tourism destination

system can be appreciated, but each of the three
elements needs further consideration in terms of
their contribution to various opportunity sets.
      This is not to argue that there are 'holiday
consumption' or 'destination-based' opportunity
sets. What is being acknowledged is that
destinations are vital, living entities subject to
change as a consequence of economic, political and
social forces both related and unrelated to tourism
activity. Accordingly this will have an impact on
tourists and the industry which is likely to change
the nature of opportunity sets in origin areas. In
a sense by studying a specific place as a tourism
product, insights into the composition, and, of
more significance, changes in the composition of
opportunity sets can be gained. In particular a
detailed examination of a destination area can
contribute to the development of destination area
sets and/or sub-sets of dimensions which hitherto
might not have been conceived of. This chapter
therefore considers the Languedoc-Roussillon region
in southern France, the subject of a joint
Groningen-Reading Universities study, in which
perceptions, attitudes and use of resorts were
investigated. The region as a tourist destination
opportunity set is place-specific. In so far as it
offers holidays similar to those elsewhere,
essentially summer sun, the region provides an
appropriate illustration of how a destination area
set can be constructed, and perhaps reconstructed,
from the destination viewpoint. Such a destination
area set suggests a local tourism industry or
facility set, comprising the attractions and
activities available in the destination.

LANGUEDOC-ROUSSILLON TOURISM REGION

      The holiday resort region of Languedoc-
Roussillon is an appropriate tourism destination to
study because of the wide differences that exist
both between its holiday resorts and the way these
places are experienced by tourists visiting the
region. An introduction to some of the dimensions
of the region's variety in holidaymaking is
contained in Ashworth and Stabler (1988); aspects
of resort images are treated in Stabler (1988a) and
the full results of the resort analysis can be
found in Ashworth and de Haan (1988).
      The Languedoc-Roussillon region has a
Mediterranean coastline stretching 200 kilometres

from the Rhône to the Pyrénées. It contains the five departments of Aude, Gard, Herault, Lozère, and Pyrénées-Orientales covering 27,500 square kilometres (five per cent of the area of France) containing almost two million people (four per cent of the population of the country).

In the 1950s tourism in the Languedoc-Roussillon region was weakly developed, and largely local, attracting annually about 300,000 visitors, fewer than half of whom came from outside the region (Pearce, 1981). As late as 1969 the Languedoc coast was classified as of only regional, rather than national importance (Cribier, 1969).

In the immediate post-war period French planning was characterised by the initiation of imaginative and grandiose projects designed to modernise the French economy (Ardagh, 1982). Centralised state direction and large public investments in infrastructure typified such schemes. The lagging economy of Languedoc-Roussillon was an obvious target for such planning and given the natural features of the area the development of tourism appeared to be the most feasible instrument for stimulating growth. The first systematic central government intervention in the area was in 1955 when the Societé Mixte de Bas-Rhône/Languedoc was established. Its main objectives for the development of the region were:

(i) diversification of the economy to provide new employment in order to reverse the emigration trend;
(ii) to raise the level of regional incomes;
(iii) to meet the rising demands for tourism facilities from French and foreign visitors.

This would relieve pressure on the Côte d'Azur and it would help to correct France's growing adverse international balance of tourism payments.

In 1963 an inter-ministerial commission, Le Mission Interministerielle, was established to encourage the development of integrated tourism resorts. The Mission had a comprehensive character and was composed of representatives of central government ministries, of the five departments previously mentioned and of four specially created development companies, composed of public and private interests. The roles of the Mission were the coordination of the concerned government departments and the maintenance of the unity of the project and its implementation.

The product 'Languedoc'

Five clusters of resort units were planned by the Mission, separated by open conserved landscapes, a sixth unit was planned to be built later. The three units which were the subject of the Groningen-Reading research in 1986 can be seen in Fig. 9.1 (tourist units 1, 2 and 3).

The destination as a facility set

The Languedoc region can be described in terms of an opportunity set composed of a number of sub-sets of resorts which in turn contain a range of tourism facilities on offer. As argued earlier, however, such a regional set is necessarily wider than the 'industry' set described in Chp. 2. Inventories of accommodation, catering, entertainment and many more types of facilities can, and have been constructed, (Ashworth & de Haan, 1988). The significant conclusions drawn from these analyses were that in the region a number of distinctly different types of destination resorts existed, offering particular packages of facilities, either to specific segments of the holiday market or to the same market at different points of time in the holiday experience. This can be illustrated by reference to examples of categories of resort which were identified:

(i) the 'Mission' resorts, typified by modern purpose-built apartments, extensive boat marina development, a very dominant accent on tourism and only a few other city-functions (e.g. La Grande Motte, Le Cap d'Agde and Gruissan);
(ii) the 'autonomous' resorts typified by organic growth usually in response to local leisure demands and initiatives, and by a usually more multifunctional 'mature' composition of city-functions (e.g. Narbonne Plage, Carnon and Palavas);
(iii) the multifunctional towns which offer a whole range of shopping, catering and other urban functions principally to residents but incidentally available to visitors (e.g. Sète, and, to a lesser extent, Agde);
(iv) the inland historic 'gem' towns like Aigues Mortes, Carcassonne and Arles, offering historic attractions and catering and shopping services dependent upon such an historic atmosphere.

Figure 9.1: The Languedoc-Roussillon resorts

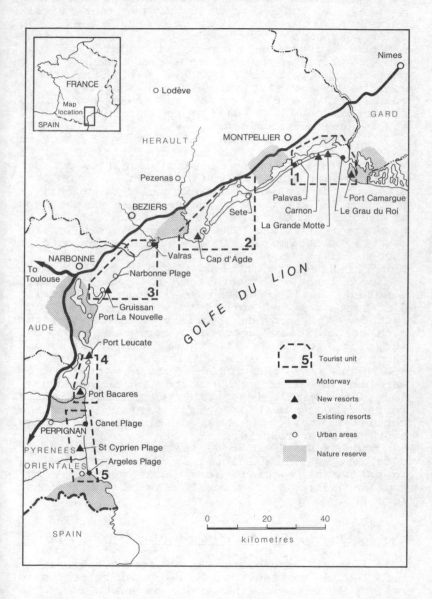

The product 'Languedoc'

Holiday accommodation in the Languedoc region is dominated by self-catering which, including camping, accounts for half (52 per cent) of all accommodation. If staying with friends and relatives and boat accommodation is included, this proportion increases to nearly two-thirds (65 per cent). Thus the region caters predominantly for a particular type of holidaymaker but there remain considerable variations between resorts. Such variations in type, cost and even ownership structure, make it difficult to conceive of a single accommodation set.

The newest resorts are dominated by tourism and do not have many other city-functions. The Mission resorts are the clearest examples of such nearly monofunctional cities. In contrast the older the resort, the more additional functions can be found and the greater the variation in the type of tourist accommodation, leisure possibilities and catering facilities. The process of ageing of the resorts is accompanied by the tendency for them to become fully fledged towns. However, it is the tourist-historic cities which have the most balanced functional character, i.e. are the least monofunctional. Their role in tourism is quite different from and more complex than, the beach resorts. They provide a variety of urban functions such as public and commercial services, banks and shopping, together with their related cafés and lunch rooms in the inner cities. In most of the built-up area the accommodation sector is of marginal importance. The historical architecture, the places with a beautiful view attract tourists for a relaxing meal or a drink, which gives the tourist-historic cities a distinctive advantage over the newer resorts.

The essential point is that the destination as a facility set is difficult to reduce to a limited inventory of specialised tourism services, and equally difficult to generalise on at the regional level.

The destination and tourist behaviour

A distinctive pattern of visitor behaviour was revealed in the resort study which can be stated to reflect that for the Languedoc as a whole. This was typified by a concentration on beach activities like sunbathing and swimming and on the resort boulevard activities such as sitting at terrace cafés and eating in restaurants. Visitor behaviour was basically passive rather than the active pattern suggested by the brochures produced by the holiday destinations.

The conclusions drawn from research into visitors' use of resort facilities were relatively clearcut. The beach as the central feature of the resort understandably is used by nine-tenths of the visitors, although it is still perhaps remarkable that 10 per cent of the visitors claim to make no use of this feature. Food shops (70 per cent) and restaurants (60 per cent) are similarly well patronised with a large proportion of visitors making use of both sets of facilities. Other facilities were of minority interest. Souvenir shops were rejected by about three-quarters of the visitors as were sport facilities. Other possibilities of use of facilities were hardly mentioned. The picture emerges of tourists moving continuously between the beach and the food purveyors with few other intervening activities. It should be added that this general pattern of behaviour was not significantly influenced by the origin, age, or group composition of visitors.

However, differences occurred among the resorts, which can be best described by considering excursion behaviour. In order to assess the role of the wider region in the recreation behaviour of visitors, respondents were asked about excursions to other places during their stay. Just under two-thirds of the respondents (65 per cent) took or expected to take at least one excursion out of the resort. A wide variety of places offering very different recreational activities were visited. Two sorts of destinations could be distinguished, viz. inland towns and coastal resorts. The towns could be further subdivided into large multifunctional towns like Montpellier, Béziers, Narbonne and the like, and the smaller towns. The large towns offer generally a single attractive phenomenon such as an historic feature, like medieval fortified Aigues Mortes and restored Carcassonne, or a cultural attraction, such as Arles with its Van Gogh association and its Roman relics. As a living expression of the regional distinctiveness of Languedoc, smaller inland market towns, for instance Agde and Marseillan, attracted visitors.

The second group of destinations were other seaside resorts both within and outside the Languedoc study area. A sharp distinction existed between excursions to the three resorts of Sète,

Cap d'Agde and La Grande Motte and the area's other resorts that attracted almost no visitors.

From the nature of the places visited it can be concluded in general that excursions are taken in order to experience the services offered by the large cities, the historical and cultural attractions of both the large cities and the conserved small towns and to sample the beaches and attractions of other resorts. The natural landscape attractions of the surrounding countryside are notable omissions from this list. However, it is likely that respondents only mentioned urban destinations for their excursions, even though the trips may for a large part have included rural experiences en route.

Differences in visitor behaviour between resorts can be shown by drawing a distinction between what might be termed the 'self-contained resorts' and 'touring resorts'. In the former a lower than average proportion (63 per cent) took excursions, for example Carnon (43 per cent), Gruissan (43 per cent) and Palavas (46 per cent). Whereas in the latter, like Cap d'Agde (85 per cent), Narbonne Plage (70 per cent), Port Camargue (69 per cent) and Grau d'Agde (69 per cent), the proportion taking excursions was higher than average.

There is thus an identifiable generalised pattern of usage of the tourism region which is strongly influenced by the character of its resorts, cities, towns and rural environment. This usage will give rise to distinct impressions which will determine future behaviour both while in the region and in planning future holidays. There will thus be a feedback effect on the region and in the provision of tourism services.

The destination and tourist perception

Consumers' perceptions of the resorts largely reflect, not unsurprisingly, the nature of the facilities on offer. Visitors' opinions of the resorts and of the region as a whole were investigated through pairs of descriptive adjectives. Considerable differences were revealed between resorts. Some were seen as 'modern' (Port Camargue, La Grande Motte), some 'historic' (Sète), others as 'unpretentious' and 'peaceful' (Carnon, Narbonne Plage, Valras, Grau du Roi), or 'sophisticated' and 'exciting' (La Grande Motte,

Cap d'Agde, Port Camargue)(Ashworth & Stabler, 1988).

Spatial scale plays an important and not self-evident role in the perceptions of visitors. While acknowledging at a general level an environmental dimension, there are four main scales at which destination images can be detected for place-specific destination area sets:

(i) Images of the Mediterranean. The decision to go on holiday is a decision for a certain type of holiday experience which itself may be strongly associated with particular regions. The Mediterranean is for western and northern Europeans an area strongly associated with an image of continuous sun, wide sandy beaches and blue seas.

(ii) A second spatial scale in the destination image is southern France. This image is composed partly of the general Mediterranean image together with an image of French life-styles.

(iii) The third spatial scale is the Languedoc region itself, in part French Mediterranean, but different from the Côte d'Azur in being less expensive and in terms of its image, the type of holiday that can be expected, and as an area with a different hinterland.

(iv) The resort itself is the fourth level at which destination images can be detected: the local image. A 'modern exciting' resort like La Grande Motte promises a totally different holiday from a resort like the 'beautiful but unpretentious' Narbonne Plage.

The overall conclusion that emerged from the analysis of received images in the 1986 research was that of pleasant, simple, peaceful resorts, which may or may be not exciting. When the description of the particular resort is compared with the image of the Languedoc as a whole, the most obvious finding is the measure of agreement between the local and the regional image. At no point was there a sharp divergence of opinion. The resort is clearly seen as a microcosm of the region, or the region as an extension of the resort. Actually this was rather surprising as there were considerable differences between the resorts with respect to the nature of the facilities and images projected by the local tourism industry and information centres. An explanation for this apparent discrepancy between the image received and projected and perhaps reality, is that visitors, especially staying visitors, have a very limited knowledge of other resorts on the coast and of the hinterland and merely project the image of their own resort onto the wider perspective.

A notable discrepancy is that found in the variation in perceptions that different groups have of the same resort. It could be argued that differences in images held by visitors should be related to their personal characteristics or holiday experience. Day-visitors may see the resort differently, because they spend less time at it and visit it more frequently than staying visitors. However, the differences between the various types of visitors proved to be small. Holidaymakers tend to be more positive in their opinion while day-tippers, and, to a lesser extent visitors on a long weekend, are rather more likely to be negative. Only four per cent of the holiday-makers found the location of the interview, the resort, ugly compared with 10 per cent of the day-visitors. There was a similar pattern of perceptions for the coast as a whole.

The effect of the place of origin of visitors on the images they held was also tested. Three populations were distinguished, visitors from the region itself, visitors from elsewhere in France and foreigners. Expecting that each category would have their own preconceptions based on different experiences, expectations and standards of comparison, there proved to be only marginal differences in image of the individual resorts. When considering the opinions about the region as a whole, only the people from the Languedoc-Roussillon region itself were more likely to see the region as modern, while at the opposite extreme foreigners were more likely than average to see it as historic. This confirms the idea that people from the region, who are predominantly day-trippers make greater use of the more ubiquitous facilities of the beach, while those from further away on infrequent visits are more attracted to the unique features of the region, such as the historic and cultural attractions. Each group's image therefore seems to be a reflection of its distinct pattern of activities.

OPPORTUNITY SETS AND TOURIST DESTINATIONS

Tourism as a subject of serious academic study has suffered from the serious problem caused by its very diversity on both supply and demand sides. This has made the construction of general systems of analysis extremely difficult. The temptation to simplify an otherwise excessively complex situation by attempting to isolate specifically tourism resources, facilities, activities, industries and places is therefore strong. Such attempts to create models of a strictly tourism system, however, generally fail, as the very isolation of the tourism phenomenon denies its integral relationship with other resources, facilities, motivations, activities and the like.

Tourist destinations are typical examples of this dilemma. In order to pursue a systematic investigation of tourism, its function within destinations must be separated out for study, but such a separation denies the very multifunctional nature of places and conceals the relationship between tourism and other place dimensions. Opportunity sets appear to offer, if not actual solutions to this paradox, at least a method of analysis that does not require the abandonment of the essential characteristics of places as a precondition. The focus of attention is upon the link between supply and demand, however defined, and upon the nature of the transaction that forms such a link. However, it is the argument of this chapter that the shift of focus from the tourism 'industry' and from consumer choice in origin areas to the destination involves a radical redefinition of the main terms of the model. In particular this transaction, which forms the central focus of opportunity sets, is fundamentally different if the analysis arises from a destination-based study.

The opportunity sets concept has in turn suggested the direction in which future research in the Languedoc should take place. It is clear that a study of the image projected and the marketing of the Languedoc in tourist-generating areas, both in foreign countries and in France, needs to be undertaken to assess the effectiveness of the promotion of the region by the regional tourism authorities. In terms of opportunity sets analysis a comparison can be made between the Languedoc destination area opportunity set received in generating areas with that projected by the Languedoc tourism industry to ascertain how closely they match. Recalling that the overlap of the industry's opportunity set with consumers' perceived and attainable sets forms the realised opportunity set (see Chp. 2), then if the projected image of the Languedoc is defective, this overlap will be reduced. Alternatively stated, if holiday opportunities in the Languedoc are less well represented in realised sets then potential tourists are less likely to choose a holiday in the region.

Another direction of research which could be usefully undertaken in Languedoc is to consider the composition of its opportunity set matrix by a re-interpretation of the functional analysis data and promotional material emanating from the region. One specific dimension to which reference has already been made, accommodation, warrants a more detailed study since it is a key feature of the holidays on offer in the region. Moreover, given the dynamic nature of tourism, it would be constructive to compare the capacity with occupancy rates to establish whether the type of accommodation matches consumer perceptions and preferences. In the wider context the study area needs to be functionally related to the interest of the region and not to be confined to the coastal resorts. Any assessment of visitor behaviour and opinions should attempt to capture the many complex facets of the link between the tourism experience and the tourist destination which tend to be overlooked or simplified away in the more narrowly focused 'industrial' approaches at any one point in time. Of particular importance are the changes in the destination which occur as the season progresses. The authors of this chapter acknowledge that the study took place in the early season and thus the supply response was different from that prevailing in the high season. Moreover, the investigation of visitor excursion behaviour emphasised places visited rather than the routes followed. Future research in the region should concentrate on compiling a profile of facilities, which constitute an objective set, and attempt to establish how the perceptions with which tourists arrive are influenced by locally provided information, contact with other holidaymakers and residents and features and facilities discovered while on holiday.

REFERENCES

Ardagh, J. (1982) <u>France in the 1980s</u>, Penguin, Harmondworth, Middlesex

Ashworth, G.J. & de Haan, T.Z. (1988) <u>Regionalising the Resort System: Tourist Regions on the Languedoc Coast</u>, Sociaal-Geografische Reeks, Faculteit der Ruimtelijke Wetenschappen, Rijksuniversiteit, Groningen

Ashworth, G.J. & Stabler, M.J. (1988) Tourism development planning in Languedoc: Le Mission impossible? pp 187-197 in B. Goodall & G.J. Ashworth (Eds) <u>Marketing in the Tourism Industry</u>, Croom Helm, Beckenham

Cribier, F. (1969) <u>La Grande Migration d'Eté des Citadins en France</u>, Mémoires et Documents du CNRS, Paris

Pearce, D.G. (1981) <u>Tourism Development</u>, Longman, Harlow

Stabler, M.J. (1988a) The image of destination regions: theoretical and empirical aspects, pp 133-161 in B. Goodall & G.J. Ashworth (Eds) <u>Marketing in the Tourism Industry</u>, Croom Helm, Beckenham

Stabler, M.J. (1988b) Modelling the tourism industry: the concept of opportunity sets, paper presented at Leisure Studies Association 2nd International Conference, University of Sussex, Brighton

operational factors (time/cost), regulatory measures;
(iv) images of the destination, which influence prospective tourists' expectations - all tourists have mental pictures of potential destinations, normally based on historic rather than current events, which destination area agencies seek to maintain or improve;
(v) total price to the consumer of the complete holiday package.

The first two are integral components of any **tourism place product** whereas the latter three are really attributes of those place components.

The place components may or may not be highlighted when marketing the TTP. There is no single way in which the individual components fit together to form a TTP suitable for all potential tourists. All the components together contribute to the tourist's satisfaction with the holiday, but in differing degrees for different tourists. Destination tourism agencies must therefore seek to promote an overall image of that place which is attractive to potential tourists. However, all the individual components are seldom under the control of one organisation: each component is normally controlled and often marketed by a separate organisation. Many attractions, facilities and services (e.g. theme parks, hotels, restaurants, car hire) are run by private businesses for profit; others (e.g. stately homes, zoos, and museums) may be operated by private businesses, voluntary organisations, or public agencies; and yet others (infrastructure such as roads and public utilities) provided by public agencies and local government. Even where certain of the components - travel, accommodation, meals, excursions - are combined as ITs by independent tour operators or the owners of one of the components (e.g. airline, ferry operator, or hotel group) problems can occur with respect to the control of standards or quality of certain components. What control, for example, does a tour operator exercise over the time its holidaymakers spend at airports and the service received there, the operating standards of the charter airline, the transfers to the hotel and back to the airport, the hotel itself and its surrounding neighbourhood? 'Naturally a wise tour operator will have some impact on the quality' of the components but 'an honest one will also admit that his influence is limited' (Delaney-Smith, 1987). The tourist will, of course, hold the tour operator responsible!

Do the interests of destination tourism agencies and of tour operators coincide? Where a tour operator uses a particular destination there would appear to be a common interest in the quality of the product and the market segments served. However, even acknowledging that neither tour operators nor destination tourism agencies are directly responsible for the quality of all the individual product components, there is an essential difference. Tour operators are selling their own products, namely ITs to one or more destinations, whereas destination tourism agencies are usually concerned with promoting a 'place image' which largely comprises other firms' products. Such destination agencies, outside of Eastern Europe and certain Third World countries, therefore have no product <u>per se</u> to sell and, moreover, may represent only a proportion of all tourism businesses in the destination. Tour operators choose destinations on the basis of the latter's attractions and are even more selective in their use of destination facilities, e.g. accommodation. Therefore the IT, viewed as a TTP, embraces certain place components but is more often than not marketed as a holiday type, e.g. a summer sun, winter sports, or sea cruise package. ITs as standardised, repeatable products are susceptible to modern marketing techniques (Allen, 1985).

MARKETING THE TOTAL TOURISM PRODUCT

What is marketed - holiday places, holiday types or a combination of both? Destination tourism agencies must emphasise place whilst parading the range of holiday activities possible there. Tour operators have a choice but their advertising favours holiday type, allied to the range of possible destinations. Potential customers are targeted at different stages of the holiday choice process. Destination tourism agencies implant ideas about where to holiday during the early stages of choice whereas tour operators are concerned with the 'hard sell' at the decision-making stage, viz. holiday there (or somewhere else) with this particular operator.

ITs are assembled from the five basic elements of the TTP plus certain 'value added' by the tour operator in the form of price guarantees, etc. (Middleton, 1988). They are marketed to the general public at a published, inclusive price in which the costs of the components cannot be separately identified (see Chp. 5). The IT, being primarily a holiday, is not place-specific in being tied to a single destination (although a particular environment, such as a seaside resort or health spa, is a necessary component).

There is near perfect substitutability between destinations within many IT opportunity sets, such as summer sun, and neither the IT product nor the quality of the holiday experience are materially altered by the destination at which the holiday is taken. Such substitutability applies not only to IT products offered within a given tour operator's holiday programme but also between IT programmes of competing tour operators. ITs appear increasingly homogeneous to the consumer (Goodall et al., 1988) even though individual tour operators seek to differentiate their product from those of rivals. Thus the mass tour operator, in particular, is marketing a **holiday brand image**, emphasising the quality of service of that operator, and in which the image of a holiday in a <u>given</u> destination is unlikely to figure prominently. Indeed, if 'destination' is a selling point for the mass tour operator it is much more likely to be the range of destinations from which to choose, rather than the availability of a given destination, which is important. Place, however, may be a basis for IT product differentiation since smaller tour operators may specialise by destination, e.g. only offer resorts in a given country. All tour operators include destinations in their IT programmes which support their brand image: destinations are added to and dropped from a tour operator's programme as commercial factors dictate.

Of course the way in which a tour operator presents a destination can influence the likelihood of a prospective holidaymaker choosing that destination rather than another in the operator's programme but the essential point is that, first and foremost, the tour operator is selling an IT holiday. If the customer is uncertain about one destination the tour operator will offer an alternative rather than risk losing that customer to a rival. Are destination attributes represented accurately by tour operators, and in a way which meets with the approval of destination tourism agencies?

The destination tourism agency seeks to market a place-specific TTP, i.e. a fixed location which has a (changing) comparative advantage for one or more types of holiday. The agency must be aware that selling the 'place' is often more difficult than selling a holiday. Marketing the place-specific TTP to consumers scattered in many countries poses major economic difficulties and if the agency is successful in creating an awareness of that destination as a possible holiday base (e.g. by informative advertising) the question for many would-be holidaymakers becomes 'What ITs do tour operators offer to that destination?' Destination tourism agencies therefore need to get their message across, in addition, to tour operators (e.g. by persuasive advertising and especially other forms of promotional activity). Even where a destination is included in a tour operator's programme it has to face competition from other destinations in the programme offering similar holiday opportunities.

The tour operator's vital marketing tool is its holiday brochure which, at the point of sale - usually a travel agency (see Chp. 14) - substitutes for the product, which cannot be inspected before purchase. The prospective holiday is therefore represented in an intangible form by the brochure. How a destination is 'marketed' in such brochures is crucial for the volume of holidaymakers attracted to that destination, especially if catering for mass tourism.

TOUR OPERATORS' BROCHURES

Tour operators generally produce elaborate, glossy brochures which describe in detail the otherwise intangible IT product (Burkart & Medlik, 1981). Whilst these brochures appear to be 'mines of information' their purpose is not simply to inform but to persuade potential holidaymakers to purchase. Tourism marketing relies on brochures to a much greater extent than other forms of consumer marketing (Middleton, 1988). As well as being an advertising medium a brochure is the basis of a holidaymaker's contract with the tour operator. Brochures represent the product 'stock' at the retail level but, at the time of sale, the TTP is no more than an idea - the brochure establishes expectations of quality, value for money, product image and status (Middleton, 1988). For

174

inexperienced holiday buyers the brochures are especially important.

Brochures remain the principal means a tour operator has, not just of informing, but of persuading potential holidaymakers to buy its ITs rather than a rival's. Their persuasive role is usually more important than their informative one. Tour operators are fully aware of the strategic significance of their brochure(s) and, especially in the case of mass tour operators, the brochures are designed in 'in-house' advertising departments or in conjunction with their advertising agency's design studio (Holloway, 1985). The brochure conveys the key selling message and must therefore identify with the holidaymaker's needs, demonstrating in readily comprehensible text and high-quality photography the image and positioning of the IT product and its supplier. The appearance and appeal of the brochure's front cover, especially if displayed in self-service racks, is crucial in attracting the holidaymaker's initial interest. Booking forms are usually included as part of the brochure to make purchase easy.

Each tour operator develops a 'house style' for its brochure(s) and, more and more, distinctions between tour operators rest on brochure style, as well as on price. At the extreme the brochure becomes a 'designer product', e.g. Thomson's Freestyle (Middleton, 1988). Tour operators who sell holidays 'market dreams' (National Consumer Council, 1988) and the brochure is their tool - the expectations created must be matched when the product is consumed!

With respect to ITs, Holloway (1985) lists the information that should be included in a tour operator's brochure:

(i) name of the firm responsible for the IT;
(ii) transport mode(s) used, - for air travel the carrier's name, aircraft type and use of scheduled or charter services;
(iii) details of **destinations**, itinerary and travel times;
(iv) duration of each IT (number of days'/nights' stay);
(v) description of the **destinations** and type of accommodation provided, including meals;
(vi) whether services of a tour operator's representative are available at **destinations**;
(vii) price of each IT, with extras charged clearly indicated;

(viii) details of special arrangements and facilities, e.g. hotel baby-sitting service, availability of ski packs, etc. and any associated charges;
(ix) full booking conditions, including cancellation terms;
(x) any optional or compulsory insurance cover;
(xi) documentation required for travel to the **destinations** featured and any health hazards or inoculations recommended.

Destination is mentioned four times in the above list including a description of the destination's attractions and facilities. Place information forms only part of the total information required by the holidaymaker and is meant to aid the holidaymaker's choice of destination but this is very much a secondary purpose of the brochure. Destinations are presented in a way which supports the tour operator's brand image: the destinations' positive features are emphasised, their negative ones neglected.

Holiday brochures contain marketing messages, in an informational form readily absorbed by potential tourists, designed to create and reinforce the tour operator's image of supplying a quality and reliable product. The tour operator is also under pressure to strike a strategic balance between the need for separate brochures to appeal to different market segments and the incentive to keep costs down by reducing the number of brochures. Paper quality, use of colour, density of copy, graphics, and style and density of photography are altered to suit the product image to the target market (Middleton, 1988).

The marketing message transmitted by the tour operator's brochure is clear and persuasive but is it accurate from the destinations' viewpoint? The glossy colour photograph illustrating the 'good beach life' on a summer sun IT at a particular resort will not have been taken at the peak season when the beach may well be overcrowded! Likewise the photograph of the skier with the piste to him/herself! A study of how destinations are represented in tour operators' brochures is presented below for skiing ITs: it demonstrates that tour operators can view the same destination attractions and facilities rather differently.

A CONTENT ANALYSIS OF SKIING BROCHURES

Tour operators' brochures present the TTP in a particular form - the inclusive tour (IT). Since ITs are primarily holidays the brochure presentation makes an initial distinction between the characteristics of the IT, such as travel mode(s), accommodation arrangements, holiday activities, etc. and information about the individual destinations (including named hotels, etc.) at which holidays may be taken.

Any product can be viewed on three levels - core, tangible and augmented (Kotler, 1984) - and the presentation of general IT characteristics in brochures is no exception. The core product identifies with the holidaymaker's perceived need, in the case of skiing for a fun-filled, action-packed, exhilarating experience, and the text and photographs are designed to confirm this, as well as encouraging the purchasing decision. The formal offer of a specified holiday of given duration, taken at a particular time, to a selected destination, for a specified price constitutes the tangible product whereas the augmented product 'expresses the idea of value added over and above the formal offer' (Middleton, 1988) and is one way tour operators can differentiate their ITs from those of competitors. In the case of skiing ITs examples of augmentation include the 'snow promise' (or 'no snow guarantee'), free carriage on aircraft of the holidaymaker's own skis, free ski guiding, free parking at departure airports, free child-minding, and discount offers at dry-ski slope facilities or ski clothing shops. The distinction between the tangible and augmented IT may be blurred where special holiday offers, such as 'learn to ski weeks' or 'skiing house parties', are promoted as part of the operator's product image. Details of booking conditions and insurance, plus further price information related to group and children's discounts also appear in the general characteristics section of the brochures.

The database

For the 1986/87 winter holiday season brochures were obtained from all the mass tour operators retailing skiing ITs in the United Kingdom (UK) and The Netherlands and in addition, in the case of the UK, from a 50 per cent sample of other tour operators, including specialist and direct sell ones. The brochure data set covered 72 UK (12 of which were mass tour operators) and seven Dutch tour operators who between them offered skiing holidays to a total of 454 resorts in 13 European countries.

Each brochure was subjected to a content analysis to extract two data sets. The first concerned the brochure as a whole, recording the number and proportion of pages devoted to IT product information relative to resort descriptions (and, if appropriate, to advertisements and non-skiing holidays). The form in which price information was presented was also noted: whether grouped in the general section or set out individually for each resort as part of the resort description. The general IT product information was further analysed, using a regular 100-cell grid, to determine the proportion of each page devoted to headings, text, photographs, maps, tables and 'white' (unused) space.

The second data set established for each resort in the brochure the number of pages occupied by the description of its attractions and facilities and, using the same grid-cell approach, the proportion of page space devoted to headings, text, photographs, tables, maps and white space. A detailed analysis of the text identified the proportion devoted to skiing conditions and facilities, après-ski, accommodation and price/travel information. Photographs on the resort pages were also analysed via the grid-cell technique to demonstrate their relative coverage of skiing activities, après-ski, and accommodation. Each resort was also measured against two check lists to determine what information was given about a resort's attractions and facilities. The first list concentrated on information which potential skiers would require about conditions, e.g. snowfall, resort height, length of season, aspect, vertical extent of skiing; about facilities, e.g. prepared pistes, lift systems, ski schools; and about activities, e.g. ski tests, ski races, mono-skiing, heli-skiing. The second considered après-ski and facilities for other winter activities, e.g. indoor swimming and tennis, bowling, squash, sleigh rides, etc.

These data sets were used to compare tour operator brochures and especially resort profiles, in particular whether the same resort, used by two or more tour operators, is represented differently.

The product image

As suggested above the brochure is the tour operator's first-line weapon in the hard sell and their brand image must stand out in the pages describing their skiing IT(s). Whilst factual information about skiing activities, accommodation types, alternative travel modes and tour operator resort services is given it 'sprouts' a slogan-laden veneer designed to persuade the potential holidaymaker that this tour operator is 'The best in the business', 'The people to ski with', or offers 'The experience that guarantees great holidays'. Whilst mass tour operators may claim 'something for everyone', the marketing message is often targeted selectively, e.g. 'Skiing made easy' at first-time skiers, or 'Top value skiing at low low prices' at the young budget-conscious skier. Attention is drawn to the tour operator's experience of operating skiing ITs (i.e. reliability) and on the quality of their resort staff - 'friendly efficient resort representatives, knowledgeable ski guides, super chalet girls, caring child-minders' - in order to support such claims as 'At your service', 'We care', and 'We take more care'. Destination characteristics are rarely mentioned as part of the product image.

Length of brochure varies from four to 180 pages: generally, the longer the brochure the greater the proportion of pages devoted to resort description. The longest brochures are therefore produced by tour operators offering the greatest choice of destinations: these are primarily British and Dutch mass tour operators (although a few UK specialist tour operators rival them). As Table 10.1 shows, brochures of mass tour operators are over twice as long as the average length of brochure and the similarity of presentation between British and Dutch mass tour operators' brochures is striking. Not surprisingly the proportion of pages devoted to product characteristics and image is greatest for smaller and highly specialist tour operators who target particular market segments and offer an IT programme based on a few resorts. Direct sell tour operators devote most space - nearly half of their pages - to product characteristics and image. The single purpose intent of skiing brochures is obvious from Table 10.1 since the use of advertisements (e.g. for skis or ski clothes) is very restricted. The only tour operators to promote other holiday opportunities

Table 10.1: Product, resort and price information in skiing brochures

Tour Operator Type	Av.No pages	% of Pages Devoted to			Non-Ski	Prices (% on Resort page)
		Product	Resorts	Ads		
UK mass	98	22	76	1	1	75
Young market	33	36	60	4	–	100
Direct sell	21	46	53	–	1	56
Specialist	38	37	52	1	–	69
Foreign-owned	38	35	48	–	17	64
Av. all UK	42	38	57	1	4	70
Dutch mass	105	20	79	1	–	50

Table 10.2: Presentation of general inclusive tour information in skiing brochures

Tour Operator Type	Information Format (%)					White Space
	Heads	Text	Photos	Maps	Tables	
UK mass	7	34	30	2	15	12
Young market	7	34	30	1	16	12
Direct sell	10	36	28	4	12	10
Specialist	8	30	33	2	11	16
Foreign-owned	6	36	24	3	18	13
Av. all TOs	8	35	27	3	13	14
Dutch mass	8	33	27	7	12	13

are UK-registered subsidiaries of foreign parent companies, e.g. Club Méditerranée where two-thirds of the brochure is devoted to non-skiing holidays.

Tour operators usually devote some 13 pages to their IT brand image and holiday information. These pages are dominated by text and photographs, as Table 10.2 demonstrates, and only in the case of specialist tour operators does space taken by photographs exceed that taken by text. This general information is interspersed with colour, action photographs of skiers, especially where text deals with the operator's services such as ski guides, ski schools, ski hire, etc. Text also deals with travel arrangements in some detail, often illustrating this section with photographs of coaches and/or aircraft and using tabular presentations for resort access relative to departure airports. General descriptions of the type of accommodation used are given, along with photographs. The formatting of this general product information does not differ markedly between brochures of the different categories of tour operator: in only one instance is there a striking difference - Dutch mass tour operators' greater use of maps to show choice of resort.

The resort profile

Each resort, in each brochure, is the subject of a short focused overview which attempts a detailed description of its attractions and facilities:

(i) the skiing available. This will include the 'vital' statistics of the resort as a skiing area, e.g. number and length of pistes, number and type of lifts, availability of lift passes, ski school details. It is now common to find ambitious piste maps showing lifts and runs, the latter usually colour-coded according to severity;
(ii) the après-ski opportunities. Eating and drinking, dancing/discos, and other sporting activities and excursions are covered. Mention may well be made of opportunities for any non-skiers in a holiday group;
(iii) each (named) accommodation unit, i.e. hotel, chalet, etc. Size, location within the resort, interior decor, general and en suite facilities and meal arrangements are noted. Where accommodation is on a self-catering basis a plan of the unit's layout is frequently included.

These 'resort snapshots' should correspond to place images but the emphasis is on the positive features. This is reflected in use of headings and summary panels in some brochures where value-laden judgements (such as 'lively après-ski - lots of British!' or 'one of those few places that has to be taken seriously - on and off the slopes') transmit eye- and phrase-catching messages to the potential holidaymaker.

Table 10.3: Presentation of resort information in skiing brochures

Tour Operator Type	Information Format (%)					
	Heads	Text	Photos	Maps	Tables	White Space
Mass	7	26	38	13	11	5
Young market	8	19	42	8	12	11
Direct sell	8	26	35	10	4	17
Specialist	5	22	45	7	8	13
Foreign-owned	7	21	40	10	13	8
Average	7	24	36	9	10	14
Range	2-16	8-67	0-58	0-20	0-25	0-62

The resort base of the skiing IT programmes offered by the tour operators studied varied from a single resort to 120 resorts. Excluding the 17-page brochure of the tour operator specialising in one resort, the number of pages devoted to each resort in the brochures varied from as little as 0.4 to a maximum of 5.0 pages. Presentation of information on the resort pages was examined using the same method as for the IT product pages: the results are shown in Table 10.3 (in which British and Dutch mass tour operators are grouped together). Variations in resort page layout exist between types of tour operator: for example, tour operators who target the young market make greater use of photographs than do either mass or direct sell tour operators. However, the averages presented in Table 10.3 mask considerable differences between tour operators within each category because some include price information on resort pages whilst others do not, some use piste and/or resort maps and others do not, and in one case no photographs are used.

Table 10.4 examines the use of text and photographs to describe resorts. As expected skiing activities and facilities are most prominent, accounting for nearly half of the photographic space and two-fifths of the text, although description of accommodation units occupies the same proportion of text. The space devoted to accommodation confirms its importance as a major factor influencing a holidaymaker's choice (as already hinted by Kent in Chp. 3). Again, however, the average figures are not representative

Table 10.4: The use of text and photographs in resort profiles (percentages)

Coverage of:	Text Average	Range	Photographs Average	Range
Skiing	38	0-87	47	0-100
Après-ski	14	0-51	11	0-47
Accommodation	38	0-100	32	0-100
Other	10	0-55	10	0-30

of all brochures as the percentage ranges in Table 10.4 demonstrate. For example, overall the representation of après-ski is limited but in brochures designed to appeal to the young singles market the emphasis on après-ski may be up to four times higher than the average.

Comparison of destinations for (and by) skiers is difficult since 'every resort is somebody's ideal resort but none suits everyone' (Gill, 1986). Many resorts are unsuitable for certain types of skier, e.g. they lack nursery slopes and easy pistes for beginners in some cases whilst in others there is an absence of challenging pistes ('black runs') for advanced skiers. The skiing information given on the resort page may not be the most helpful in selecting a destination: length of pistes of varying grades is of little use to someone contemplating an early or late skiing holiday if there is no mention of the resort's snow record. Do tour operators provide similar skiing information about the resorts included in their brochures? Do they recognise the differential suitability of resorts for skiers of different ability levels and how do they present this information in their brochures?

For ten French Alpine resorts, which appeared in the brochures of at least eight British and Dutch tour operators, a comparison was made of the characteristics of skiing areas and facilities listed in the resort profiles. The analysis proceeded on a presence or absence basis for each characteristic in the case of each resort in each brochure: the results presented in percentage form in Table 10.5 show for each resort the proportion of tour operators detailing each characteristic. These characteristics are not exhaustive of the skiing information contained in brochures but they are representative of the information that skiers

Table 10.5: Resort profiles for popular French ski resorts (percentage of times a characteristic is mentioned in TO brochures)

Skiing Facilities	A	B	C	D	E	F	G	H	I	J	Av.
Resort height	84	79	90	88	79	83	79	83	76	67	81
Vertical extent	84	86	80	100	89	88	86	83	72	83	85
Snowfall	5	7	10	25	5	13	38	11	4	11	13
Piste length/No	79	86	50	88	79	63	86	61	60	67	72
Piste grades	74	71	90	100	84	71	86	78	60	72	79
Piste maps	63	79	50	88	74	79	71	61	64	67	70
Nursery slopes	21	21	20	38	26	29	50	22	28	22	28
Slope aspect	37	21	30	38	37	33	29	32	60	22	34
Lift capacity	26	21	30	25	32	29	43	22	16	28	27
Lift types	63	50	70	63	79	42	86	61	68	50	63
Lift pass	68	79	50	75	74	50	64	44	60	50	61
Ski school open.	32	29	10	25	37	25	21	28	20	17	24
Ski school lang.	32	14	10	38	21	33	29	44	24	22	27
Ski bus	16	50	10	38	32	25	0	61	60	6	30
Ski guiding	26	14	30	50	37	42	14	28	20	28	29
Off-piste	32	57	40	88	63	58	57	78	60	28	56
Langlauf	63	71	50	75	53	54	43	39	52	44	54
No of TOs	19	14	10	8	19	24	14	18	25	18	-

Note: A = Avoriaz; B = Chamonix; C = Courchevel; D = Flaine; E = La Plagne; F = Les Arcs; G = Les Deux Alpes; H = Tignes; I = Val d'Isère; J = Val Thorens

need in order to choose between resorts. However, no single characteristic is mentioned by all tour operators for all resorts. Generally the more tour operators offering a resort the lower is the maximum proportion of operators including a given characteristic. The only cases of 100 per cent representation - piste grades and vertical extent of skiing at Flaine - are for the resort served by fewest tour operators.

The relative importance of these skiing characteristics can be established from the average representation of each characteristic in the 10 resorts (see final column of Table 10.5). This percentage can be used to rank the importance of characteristics as seen by tour operators: the vertical range of skiing ranks first, closely followed by resort height and piste gradings. Information on piste lengths and location, lift facilities, off-piste and langlauf (cross-country) opportunities form a second group of characteristics represented in between one half and three-quarters of cases. Other characteristics appear less frequently, e.g. slope aspect, nursery slopes, ski-guiding, etc. in just a quarter to half of the cases. The lowest rank is for snowfall at the resort! (Where given this is the amount of snowfall rather than the snow record of the resort.)

The same resort can therefore exhibit variable, but overlapping profiles in different brochures. The profile coverage includes, at its most extensive, 20 or more skiing characteristics in certain brochures and as few as five characteristics, at its least extensive, in others. Such differences cannot be attributed simply to brochures targeting different market segments, although it is recognised, for example, that only brochures aimed at first-time skiers need to comment on the presence and quality of nursery slopes. The differences are primarily a reflection of the tour operators' 'house-styles' and their judgement of the characteristics they consider important to skiers deciding between resorts. There is a preoccupation with basic facts, i.e. number of lifts of different types, lengths of marked piste of differing severity, numbers of ski school instructors, etc. although certain factors, such as lift capacity, are neglected by some three-quarters of tour operators. For destination areas, coverage of a resort's skiing characteristics therefore depends on which tour operators offer skiing ITs to that resort.

Tour operators may not be consistent within a brochure - the coverage of characteristics is not the same for each resort. This is to be expected where facilities differ between resorts - langlauf opportunities may be present in one resort but not in another - but it also applies to basic information, such as resort height or lift capacities. Differences between resort profiles in brochures would be magnified if the analysis were to be extended to après-ski opportunities.

How accurate is the information presented? Further research is required. It was noted above that the information is not consistent within a single brochure - in at least one case the length of marked piste at Avoriaz is given as three times longer on the resort page than in a comparative resort table on another page. Nor do numbers quoted always tally, e.g. in one brochure the total

number of lifts quoted differed from that obtained
by summing numbers for cable cars, gondolas, chair
and drag lifts in half of the French ski resorts
examined. There is a lack of agreement between
operators' brochures in respect to the skiing
characteristics of common resorts although,
generally, there is agreement on figures for height
of resort and overall length of marked piste.
Confusion rules, however, in other comparisons:

(i)   on number of lifts of different types,
e.g. for Les Arcs four tour operators quoted
53, 52, 35 and 34, respectively for the total
number of lifts. All agreed there were two
cable cars; three operators had no gondolas
but the fourth had five; for chair lifts 14,
16, 16 and 17 and drag lifts 19, 34, 17 and 34
were the quoted numbers (in the same order as
the original totals!);
(ii)   on numbers of pistes of differing
severity, e.g. two British mass tour operators
agree the overall length of marked piste at
both Tignes and La Plagne but at Tignes have a
threefold difference in both the number of
green (easy) runs and red (intermediate) ones
and at La Plagne a fivefold difference on
green runs and a threefold one on red runs;
(iii)   on numbers of English-speaking ski
school instructors, e.g. at Les Arcs there is
a 100 per cent difference in the number quoted
by two tour operators.

These examples are sufficient to suggest that
the information quoted in brochures is rarely 100
per cent accurate. As a result destination areas,
in addition to receiving only partial coverage, may
be under- or over-presented with respect to their
'vital' skiing statistics, i.e. the place product
is not represented in the same way as if promoted
by destination tourism agencies.

Resort gradings

Tour operators do not present resorts in a
neutral or purely factual way. Brochures are
designed to sell their products and textual comment
provides a positive interpretation of the skiing
opportunities in each resort. This is frequently
done by assigning resort gradings: half of the
brochures studied attempted some formal grading of

resorts' suitabilities for different types of skiers. Grading adds another dimension to the possibility of misrepresentation of destinations and to the likelihood of differences between tour operators. For the tour operator a grading scheme is equivalent to segmenting the market within a single brochure, e.g. one resort may be best suited for first-time skiers, another for experts, yet another for a mixed ability group. But do tour operators get their grading assessments right? If they do, tour operators using the same resort would grade it identically as to skiing suitabilities.

Tour operators have their own different resort grading schemes - the only thing these have in common is that the criteria upon which each scheme is based are not made explicit in the brochure. Schemes categorise skiers as beginners, intermediates, or advanced, although most Dutch tour operators merely distinguish beginners from other skiers. Resorts are graded according to their suitability for each skier category: the grading schemes are highly variable ranging from two simple divisions (recommended, available), through word codes (excellent, good, poor), to star ratings (normally a three-point scale, although four- and five-point scales are also used).

Gradings were compared for 16 French resorts - all but one located in the Alps - to which skiing ITs were offered by at least two tour operators. Table 10.6 shows, in percentage terms, the highest number of tour operators serving each resort agreeing a particular grade of suitability for each skiing category, e.g. of the 10 tour operators using Les Arcs five (50 per cent) rated it 'excellent' for beginners, three well suited and two less suitable. The results suggest that tour operators are less likely to produce common gradings for beginners and advanced skiers than they are for intermediates - in less than one in five cases do all tour operators using a resort agree a common rating for either beginners or advanced skiers (compared to agreement in nine out of ten instances for intermediates). For any given resort, on average, one-third of tour operators rate its suitability for both beginners and advanced skiers differently from the majority. No comment is made here as to whether the majority rating is the correct one: the important conclusion is that individual tour operators interpret what is essentially the same factual base differently. Tour operators may therefore project

Table 10.6: Resort gradings - agreement between tour operators

| Resort | No of Tour ops. | Max percentage of TOs in Resort Agreeing Grading for | | |
		B	I	A
Alpe d'Huez	5	80	100	80
Avoriaz	7	42	86	86
Chamonix	5	40	60	60
Courchevel	4	50	75	75
Flaine	3	100	100	66
La Mongie	2	50	100	100
La Plagne	8	88	100	63
Les Arcs	10	50	100	60
Les Coches	2	100	100	50
Les Deux Alpes	6	50	100	67
Montgenevre	3	67	100	67
Tignes	8	37	100	100
Val d'Isère	10	40	100	90
Valfrejus	3	100	67	100
Valmorel	4	50	100	50
Val Thorens	8	75	88	88
Average	-	64	93	64
Percentage of resorts where TOs in full agreement		19	69	19

B = Beginners; I = Intermediates; A = Advanced

different images of the suitability of the same resort to prospective skiers. Is this in the destination's best interest?

CONCLUSIONS

'Brochure Speak'

Brochures are designed to sell tour operators' products. As with comparative shopping, wide choice of ITs increases total sales. Intangible IT products are compared before purchase (booking) via information in brochures, which continue to act as a product substitute up to the time of departure. Brochures supply holidaymakers with a plethora of information, especially about destinations. Frequently that information needs further interpretation: it is difficult, for example, to put to good use the 'vital' skiing statistics normally quoted for each resort. Moreover, tour operators are selective when presenting information about the destination and often it is information not given, e.g. snow record, bed/lift capacity ratio, location of accommodation within the resort, which would be of more value in assisting choice. Even where information is presented imaginatively, e.g. a piste map conveys what a ski area has to offer much better than a list of statistics, different tour operators' brochures make the same resort look very different.

Brochures are a prime vehicle for creating a brand image and Middleton (1988) argues that competition between tour operators will switch increasingly from price to product image and positioning. Where two tour operators offer skiing ITs to the same resort they start from the same objective factual base but each seeks to differentiate its product from that of their rival. This may be done in the way they present the destination, its attractions and facilities. Thus, it was shown above that tour operators rarely present exactly the same 'vital' skiing statistics for a resort, that where they do quote the same characteristic(s) different values can occur, and that where 'suitability ratings' are given there are differences of interpretation of those characteristics. In a sense it is not the resort information _per se_ which is instrumental to differentiation of a tour operator's product (and any successful alternative layout of the resort pages would soon be copied) but more the way in which the tour operator 'bundles' components to form a distinctive IT, including ways of augmenting the product.

In the case of skiing the need to 'interpret' and even supplement tour operators' brochures has generated a range of independent skiing guides (which also serve the large independent skier market). These guides claim to be independent, impartial, consistent, and perhaps most important, discriminating in that they make both positive and negative pronouncements about a resort's skiing, après-ski and accessibility - prevalence of ski lift queues, inconvenience of accommodation location within the resort, poor snow records, etc. are commented upon.

Such guides enjoy greater licence to pronounce judgements than tour operators' brochures. There is an obligation to ensure that description and information contained in the brochure are accurate since the brochure forms the basis of the holidaymaker's contract with the tour operator: 'no-one would justify knowingly issuing incorrect information but slovenly compilation itself has become a serious offence' (Holloway & Plant, 1988). The European Commission places an obligation on member states to ensure that information in brochures is legible, accurate and understandable and in the UK it is a legal requirement that brochure information should not be misleading. But that is not the same as saying it should be accurate (National Consumer Council, 1988). The effect, according to Holloway and Plant (1988) 'is to make tour operators' brochures less interesting, more coldly factual, and sadly, less helpful'.

The content analysis of skiing brochures presented above casts doubts, however, on the accuracy of the resort information they contain. Even where brochures do not falsify reality their descriptions and photographs of resorts are so selective that the actual environment is not recognisable by the holidaymaker (Lundgren, 1985). Where resorts are misrepresented or negative features are ignored the satisfaction derived by holidaymakers will be below expectations, with obvious adverse consequences for repeat visits to that resort and repeat bookings for the tour operator concerned. Indeed, research conducted by the European Commission showed a high level of dissatisfaction with ITs - about one-third of UK consumers expressing some dissatisfaction (National Consumer Council, 1988). Holidays can, of course, result in disappointment for a variety of reasons, only some of which are attributable to the actions of tour operators, but it is also likely that inadequate information in brochures is a contributory cause to such disappointment and a source of legitimate complaint by holidaymakers.

Lessons for destination areas

Destination tourism agencies seek to get their resorts included in tour operators' programmes. In addition, it is in their interest to ensure that their resorts are represented fully and accurately in tour operators' brochures. This is the only way to ensure destinations reap long-term benefits from tourism. Tour operators can always drop resorts from their IT portfolios for the following season, even where the lack of success of the resort stems from the tour operator's informational error, e.g. the skiing tour operator who grades a resort suitable for beginners when it is not so. Ensuring tour operators have accurate and up-to-date information is the way a destination can avoid such a calamity.

It is also important that the descriptions of resorts in tour operators' brochures conform to and reinforce the promotional images destination tourism agencies transmit directly to prospective holidaymakers. Destination tourism agencies and enterprises need close and continuing contact with tour operators in order to distribute information on their resorts. Tour operators need to be confident that the information being supplied is accurate! Accurate transmission of information onward to tour operators is especially important where the latter are interested in a resort because it fits into their market segmentation programme. For example, a skiing resort being marketed to young, single skiers must have appropriate skiing for intermediates and experts, accommodation preferably in the form of chalets, and suitable après-ski facilities such as discos. Destination tourism agencies need to improve their contact with tour operators at the latter's initial planning stage. If successful contact is established they may be able to contribute to the augmentation of the tour operator's product, e.g. in arranging for skiing tuition to be organised as an integrated part of a skiing IT.

REFERENCES

Allen, T. (1985) Marketing by a small tour operator in a market dominated by big operators, European Journal of Marketing, 19, 83-90

Burkart, A.J. & Medlik, S. (1981) Tourism: Past, Present and Future, 2nd edition, Heinemann, London

Delaney-Smith, P. (1987) The tour operator - new and maturing business, pp 94-106 in A. Hodgson (Ed) The Travel and Tourism Industry: Strategies for the Future, Pergamon, Oxford

Gill, C. (Ed)(1986) The Good Skiing Guide, Consumers' Association and Hodder & Stoughton, London

Goodall, B., Radburn, M. & Stabler, M. (1988) Market opportunity sets for tourism, _Geographical Paper 100: Tourism Series_, 1, Dept of Geography, University of Reading, Reading

Holloway, J.C. (1985) _The Business of Tourism_, 2nd edition, Pitman, London

Holloway, J.C. & Plant, R.V. (1988) _Marketing for Tourism_, Pitman, London

Kotler, P. (1984) _Marketing Management: Analysis, Planning and Control_, 5th edition, Prentice-Hall, London

Lundgren, D.E. (1985) _The Tourist Business_, 5th edition, Van Nostrand Reinhold, New York

Medlik, S. & Middleton, V.T.C. (1973) Product formulation in tourism, in _Tourism and Marketing_, Vol. 13, AIEST, Berne

Middleton, V.T.C. (1988) _Marketing in Travel and Tourism_, Heinemann, Oxford

National Consumer Council (1988) _Package Holidays: Dreams, Nightmares and Consumer Redress_, PD 18/88, National Consumer Council, London

III

FROM PRODUCT TO ORGANISATION

The tourism product, however this has been defined in the preceding chapters, is shaped from a variety of urban elements, whether these be the existing commercial and public services originally intended for residents, the relict artefacts and historic associations which can be interpreted as 'heritage', or facilities built specifically for tourist use. These are combined at various spatial scales with other elements drawn from the attributes of the wider region and packaged in various ways in the brochures of tour operators. In all of these the role of intermediary organisations was apparent. The selection, combination, interpretation and packaging are all the result of conscious goal-directed decisions made within organisations created for that purpose. It is therefore both logical and necessary to shift the focus of attention from the product to the organisation that created it.

In most studies of tourism development this self-evident necessity has proved so difficult to implement that it is frequently not attempted in any systematic manner. The organisational element is introduced only in the description of the later stages of the marketing process, as a more or less unique set of instruments for placing a pre-determined product upon a pre-selected market. The dangers of such an approach are evident in most of the above chapters where not only the detailed dimensions of the product, but even more basic conceptualisation of the nature of the holiday product, have been shown to be dependent upon the initial institutional framework of the analysis. It is equally tempting to respond to the diversity of organisational structures by treating each as uniquely different, and thus to be individually described in each case. The foregoing chapters however have eschewed this approach when related to tourists, tourism resources and even tourism places, and attempted instead to categorise and theorise with the intention that more generally applicable conclusions can be drawn. It would be inconsistent having treated the other elements in the tourism marketing process in this way, then to regard each organisation as a unique phenomenon to be described as such.

The difficulty as in all such attempts to generalise is the sheer diversity of organisations involved in the marketing of tourism. All four of the following chapters consider aspects of tourism marketing from the point of view of a unique organisation. There are however three dimensions that can be used to aid the allocation of these particular organisations to more general categories. Each of these dimensions however has limitations which must be appreciated if they are to be used as the basis of a general taxonomy of tourism marketing institutions.

The theory-application dimension

There are many explanations of the failure of a widely acceptable body of theory to emerge in tourism studies. The very disciplinary eclecticism illustrated in the contributions to this book has encouraged contributors to seek theoretical structures from within their parent disciplines rather than search for more general multi-disciplinary frameworks. In any event tourism has from its inception as a separate study been essentially applied and practical, with the concomitant and inevitable in-built distrust of the practitioner for the theoretician. This situation may or may not be intrinsically important in the long run, but it has important consequences within tourism organisations. Namely that in the absence of an agreed set of concepts, techniques, definitions or research programme priorities, organisations have tended to establish their own as a result of their confrontation with specific empirical problems. The four chapters which follow each make distinctive contributions to theory, broadly defined, which are applicable elsewhere. Examples would include van der Knijff's use of site evaluation criteria, or Pattinson's search for the relevant elements in regional image definition. Such contributions however, are largely incidental, in that they were not the initial purpose of the work presented and result from the search for ad hoc solutions to ad hoc problems. Any wider application would have to bear that in mind and make appropriate allowances.

The public-private dimension

An obvious distinction to draw between organisations is between those in the pub private sectors. However this distinction, blurred in practice, has become even more difficult to distinguish in the last decade. The organisations considered in detail below may be legally responsible or democratically accountable to public authorities or to private firms, or more likely to various combinations of the two. The management structure may however be less important as a distinguishing characteristic than the nature of the objectives and the methods of operation.

In the case of Carinthia considered by Zimmermann, the organisation is a complex balance of public and private bodies pursuing an equally complex mix of collective and commercial goals. The regional tourist board, described by Pattinson is pursuing essentially commercial profit-making objectives in the service of private firms, and far from including collective social or public planning goals is actually in conflict with them in a number of ways. The actual legal organisational structure of the Board, its statutory origins and its system of accountability, is of less importance in its allocation to the public or private sectors than in how it operates in terms of the working philosophy of its personnel and the goals that it seeks. The van der Knijff and Radburn and Goodall chapters can also be contrasted by their relative positions along this public-private spectrum. The Frisian case illustrates the work of a publicly responsible local authority pursuing politically defined goals, while the case of the travel agents is equally clearly a study of the operation of private commercial firms in a competitive market. Despite this both are dependent in different ways upon implicit partnerships between the public and private sectors. The provincial authority as initiator and coordinator of tourism development remains dependent upon private enterprise and investment for the detailed execution of its general plans; while for the independent travel agent the public sector is viewed as the creator of the external legal context for their operation.

The promotion-management dimension

The process of tourism marketing, which

extends from the shaping of the product to its final consumption by the customer, is rarely the responsibility of a single organisation. In particular there is a distinction between those organisations concerned with managing the product and those concerned with promoting it. This distinction results in what is in many ways a curious and logically untenable situation. Few other products are 'sold' by organisations that have no responsibility for, control over or even ownership of, their manufacture.

The explanation undoubtedly lies in the equally curious nature of tourism as an industry and the way responsibilities for it have been assumed incrementally by various authorities. The four cases described below concern themselves with quite different combinations of these two aspects of the marketing process. The regional tourist boards are promotion agencies who market the services of others, who may or may not be subscribing members, and more widely are selling resources of landscape beauty or historic atmosphere over which they have neither control nor ownership. The travel agents are in a similar position in so far as they are selling destinations as a whole but in another sense they are assemblers of packages of services which they may or may not themselves produce. The Carinthia tourism organisation however is responsible for both promotion and for the management of many tourism facilities. By contrast, the Frisian provincial planners are attempting to manage aspects of the product or to initiate and coordinate new products, but are not directly concerned with the subsequent promotion of such products.

Thus all four case studies illustrate in detail different aspects of each of these dimensions and their location in particular national contexts, whether the United Kingdom, Austria or The Netherlands, is less important than these generic characteristics, which could be reproduced in examples from elsewhere.

Chapter 11

THE ORGANISATION OF TOURISM IN AUSTRIA: MARKETING AT THE PROVINCIAL LEVEL

Friedrich Zimmermann

INTRODUCTION

This chapter discusses the Austrian attempt to reorganise the basis of tourism marketing at the provincial level. Until recently tourism marketing was undertaken by Provincial Tourist Offices, functioning as part of the provincial administration. Developments in tourism made it desirable to separate these marketing activities from administration to make the organisation better balanced and more effective. Although the structure described below may seem too complex to work flexibly, it is the structure which the Austrians, after long discussion, see as having the best chance of success.

TOURISM IN AUSTRIA

Structure and processes

The economic importance of tourism in Austria can be demonstrated by the following facts: Austria is visited by about 15 million foreign tourists, who spend 85 million nights there each year. The receipts from international tourism in Austria in the mid-1980s are about £11,500 million per year. This compares with £7,700 million in the United States, £5,000 million in Italy, £8,500 million in Spain and £7,500 million in France.

Domestic tourism is of the order of about 5.5 million guests who also make an important contribution to the total receipts of the tourism industry; Austrians account for 28 million overnight stays per year.

The organisation of the tourism industry in Austria can be characterised as small to medium scale, while the sources of capital are mostly private and family enterprises are dominant. There

199

has been only limited multinational investments, and venture capital is of little importance within Austrian tourism. The supply of accommodation has developed in response to strong demand pressure dating back to the early 1960s; it had increased to about 1.2 million guest beds by the mid-1980s. A special phenomenon is the letting of rooms in private homes (30 per cent of all available beds) which contributes much to the dispersion of guests in peripheral areas.

The demand shows an extremely high proportion of foreigners, viz. 76 per cent, and a clearly marked dominance of visitors from the Federal Republic of Germany (two-thirds of all overnight stays of foreigners, followed by the Netherlands with 11 per cent and the United Kingdom with 5 per cent). Marked changes in travel behaviour show in the reduction in summer tourism, which declined from 78.2 to 66.8 million overnight stays between 1981 and 1987. The product **Summer in the Alps** in its traditional form does not seem to be attractive any longer, and is subject to widespread international competition. Winter tourism, which was a growth area up to the early 1980s (with overnight stays increasing from 23 to 43 million between 1971 and 1981; 1987 - 47 million) now shows a marked tendency to decrease. This is an indication that a certain phase of maturity has been reached in certain winter-sports products. Furthermore, main holiday stays have been extensively replaced by visitors taking short holidays and seeking recreation in nearby places. These changes are also marked by a clear and increasing regional concentration, tendencies towards centralisation and a steady increase of the west-east tourism gradient. The percentage of overnight stays in the western provinces of Salzburg, the Tyrol and Vorarlberg increased from 40 per cent in the early 1950s to 66 per cent in 1986.

Tourism policy and organisation: the legal aspects

Under the Austrian Constitution, tourism is the responsibility of the provinces (Länder) which until recently included a Provincial Tourist Office as an integral part of the provincial administration. Provinces together with the Federal Government, shape the framework of tourism policy, the main objectives of which are:

(i) to encourage patriotism and regional identity;
(ii) to make people more aware of environmental problems;
(iii) to ensure that tourism provides visitors with positive emotional feelings;
(iv) to take advantage of old and new segments of the tourism market;
(v) to intensify promotional activities;
(vi) to improve marketing.

Another institution which influences tourism policy in Austria is the Austrian Tourism Congress, which meets every four years. This is organised by the Ministry for Economic Affairs and the Board of Trustees of Austrian Tourism, an institution which has the task of discussing and coordinating decision-making for Austrian tourism policy. At its 1989 meeting nine committees discussed tourism and the environment, man and tourism, education, training and information, the tourism economy, infrastructure, tourism supply, traffic and communications, public relations and marketing, and future trends.

It is very difficult to evaluate the effectiveness of overall tourism policy in Austria because of the very different frameworks which are operated to assist the tourism industry at the various levels of government. In particular the influence of the Federal Government is very limited compared to that of the provinces. In 1981, the Austrian Regional Development Conference published the Austrian Land Use Concept, which is being phased in over a period of 10 years and covers the following aspects of tourism:

(i) further improvements in the quality of accommodation;
(ii) development of special packages to extend the seasons;
(iii) special development strategies for peripheral regions;
(iv) conservation of the environment and local culture, and improved presentation of the cultural heritage;
(v) restoration of environmentally damaged tourism sites;
(vi) development of tourism supply without technical infrastructure, the so-called 'gentle tourism', which is more environmentally sensitive and pays more

attention to the living space and life styles of the native population.

Based on present tourism trends and developments, the question arises as to whether the existing legal and organisational framework for tourism in Austria with the extensive authority of the provinces can cope with future problems. The province of Carinthia will be used to demonstrate how implementation of the reorganisation of tourism management has progressed at the provincial level.

TARGETS AND STRATEGIC CONSIDERATIONS

In view of its achievements as well as its importance in the national and regional economies, the future long-term development of Austrian tourism must aim to optimise both economic and individual benefits from tourism whilst safeguarding the environment from damage. This overarching objective must be integrated into the processes of reaction and adaptation, which are constantly necessary in an economic sector as sensitive as tourism, where innovation cycles are becoming shorter and shorter, in order to achieve a transition to a 'rolling plan' principle. This will entail a highly flexible set of measures to create the 'landscape of tourism', as well as require the setting up of an information and early warning system. However, these arrangements must be considered utopian under the present legal and organisational framework.

In the course of any administrative restructuring certain strategies must be defined. The following measures are seem as desirable:

(i) Removal of tourism publicity and sales promotion from the provincial administration.
(ii) Creation of a flexible marketing structure organised by professionals at the provincial level: such a body should coordinate the activities within each region. The aim is to increase considerably the competitiveness of marketing in the international arena.
(iii) Professionalisation of the area-specific organisational structure for the entire marketing and planning of tourism, with units acting as managerial experts on a regional basis. A full-time managing director,

with advisory committees and a branch office structure might well be necessary to make effective use of existing resources.

(iv) A system of leading zones (leading regions) is required to achieve a better match between supply mix and real market conditions. Lead establishments should be installed within each region to guarantee vertical as well as horizontal exchange of information.

(v) Such a hierarchical marketing organisation would be of great importance, not only where it functions as a coordinating body but also with regard to the diffusion of information, advice and support relating to tourism supply to regional and community agencies as well as to individual businesses.

(vi) Marketing concepts have to be elaborated which further coordinate tourism supply with its targeted visitors.

(vii) Models for tourism development based on long-term interdisciplinary cooperation and graduated hierarchies need to be elaborated. These will serve as guidelines for provincial and regional action. The required analyses should be subject to tender and should encourage endogenous development and public participation to ensure public acceptance of proposals.

(viii) Plans and projects for improvement will be prioritised within the rolling plan as part of a flexible supply mix. Emphasis will be placed on existing tourism regions in order to maintain competitiveness.

(ix) All individual projects would be subject to an integral cost-benefit analysis, paying special attention to the impact on local population and environment (applying tests of social and environmental tolerance).

(x) A quality tourism product is central to local tourism success but must also be related to social, cultural and environmental matters.

CHANGING THE ORGANISATIONAL STRUCTURE

Reorganisation of the Austrian provincial administration for tourism will now be illustrated by reference to the changes recently introduced in the Province of Carinthia.

Marketing at the Provincial Level

The present organisation

The basis for the promotion of tourism by
government agencies can be traced back to 1974.
According to the existing legal position it is the
responsibility of the province, viz. the competent
member of the provincial government as well as the
Department of Tourism within the Provincial
Government (Tourist Office), to promote tourism.
This includes the following tasks:

(i)   tourism publicity and sales promotion;
(ii)   the support of events which promote
tourism;
(iii)   measures to improve the quality of the
tourism product as well as measures to
maintain and improve the basic structures of
tourism;
(iv)   assistance to private sector tourism
establishments.

These tasks can be assisted via government
grants, financed from the province's share of the
tourist tax. Publicity measures in particular are
financed by the taxes levied for overnight stays.
The 1974 attempt to introduce and concentrate
provincial tourism administration and marketing was
not wholly successful because:

(i)   A lack of flexibility in the Office of
the Provincial Government prevented quick
decisions, especially in the field of
marketing.
(ii)   Limited coordination and cooperation
existed between provincial, regional and local
tourism organisations, and the private sector.
(iii)   The limited decision-making
responsiblity for tourism of the local and
regional tourism organisations.
(iv) The failure to give enough scope for
decisions to experts in the field of marketing
within the framework of the Office of the
Provincial Government.

Reorganisation of tourism administration in Carinthia: The Carinthia Tourism Company Ltd

The basic principles, according to which
tourism is to be conducted (types of promotion,
publicity plans, preview of future development,

basic deliberations concerning policies of tourism) shall no longer be carried out by the Provincial Tourist Office without consulting experts and enterpreneurs. A marketing organisation is therefore to be established which will operate independently - a limited liability company is proposed. The partners are the Province of Carinthia, the group of experts specialising in tourism at the Chamber of Commerce, the Chamber of Workmen and Employees as well as the Chamber of Agriculture. The role of the company is to instigate measures in the interest of Carinthian tourism, especially the coordination and execution of all marketing activities. These include:

(i) Image creation and sales promotion, as well as general publicity for tourism in Carinthia.

(ii) Measures to promote and put into effect tourism innovations including the commercialisation of relevant results, ideas and experiences.

(iii) Market research, especially in the fields of publicity and sales promotion but also research in basic product structures.

(iv) Promotion of tourist events as an integral part of tourism marketing.

(v) Coordination and realisation of large scale events, which will benefit Carinthian tourism.

(vi) Presentation of tourism offers involving major publicity.

(vii) Coordination of regional and local marketing activities of Carinthian tourism facilities.

(viii) Consultation and promotion of regional and local tourism agencies as well as individual tourism businesses.

(ix) Coordination and cooperation with the Provincial Tourist Office.

(x) Cooperation with the national efforts to publicise tourism in Austria.

(xi) Participation in and establishment of tourism businesses within the framework of the company's terms of reference.

At the present time the Province of Carinthia has at its disposal income from the taxes levied on overnight stays (16 million overnight stays in 1988 generated £2 million) for any tourism publicity and sales promotion carried out on a supra-regional basis. Two-thirds of the provincial share in the national tourist tax can be added to this amount. Since the Provincial Tourist Office no longer carries out any marketing activity the provincial administration makes the funds available to the Carinthian Tourism Company, i.e. subsidises its marketing activities. The Company has wide powers to engage, not only in marketing activity, but also in supplying local components of the tourism product. The approval of the General Meeting (which functions as a Board of Directors) must be obtained where the Company is acquiring, selling or mortgaging real estate; acquiring and selling interests in local tourism businesses; obtaining trade licenses and taking up loans, funds and credits exceeding certain threshold amounts.

The Company's marketing function

The marketing activities of the Company rely heavily on a Marketing Advisory Board consisting of some 20 tourism experts. The right to nominate members to the Marketing Advisory Board rests with the partners of the Company, but, in order to integrate other important decision-makers, further representatives are drawn from the Carinthian Tourist Conference, the Austrian Association of Hotel-Owners, the Austrian Union of Communes, the Austrian Union of Towns, the Austrian Trades Union, the Camping-Sites Business Group, etc. The Chairman of the Marketing Advisory Board is nominated by the Provincial Government and in order to guarantee coordination, cooperation and diffusion of information, the member of the Provincial Government with responsibility tourism, will be vice-chairman. The Marketing Advisory Board:

(i) approves the Company's publicity strategy for the coming two years and the preview for the next five years;
(ii) deliberates on the proposals submitted by the Tourist Conference (see below) and makes recommendations on these to the Company;
(iii) has the right to make recommendations regarding all matters handled by the Carinthia Tourism Company;
(iv) has the right to establish, with the agreement of the Company, expert committees to examine special problems associated with the provincial tourism industry.

The Carinthian Tourist Conference

The Carinthian Tourist Conference which meets every year is essentially a forum for information exchange and policy debate. Its members are tourism and spa managers of Carinthia, plus entrepreneurs from the tourism communes. The latter are represented according to the number of overnight stays (with overnight stays of under 100,000: 1 delegate, from 100,001 up to 500,000: 2 delegates, with more than 500,000 overnight stays: 3 delegates). In addition the Provincial Expert on Tourism, the members of the Marketing Advisory Board, the director of the Provincial Tourist Office, the manager of the 'Regional Care' Department, the manager of the Carinthia Tourism Co. Ltd., are co-opted. The Conference seeks to coordinate information on the structure of and developments in tourism, and on the activities of the Carinthia Tourism Co. Ltd, as well as making recommendations for tourism marketing and tourism policy which are binding upon the Marketing Advisory Board.

Alongside the departments of marketing, 'public relations', 'advertising', 'sales promotion', etc., a department of 'regional care' is to be established as part of the company. This department will serve as a liaison office for the various regions in order to guarantee constant contact with the 'reality of tourism' in the communes and regions and, consequently, to safeguard 'internal marketing'. It will administer all measures relating to coordination and cooperation between the Tourism Company, regions, communes and tourism businesses; it will be a contact office for enquiries and information as well as the contact point on all marketing matters. The regional tourism industry is thus continually involved with decisions in tourism marketing, and can for its part make an important contribution towards the improvement of tourism marketing in Carinthia.

ROLE OF THE PROVINCIAL TOURIST OFFICE

When the tasks of marketing are handed over to the Carinthia Tourism Co. Ltd., the Provincial Tourist Office will still retain responsibility for:

(i) tourism policy including, consultation on projects and evaluation of projects for tourism development at commune and regional levels so as to achieve optimal utilisation of resources;

(ii) tourism planning and financing of tourism facilities (a coordinating function between Province and Federal Government);

(iii) financial support for special measures or activities on the regional and commune level as well as for establishments;

(iv) administrative coordination - where planning of and consultation on projects is concerned - between the Provincial Tourist Office, Department of Communes, Provincial Planning Authorities and the Department for Environmental Matters.

OUTLOOK

The demands to carry out a restructuring of Carinthia's tourism organisation must lead to a number of problems arising from the nature of the political environment and from conflicts of interest within both public and private sectors of the regional tourism industry. In spite of these problems and, especially, in view of the international development of tourism which since the early 1980s has by-passed Carinthia, it seems to be high time to change existing structures, to improve decisively the marketing situation and to capitalise upon existing potentials for innovation and investment in order to regain and maintain international competitiveness.

Although the centralisation of marketing has not gone uncontested it shows that the development of tourism in Carinthia cannot be left to its own momentum, as has been the case so far, as every individual decision in such a complicated commercial domain may produce unpredictable and, very often, irreparable changes.

Chapter 12

PLACE PROMOTION BY TOURIST BOARDS: THE EXAMPLE OF 'BEAUTIFUL BERKSHIRE'

Gill Pattinson

REGIONAL TOURIST BOARDS IN ENGLAND

The Development of Tourism Act, 1969, which set up the British Tourist Authority (BTA) and the national Tourist Boards for England, Scotland and Wales with defined powers, structures and functions, also provided a powerful stimulus to the development of a regional organisation for tourism in Great Britain. The National Tourist Boards, especially the English one, gave high priority to the establishment of a regional organisation which provided a complete and comprehensive cover of their respective countries. The result was the creation and growth of non-statutory **Regional Tourist Boards** in England during the first half of the 1970s. In some parts of the country regional boards were based on existing local or regional tourism organisations but in other parts where no such local body existed and where there was a lack of indigeneous support, especially from local government circles, the successful formation of such Regional Tourist Boards took a considerable time (Bowes, 1988).

Since Regional Tourist Boards are autonomous administrative organisations their structure and roles may differ between the various English regions, reflecting in large part the differences in the importance of tourism across the country. Although some financial support comes from central sources, such as the English Tourist Board, the Regional Tourist Boards are increasingly expected to draw funds and members from the local authorities and commercial tourism interests within their respective areas. Each Tourist Board region needs to be of a size which will support a viable and effective organisation. All the Regional Tourist Boards had been established before the 1974 reorganisation of local government in England but, in most instances, the tourist board regions correspond to groupings of the new counties. Other organisations such as the National Trust and the British Hotels, Restauranteurs and Caterers Association have re-aligned their regional boundaries to match the tourist board areas because of the marketing advantages they derive. However, the tourist board groupings of counties do not always correspond to standard economic regions and statistics available for the latter, e.g. on employment, cannot be used for tourist board regions without being regrouped.

Within each designated Regional Tourist Board area it must be recognised that the local authorities (county, district and borough councils) are the destination organisations with powers to develop and promote tourism in their respective areas through the activities of their leisure and recreation departments, their structure and local plans, and their planning control decisions.

Regional Tourist Boards therefore provide a link between national and local scales, improving cooperation between local authorities and commercial tourism interests and interpreting national tourism policies at a specific spatial scale. The general objectives of Regional Tourist Boards may be summarised as:

> (i) to produce a coordinated regional tourism strategy in liaison with local authorities and consistent with the broad aims of the English Tourist Board;
> (ii) to offer advice to both commercial tourism businesses and local authorities on tourism planning;
> (iii) to encourage the development of tourist amenities and facilities which meet the needs of a changing market;
> (iv) to administer the national financial aid scheme for assisting tourism development;
> (v) to represent the interests of the region at the national level and the interests of the tourism industry within the region;
> (vi) to market the region by providing reception and information services, producing and supplying suitable literature, and undertaking promotional activities.

These objectives are not accorded equal priority and may be ranked differently by different Regional Tourist Boards. However, first and foremost,

Regional Tourist Boards may be regarded as marketing agencies: their role is to promote places, i.e. attract visitors to destinations in their areas. Their development role is of increasing importance, as is a management role in respect to tourism in their areas. The marketing activities of one Regional Tourist Board, the Thames and Chilterns, and its development of one particular place campaign - **'Beautiful Berkshire'** - is the focus of this chapter.

PLACE PROMOTION AND THE THAMES AND CHILTERNS TOURIST BOARD

The Thames and Chilterns Tourist Board (TCTB) is one of the twelve English Regional Tourist Boards and its constituent counties are Bedfordshire, Berkshire, Buckinghamshire, Hertfordshire and Oxfordshire (see Fig. 12.1). The Board's marketing strategy and its promotion of particular places has evolved throughout the 16 years it has been in existence. A series of studies undertaken in the mid/late 1970s for each of the English tourist regions served as a basis for the preparation of regional tourism strategies. The strategy for the Thames and Chilterns area (English Tourist Board/Thames & Chilterns Tourist Board, 1979) acknowledged the importance of certain national tourism policy objectives - namely, increased foreign exchange earnings, relief of visitor pressure on London and the spreading of tourism to economically weaker parts of the country. Within this policy context the principal aims of the Thames and Chilterns Tourist Board's regional tourism strategy were (and still are) the generation of employment, and the conservation and enhancement of resources and environment. The strategy argued for selective growth within the region, recognising the strength of tourism in parts of the region as well as acknowledging the strong general demand for resources consequent upon the region's buoyant economy. The region's growth potential for overseas and business tourism was highlighted.

In line with the general objectives of the regional strategy the marketing of the region as a tourist destination also sought to be selective, as well as seeking to maintain and improve the viability of tourism enterprises within the region. Priority markets were identified as business and

Figure 12.1: Thames and Chilterns, Berkshire, and the English Tourist Board regions

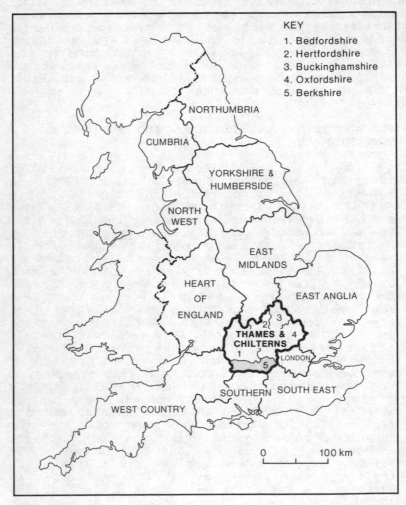

KEY
1. Bedfordshire
2. Hertfordshire
3. Buckinghamshire
4. Oxfordshire
5. Berkshire

conference travellers, overseas visitors and domestic tourists taking off-peak short breaks. The Board's general marketing activities have been described elsewhere (Bowes, 1988) and attention is focused here on the promotion of one place within the Board's area, Berkshire.

Berkshire epitomises the nature of the region's tourism development and the problems of place promotion within the Thames and Chilterns area. In the current economic climate, this is a booming area enjoying almost full employment and house prices only topped by those in Greater London. All businesses including hotels and tourist attractions are experiencing a very profitable period. Pressures for development of all types - industrial, commercial, housing, leisure, etc. - are high and the TCTB is frequently approached by companies seeking to develop hotels in the region and in the M25 and M4 peak property areas in particular.

No doubt those involved in tourism in other parts of Britain still unaffected by the increases in employment and economic prosperity will see the Thames and Chilterns region as being in a covetable position. This may be true if one only looks at hotel occupancies from Monday to Thursday but there is still much to be done in terms of selling the region as a leisure destination. Although the region contains some of the country's most famous places, such as Windsor and Oxford, many parts of the region are not identified by the travelling public as holiday places.

Tourist activities - whether individual or group holidays, day trips, business conferences, etc. - are place-specific, i.e. located in particular destinations. Many destinations may be suitable locations for such activities: they are competing for visitors, both business and leisure. The task of the TCTB is to promote places within its region, to transmit an image of the leisure opportunities to be found there in order to attract visitors to this region rather than have them go elsewhere. Berkshire has its well-known tourism resources, particularly Windsor and its association with the Royal Family and the River Thames but potential exists elsewhere in the county, e.g. associated with the restoration of the Kennet and Avon canal, the North Wessex Downs Area of Outstanding Natural Beauty. Furthermore, the 1974 local government reorganisation deprived Berkshire of a major feature previously associated with its tourist image - the White Horse and associations with King Alfred. Thus, Berkshire, especially in the tourism field, needed a new image.

From the late 1970s the employment potential of tourism was recognised by both the Government and local authorities (Cabinet Office, 1985; Morrell, 1985; Parsons, 1986; Goodall, 1987). This led to the development of tourism strategies and campaigns instigated at county and district level

213

rather than regional level as had previously been the case, involving greater cooperation between Regional Tourist Boards and local authorities.

THE BEAUTIFUL BERKSHIRE CAMPAIGN

The **Beautiful Berkshire** campaign is illustrative of this development: it is a marketing or promotion exercise designed to raise the image or profile of the county in both the business and holiday tourism arenas. The idea for the campaign originated within the Tourist Board and can be viewed as a natural progression from the regional tourism strategy and its ideas for Berkshire. The campaign provides a means of implementation.

Thus in 1982, with the help and support of the Thames and Chilterns Tourist Board, the **Beautiful Berkshire** campaign was initiated. Its sponsors are Berkshire County Council, Newbury Borough Council, Reading Borough Council and the Royal Borough of Windsor and Maidenhead, with Berkshire County Council providing office accommodation for the scheme within its headquarters at Shire Hall, Reading. The campaign now employs three full-time (one jointly funded by the Tourist Board) and two part-time staff. It reports to a Steering Committee which comprises representatives of the Tourist Board, local authorities, and the hotels and tourist attraction sector. A logo for the campaign was designed (by Harrison Cowley Advertising) to create the impression of countryside incorporating trees and water to symbolise the Thames and using a gold colour to symbolise the county's Royal status.

Initially both the BTA and TCTB made cash contributions whilst the campaign established itself. Annual contributions are made by the local authorities but an increasing proportion of the campaign's funding is from the subscriptions of participating members. Depending on the size and nature of the member's business, an annual fee is paid which includes all the promotions undertaken during the year, entries in all brochures and representations at any exhibitions. The fee, which currently ranges from £395 to £760, is reviewed annually by the steering committee in line with inflation. Member's subscriptions now account for over half of the campaign's funding (see Fig. 12.2).

Figure 12.2: Sources of funding for the Beautiful Berkshire campaign

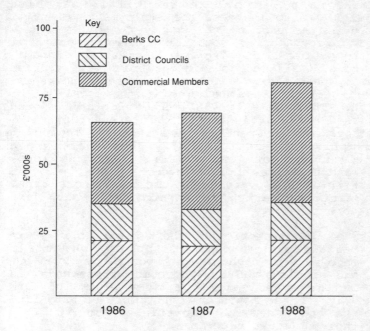

It has always been a condition of membership of the **Beautiful Berkshire** campaign that establishments were already commercial members of Thames and Chilterns, in order that the Tourist Board did not 'compete' for subscriptions, and the two organisations therefore worked to complement each other's efforts. The campaign began with only 35 members in 1982 but members have steadily increased to a current total of 82, out of a total of 120 TCTB members in the county of Berkshire. Nearly half the participating members are hotels and nearly a third tourist attractions, the remainder being travel/transport organisations, conference centres and local government: smaller tourism businesses (guest houses, bed and breakfast, etc.) which are TCTB members are less likely to be able to afford the subscription to the campaign.

215

Aims and objectives of the campaign

The main aim of the Beautiful Berkshire campaign was to increase the employment potential of tourism as part of the County Council's wider-ranging programme of combatting unemployment. It was the potential for the future creation of semi-skilled or unskilled jobs in the travel and tourism industry that had particular relevance to Berkshire where there is an imbalance in the local labour market. There is a buoyant market for skilled and qualified workers: indeed in the late 1980s, skill shortages are apparent in some sectors, including ironically the hotel industry, but there are a limited number of jobs available for the local semi- and unskilled labour force.

Within this overview of employment creation, the **Beautiful Berkshire** campaign began with five main objectives:

(i) The promotion of short-break holidays in Berkshire. Throughout the region hotels enjoyed very high mid-week occupancy rates but had problems filling bedrooms at weekends and in the school summer holiday period of late July and the month of August when so many from the business and industrial community take their holidays elsewhere.

(ii) To promote the county as an excellent location for business meetings and conferences in order to keep Berkshire companies using facilities within their home county and to encourage companies and organisations world-wide to bring highly profitable conferences and incentive business to Berkshire hotels. Incentive business is travel given by firms to employees or to dealers and distributors as a reward for endeavour and a spur to achievement (Holloway, 1985).

(iii) To promote the number of visits to tourist attractions and facilities. This includes opportunities for leisure associated with the county's rivers and canals.

(iv) To concentrate promotional effort on parts of Berkshire that are less well-known than the Royal town of Windsor, which is visited by millions of people each year, and the River Thames.

(v) To promote Berkshire to the overseas market in general and North America in particular.

216

These objectives are consistent with the region's tourism strategy and reflect both Berkshire's comparative advantage in meeting certain tourism demands, e.g. business and conference, and the existence of supply capacity, such as the under-utilisation of hotels at weekends. It is, however, true to suggest that the determination of these objectives was pragmatic and intuitive rather than being based on detailed market research.

The involvement of the TCTB in the running of the campaign has been significant, providing the campaign with access to the Board's marketing distribution network. For example, **Beautiful Berkshire** has been able to take a share of the TCTB stand at the World Travel Market (an annual exhibition held at Olympia at which stand space is in great demand and therefore very costly). It has been further strengthened by the appointment of a Marketing Officer in November 1986 who is jointly funded by the Board and the **Beautiful Berkshire** campaign. The purpose of having a 'shared' member of staff is to increase the cooperation between the two organisations and to develop joint initiatives where appropriate. The post of Marketing Officer was for an initial two-year period and this will be re-negotiated according to its perceived success. The job of the Marketing Officer was to focus on direct marketing of the **Beautiful Berkshire** members and to target conference and group travel buyers in particular. Direct marketing uses various communication techniques such as door-to-door distribution, telephone marketing, direct response advertising (e.g. coupon reply advertisements) and direct mailing of known target areas selected by socio-economic neighbourhood identification. The Conference Manual and the Travel Trade Manual are mailed to known contacts at top Berkshire companies from information supplied by the County Council and to selected companies from The Times 'Top 1000' list. This, together with the contacts made at trade exhibitions over earlier years, forms the mailing list.

Since 1982 these five objectives have been re-affirmed each year by the Steering Committee with only a change in focus on the overseas marketing objective. North America is no longer seen as the primary target for overseas marketing promotion as the numbers of American visitors has fluctuated so much due to fears of terrorism in Europe, the falling strength of the US dollar and in 1988 the effect of the campaign for the Presidency. Many tourist authorities are aware that to concentrate all overseas marketing budgets on North America is too risky and that other long-haul markets should be sought such as Japan and Australia. Efforts should also be made to sell British products to the near-European markets with the opening of the Channel Tunnel in 1993 and the lowering of internal trade barriers in 1992. The **Beautiful Berkshire** campaign has identified Germany, The Netherlands and Scandinavia as target markets for their 1988/89 promotions. The campaign is therefore segmenting the market, emphasising different aspects of the Berkshire tourism product in different markets.

The individual promotions

Weekend breaks. The promotion of weekend breaks has been achieved by the publication of a full colour booklet containing details of all the hotels in the campaign, maps and information on the attractions of Berkshire and a booking form. The booklet is entitled 'Weekends in Beautiful Berkshire' and the print run has increased from 30,000 in 1984 to 35,000 in 1988 and with an increase to 40,000 proposed for 1989. At first the advertising campaign for week-end breaks was spread over local evening, national daily and national Sunday papers but experience has shown that concentration on women's magazines, both weekly and monthly, produces a more cost-effective response rate. This is because women's magazines are carefully targeted at socio-economic groups with time and money for 'extras' and because it is felt that women are the instigators for most weekend break holiday selections. These advertisements are in the form of a coupon to return for a brochure, thus forming a fairly well-targeted mailing list which contains around 4,000 names at present. Apart from mailing the weekend breaks booklet to these respondents, copies are distributed through the tourist information network and at exhibitions and trade fairs which **Beautiful Berkshire** staff attend in the winter months: for 1988 the breakdown of the distribution was 30 per cent through Tourist Information Centres, 25 per cent by direct mail, 25 per cent at exhibitions, 15 per cent in response to advertisements, leaving 5 per cent for public relations and miscellaneous purposes. In addition, individual hotels may advertise their weekend breaks independently, especially where they are part of a hotel group which offers such breaks throughout its hotel chain.

Conferences. The market for conferences and meetings has grown considerably in the last few years (Law, 1987) and the **Beautiful Berkshire** campaign has concentrated a great deal of effort into making useful contacts with both local and national companies and with conference placement agencies and organisers. The aim is to build up a 'contact list' of companies and organisations who will be kept up-to-date on the conference facilities currently available within the county. **Beautiful Berkshire** has exhibited at the International Confex exhibition for several years and made new contacts each time. Confex is also a good time to plan a familiarisation trip for overseas conference buyers. Packs of information on conference venues that were mailed to the contact list and to all Berkshire companies were replaced in 1988 by a soft-cover conference handbook and a programme of personal sales calls to leading companies was undertaken which has created identifiable business for member establishments.

Tourist attractions. The tourist attractions within Berkshire, such as Windsor Safari Park and stately homes such as Basildon Park, have been promoted by the production of a colour guide called 'Days Out in Beautiful Berkshire' which was first published in 1984. It gives a general description of leisure opportunities in the county and details of all the member tourist attractions, who, in addition to their individual entry, also had the opportunity to include a voucher offering discounts to visitors. The 'Days Out' guide is currently sold for 30p per copy throughout Berkshire in newsagents, bookshops and Tourist Information Centres, as well as through outlets at tourist attractions. Hotelier members are supplied with free copies (in 1988, minus the money-off vouchers which are reserved for the saleable copies) to distribute to all weekend guests. The guide is also mailed to the organisers of group visits from 750 clubs and societies. About 80 per cent of the copies are sold, the remainder distributed on a complimentary basis by hoteliers or to group organisers or used for other public relations purposes. The Marketing Officer has made sales calls on coach operators suggesting itineraries using Berkshire attractions and familiarisation trips have been organised. In 1986, a new free leaflet called 'Introducing Beautiful Berkshire' was produced to list all attractions (i.e. member and non-member). This has been used to saturate Tourist Information Centres in the **Beautiful Berkshire** catchment area (basically day-trip distance - West Midlands, South East, East Anglia and the West Country: with particular emphasis on the M25 zone) and copies were mailed out by hotels to potential clients, e.g. previous guests.

An exhibition aimed at schools and group organisers was held annually with members taking stands. This exhibition was initially called an Education Fair but as its emphasis has moved from schools to clubs and societies, and coach operators it has been retitled the 'Days Out Fair'. The Fair uses a different venue within the county each year, e.g. Reading's Shire Hall, Windsor's Town Hall, and the aim is to encourage visits by local groups outside the peak tourist period and on the less popular weekdays during the main summer season.

The less well-known parts of the county. Another of the campaign priorities has been to promote the less 'famous' parts of Berkshire and this has been attempted over the years by commissioning articles by travel writers to bring out aspects like literary and historic connections, and by publishing leaflets on Berkshire's racing connections. Contacts with journalists have been used to get editorial in many publications and journalists are regularly invited on familiarisation trips. In addition to a regular feature in the Evening Post coverage has been achieved in other local newspapers (Colchester Evening Gazette, Gloucester Echo) and in British (e.g. Country Times, Limited Edition) and foreign (e.g. Eikoku) magazines.

Overseas promotion. Overseas promotion by the **Beautiful Berkshire** campaign took a few years to get underway as there were limited funds to produce promotional literature. The basic publication is now an A5 leaflet describing the county's attractions and accommodation, which is jointly produced by **Beautiful Berkshire** and the Tourist

Board, in a standard format set by the BTA and used by regions and cities throughout the country. In 1985 100,000 copies of a leaflet were produced to be distributed overseas by BTA and a further 15,000 copies run off for Beautiful Berkshire to use. At that time, North America was the target market so the BTA leaflet was only produced in English and a firm of marketing consultants were appointed to represent Berkshire in the USA, especially in the affluent areas of the south and west in the days before the oil money ran thin. Grant Reid Communications 'sold' **Beautiful Berkshire** to retail travel agents, tour operators and instigated a lot of press coverage for the county. The Campaign Co-ordinator, Grahame Handley, visited the US in 1987 and generated a lot of press interest but, as explained earlier, because the climate for promotion to the US has changed Grant Reid's contract has not been renewed. **Beautiful Berkshire** will still undertake a limited amount of promotion in North America but more emphasis will be given to the European market, e.g. by attending the European Coach Operators' and similar workshops.

AN EVALUATION OF THE CAMPAIGN

There is no doubt that the campaign has raised the profile of Berkshire as a county within Britain amongst the travel trade and has certainly made hotels in Berkshire more aware of the potential of their local attractions to boost trade. Obviously the 235 per cent growth in membership during its first six years highlights the success of the **Beautiful Berkshire** campaign in the eyes of its participating members. Moreover the resulting increase in funds available means that **Beautiful Berkshire** can now produce a wider and very high quality range of publications.

But what of the overall aim of the campaign to increase tourism's employment potential within the county and of the original five objectives by which this potential would be realised? It is, of course, extremely difficult to isolate the effect of the campaign from other factors influencing levels of tourism within the county, especially where overseas visitors are concerned. Furthermore the highly competitive situation in the mid-Thames labour market means that increased tourism in Berkshire is not reflected in any simple way in increased jobs in tourism. A shortage of labour can be met by other adjustments such as increased productivity of the existing labour force (which is likely where hotel occupancy rates are evened out) or substituting capital for labour (e.g. greater use of frozen meals and microwave ovens), as well as by attempting to extend participation in the labour force, e.g. by drawing in new part-time workers. The number of persons employed in the tourism sectors of the county's economy has increased by about 10 per cent in the 1980s (to just under 25,000 jobs) but, given the other job opportunities in the region, it is unlikely that the relative importance of Berkshire's tourism and leisure employment has changed much during the 1980s, accounting for some 7 per cent of the total employment in the county throughout the period.

With regard to the campaign's specific objectives the short-breaks promotion has certainly generated an improvement in hotels' weekend occupancy rates, although much less so in their July/August occupancy rates. Conference business is healthy although information on numbers of conferences and especially numbers of delegates is not readily available because many of the conferences/meetings are small-scale commercial ones (as the region lacks a major purpose-built conference and exhibition centre). Statistics for the number of visitors to tourist attractions within the county indicate, within a slowly growing overall total, fluctuations between types of attraction from year to year: unfortunately it is not possible to distinguish local group visits organised to such attractions. In the case of overseas visitors numbers tend to mirror fluctuations at the national level (which is not surprising in the case of North American tourists where Windsor is just one stop on their 'Milk Run' itinerary): it is probably too early to judge the effect of the switch of promotional emphasis to the European market.

Within the Tourist Board, the local authorities and amongst the participating members the consensus is that the **Beautiful Berkshire** campaign is a success. For the future the campaign must maintain its momentum since tourism is a highly competitive arena in the United Kingdom for destination areas: other parts of the country are promoting themselves to overseas visitors, conference business and domestic holidaymakers and neighbouring parts of the South East are also seeking to attract day-trippers. It is therefore likely that the **Beautiful Berkshire** campaign will have to become even more professional in its promotional activity and be even more specific in targeting potential markets.

APPLYING THE LESSONS ELSEWHERE IN THE THAMES AND CHILTERNS REGION

Following the success of the Tourist Board's joint efforts with Berkshire, the Board has taken the initiative in setting up a scheme for Hertfordshire which would involve a consortium of local authorities including Hertfordshire County Council. The proposal was to set up what is in essence a 'branch office' of the Thames and Chilterns Tourist Board in Hertfordshire where the promotion of tourism was not as advanced as in Berkshire and where no similar campaign to **Beautiful Berkshire** existed. An out-posted Marketing Officer has been appointed and based in the offices of St Albans City and District Council, backed up with secretarial assistance and able to call on all the services of the TCTB in terms of print buying, etc. Initially six district/borough councils and the County Council agreed to contribute to the 1987/88 scheme and another borough has since added its contribution, i.e. the initial funding of the scheme is the responsibility of the Tourist Board and the local authorities. It is not intended that existing commercial members will be asked to subscribe to the Hertfordshire initiative over and above their TCTB subscription. They will merely pay for guide entries and similar promotions where costs must be passed on to participants. Therefore it is not envisaged that the governing body of the initiative will include commercial members (as is the case for the **Beautiful Berkshire** Steering Committee).

Hertfordshire has similar marketing problems to Berkshire, e.g. with lack of business in hotels at weekends, but it does not have the advantages of such world-famous attractions as Windsor and the Thames, so the Hertfordshire Marketing Officer's first priority was to develop a marketing image for the county and a strategy for the promotion and development of that image. The fact that Hertfordshire was so little known prompted the use of the slogan 'England's Best Kept Secret' (which has been used before by other regions but not for several years), and a 'leafy' logo was developed to

223

put over a quiet, rural image. In addition,
Hertfordshire has a number of significant
historical associations, not least the Roman and
Christian heritage of St Albans, and a number of
literary connections. The Marketing Officer has so
far produced a range of publications including a
comprehensive accommodation guide, a leaflet
promoting spring breaks, a 'literary trail'
featuring stately homes associated with famous
writers and a guide to gardens open to the public.

In addition to creating an image for
Hertfordshire through promotional literature, the
funds have been used to take exhibition stands at
the major travel trade exhibitions during the last
12 months. Similar strategies to those used in the
Beautiful Berkshire campaign will also be directed
at conference buyers and journalists: together with
the Tourist Board the Hertfordshire Marketing
Officer will organise familiarisation trips for
these groups.

A further initiative has recently been set up
in the county of Buckinghamshire, providing the
same sort of service as in Hertfordshire, and the
Marketing Officer took up post in October 1988.

CONCLUSION

Beautiful Berkshire represents a case study of a
successful promotional exercise initiated by a
Regional Tourist Board and is an example of a local
authority collaborative tourism project taken to an
advanced and professional level.

It recognised both the strengths of
Berkshire's current tourism resources and the case
for selective growth of tourism in the county. Now
the Thames and Chilterns Tourist Board is extending
the application of this successful campaign model
to other parts of its region in a manner entirely
consistent with the regional tourism strategy,
albeit with a different administrative relationship
to the Board. The Hertfordshire and Buckinghamshire
marketing initiatives are extensions of the Thames
and Chilterns Marketing Department steered by local
funding committees but are very much part of the
Board although they are free to develop and expand
in different ways.

By using collaborative projects and by
inspiring local authorities to contribute to joint
marketing schemes over which the Tourist Board can
exercise control and influence, the Board is able

to get maximum publicity and promotion for the various parts of the Thames and Chilterns region. The Tourist Board's limited funds are therefore used as 'seed money' to generate much more activity than it could afford if it acted alone.

Destination areas everywhere are becoming more adept at marketing themselves to potential tourists and in a rapidly increasing market all destinations may attract more visitors. But it can be increasingly difficult to retain market share as competition becomes more severe and especially if market expansion falters. Whilst image creation and associated marketing activities have 'come of age' in Tourist Board activities there is another side to the coin - to ensure the quality of the tourism product measures up to the marketing image created. A high image profile, coupled with a quality tourism product which meets or exceeds visitor expectations, will ensure repeat business and a secure future for the destination and its tourism industry.

Note: The views expressed in this chapter are the personal views of the author and do not necessarily represent the policy or views of the Thames and Chilterns Tourist Board or of the Beautiful Berkshire Campaign.

REFERENCES

Bowes, S. (1988) The role of the Tourist Board, pp 75-88 in B. Goodall & G.J. Ashworth (Eds), Marketing in the Tourism Industry, Croom Helm, Beckenham

Cabinet Office (Enterprise Unit)(1985) Pleasure, Leisure and Jobs: The Business of Tourism, HMSO, London

English Tourist Board/Thames & Chilterns Tourist Board (1979) A Tourism Strategy for the Thames and Chilterns, Thames & Chilterns Tourist Board, Abingdon

Goodall, B. (1987) Tourism policy and jobs in the United Kingdom, Built Environment 13(2) 109-123

Holloway, J.C. (1985) The Business of Tourism, 2nd Edition, Pitman, London

Law, C.M. (1987) Conference and exhibition tourism, Built Environment 13(2) 85-95

Morrell, J. (1985) <u>Employment in Tourism</u>, British Tourist Authority, London
Parsons, D. (1986) <u>Jobs in Tourism and Leisure</u>, report by the Institute of Manpower Studies, University of Sussex, English Tourist Board, London

Chapter 13

RESEARCH INTO TOURISM MARKETS: SOME FRISIAN
EXPERIENCES

Ed C. van der Knijff

INTRODUCTION

In practice, feasibility studies of tourism
projects usually consist of a description of the
theme and character of the project, the location,
the market aimed at and a predictive analysis of
costs and benefits. Furthermore such studies
explore the necessary investment levels and the
financial structure of the projects. Finally they
may contain information about the likely impact of
the project on the regional economy in terms of
income and employment, which is usually the reason
why the planning of the project was initiated.

Two elements in this kind of study may curtail
the planning process: an unsatisfactory prediction
about the number of likely visitors or a failure to
convince investors of the potential profitability
of the project. Of course the latter will be
related to the former element. Thus an in-depth
analysis of the market appears to be the critical
element in such a study. Its format, however,
differs from one study to another. Generally two
forms can be distinguished. Some commercial
institutions have developed a standard market
analysis, based on a type of potential analysis of
the location in relation to concentrations of
population. Others do not consider a thorough
market analysis to be an important issue. They
trust their own intuition or the market experience
of the investor who commissioned the study. This
latter approach is often based upon global remarks
about recent developments in the part of the market
concerned.

From the point of view of the planner the
latter cursory market analyses will not be
satisfactory: the scientific approach is to be
preferred because it should be able to predict

outcomes within certain confidence limits and avoid risks due to market uncertainties. Furthermore the planner may well be sceptical about the background of the entrepreneur's market experience or intuition.

Local and regional government administrations generally prefer an elaborate type of market research, especially when they interfere with the supply side of the tourism market by the provision of subsidies or by financial partnership. A considerable amount of the budget for stimulation of regional tourism is spent subsidising feasibility studies and market investigations. Such feasibility studies need evaluation. What do they add to already available knowledge and what value do they have for political decision-makers especially with respect to risk reduction?

This chapter cannot evaluate all such studies but, on the basis of two examples, it seeks to contribute to the discussion about the use and abuse of tourism market analysis.

MARKET INVESTIGATION AND THE FEASIBILITY OF AEOLUS

The 1984 development plan for tourism in the province of Friesland (Heidemij et al., 1984) adopted a very expansionary outlook. Some 100 new projects were proposed in order to raise the employment in tourism by about 1500 jobs. The plan, however, was formulated in a period of severe downswing of the regional economy. Tourism was considered to be an important growth industry that would at least partly compensate for the decline in agriculture, construction and other labour-intensive industries.

A major conclusion of this development plan was that Friesland lacked a large-scale leisure attraction. To fill this gap the provincial administration acted quickly: what appeared to be the most promising project out of the original 100 proposals was soon subjected to a detailed development and design study (Bureau Kappelhoff, 1984).

The proposal involved the development of the already planned construction of a large-scale experimental windmill park, and this also suggested the theme of the attraction: AEOLUS, wind as a phenomenon, to be demonstrated in all its many aspects. The leisure element of the park was thus to be combined with an educational element.

The location of the leisure development was therefore determined by the location of the windmill park. The market analysis could thus be limited to the optimal size of the project in relation to the market. This market analysis will be briefly outlined. It starts with the presupposition that in general four types of day-trips can be distinguished, each with its own sensitivity to distance:

(i)   very short and frequently repeated trips (distance 1-5 km);
(ii) one-hour recreation (distance 5-20 km);
(iii) half-day recreation (distance 20-50 km);
(iv) whole-day recreation (distance 50-100 km).

The nature, size and location of any leisure provision should be fitted into this geographical conceptualisation. This means for example that whole-day recreation provision should only be located at a site which can draw visitors from a sufficiently large number of inhabitants within a distance of 100 km. Three sizes of complex were explored in relation to possible market sizes:

An interpretative exhibition

Two groups of potential visitors are of interest: people with a special interest in the particular subject of wind power and a group comprising incidental day-trippers. The first group is estimated at 10,000 and is relatively insensitive to distance. The second group consists of people driving along the 'Green Coast Road', people holidaying in the local region, travellers passing through on their way to the West Frisian Islands and the population of the region itself. Different rates of participation must be applied to these sub-groups, varying from 10 per cent for travellers passing through to 35 per cent for the regional population. This leads to an estimated number of visitors of 50,000 a year, as summarised in Table 13.1.

Half-day leisure park

Starting from the 50,000 visitors to the interpretative centre several other groups of

229

Table 13.1: Potential number of visitors to the interpretative exhibition

Type of Visitor	Potential Population	Predicted No of Visitors
Special interest groups	10,000	10,000 (100%)
Green Coast drivers	65,000	6,500 (10%)
Regional visitors	30,000	9,000 (30%)
Travellers from and to the islands	75,000	7,500 (10%)
Local population	50,000	18,000 (35%)
Total	230,000	51,000

Table 13.2: Potential number of visitors to a half-day park

Type of Visitor	Potential Population	Predicted No of Visitors
Special interest groups	10,000	10,000 (100%)
Incidental passers-by	40,000	40,000 (100%)
Supra-regional pop.	850,000	60,000 (7%)
Tourists	30,000	4,500 (15%)
Students	150,000	15,000 (10%)
Special tourist groups	100,000	10,000 (10%)
Total	1,180,000	139,500

potential visitors must be considered: the population living within a distance of 75 km, holidaymakers in the province, pupils and students and special groups (day-trippers by train or touring coach). The market from which visitors would be drawn is now estimated to number 1.2 million people, of which some 140,000 are expected to visit the park, as Table 13.2 shows.

A whole-day leisure park

As well as including all the previous groups of staying and transit holidaymakers a whole-day leisure park would draw from a resident population living at distances of up to 100 km away. This means a target group of 5.6 million people of which

Table 13.3: Potential number of visitors to a whole-day park

Type of Visitor	Potential Population	Predicted No of Visitors
Special interest groups	10,000	10,000 (100%)
Incidental passers-by	40,000	40,000 (100%)
Day-trippers < 100 km	4,500,000	135,000 (3%)
Tourists < 50 km	136,000	20,000 (15%)
Students < 100 km	641,000	64,000 (10%)
Special tourist groups	300,000	30,000 (10%)
Total	5,627,000	299,000

some 300,000 will visit the attraction as noted in Table 13.3.

The study concluded that the whole-day leisure park was not feasible with only 300,000 visitors, but that the half-day option with 140,000 visitors a year would be. Based on this market analysis the provincial administration went ahead with the creation of a half-day educational leisure park at an investment cost of about fl.7 million (i.e. $3.8million). The park opened in the spring of 1987 and during that year only about 30,000 persons visited the attraction. Moreover there had only been 32,000 visitors in the first eight months of 1988. The park manager has asked the Province for an additional investment of fl. 3 million to make the park more attractive.

Are the market analysts at fault for this failure? Did they over-estimate the number of visitors or were some conditions of the analysis not met? Would an even more extensive analysis have predicted this result, i.e. a more commercial type of market exploration would have led to a more realistic point of view?

Of course the geographical analysis raises no doubts: the numbers of inhabitants, day-trippers and tourists within the respective areas are real and will indeed form the market potential population from which the actual visitors have to be recruited. The participation rates, however, are less certain. Reference can be made to experimental data about leisure behaviour of the resident population and holidaymakers to the market situation of existing comparable facilities. However this aspect can be seen as a weak element in almost every market analysis. To identify likely participation rates in this particular case additional research needs to be carried out, such as to ask a sample of the targeted groups whether they would be willing to pay a visit to the AEOLUS leisure park. Assumptions also have to be made about the extent and effectiveness of any promotional activities intended to make the attraction known to potential visitors.

From a more sceptical point of view one can argue that government administrations cannot operate successfully on the commercial market. Entrepreneurial risk should be shouldered by private institutions and governmental intervention on the supply side of the tourism market should be restricted to the provision of infrastructure and other merit goods. In which case the provincial administration would have confined its activity to the provision of a simplified interpretative centre at the windmill park designed to inform the public about aspects of wind energy. The possible gap in the market for a large-scale leisure park would then be left to the market sector to judge on commercial criteria.

Operation in the day-tripper market appears to be very difficult. The capital risks are high and the market seems to be saturated. Yet many local plans for leisure development are presented and applications made for a provincial contribution towards the development costs. Most of these plans are based on a marketing analysis analogous to the one described above. A more thorough marketing analysis may show at the very beginning of a feasibility study that commercial exploitation of many plans is not possible. This would mean that further investigation of the specific project is not useful. Many feasibility studies give the impression that their authors abuse this type of marketing analysis to reach their goal: the realisation of the project. The experience described above will probably lead to a highly critical judgement of future tourism plans and projects that apply for government support or participation. This is the very basic lesson to be learned.

THE LAUWERSMEER REGION AND THE TOURISM MARKET

During the spring of 1987 some 300 households were questioned as to their interest in the

Lauwersmeer region as a holiday destination. This inquiry formed part of the research into the tourism potentials of the region (Friskus & van der Knijff, 1987). Since the Lauwersmeer was separated from the Waddenzee, policy-makers have regarded tourism development as one of the major economic potentials of the area (Ashworth et al., 1984). The expected growth of holiday accommodation has however not been realised and thus far no large-scale capital-intensive project has actually been carried out. Tourism development in this area is seen as one of the most promising ways of combatting the high local unemployment rates. The main question to be answered is why expectations have been so optimistic. What are the real expectations of tourism development and what could be the role of the provincial governments of Groningen and Friesland in stimulating this development?

One question to be answered is whether the region could play a significant role in Dutch holiday patterns. It was therefore decided to measure what interest there was for holidaying in the region. About 350 brochures prepared by the Lauwersmeer Tourist Office were sent to a representative sample of Dutch households. Two weeks later the housewives were questioned about the information in the brochure and their impression of the region as a holiday base. The housewives were approached because it was clear they were the decision-makers when it comes to choosing holidays. The results may be summarised (see also Table 13.4):

(i)   29 per cent of the respondents had visited the region at least once before, especially those who live in the north of The Netherlands;

(ii)   40 per cent showed an interest in the region as a holiday destination. This is even higher for the people who live in the northern part of the country, people without children and people in higher social classes;

(iii)   30 per cent expressed an intention of making a visit within the next 3 years.

Aquatic sports facilities, nature, the quiet surroundings and the presence of historic buildings, museums and exhibitions were mentioned as the most attractive elements of the area. An important result of the inquiry was that persons

Table 13.4: Interest in Lauwersmeer region as a holiday destination

	Visited Before	Interested in a Visit	Visit Within 3 Years
By region of origin	%	%	%
North	78	50	39
East	37	34	32
West	21	43	30
South	13	37	24
By social class			
Higher	33	40	40
Middle	28	27	27
Lower	27	43	25
Family situation			
No children 35+	32	44	38
No children 35-	20	50	27
Children	31	36	28
Age			
< 34	26	44	29
35-49	32	35	28
> 50	50	44	24
Total (N = 300)	29	41	30

who have previously visited the region view it differently from people who have not visited it before. In the first place they express more interest in holidaying in the region and are more willing to visit the region again. They also have a better knowledge of the disadvantages of the region: its open, windy character, few leisure facilities for children and especially the lack of 'all-weather' facilities. The relatively low interest of people from the southern part of the country demonstrates clearly the influence of distance.

These results partly explain the disappointing growth of tourism in the area because in particular it does not yet appear to be an attractive holiday destination for families with small children and this is an important segment of market demand.

What is the function and value of such an inquiry? It has no predictive value in the sense that it indicates what would be the effect of sending all Dutch households a copy of the brochure. However, the results of this inquiry can be used in the process of planning facilities and accommodation. In this planning process the aim is to provide for groups with a relatively high interest in the region. Shortcomings that are recognised can be compensated for and promotional activities can be targeted at the appropriate groups with a better chance of success. The relative attractiveness of this region becomes clearer when it is compared with another region. During the same period a similar inquiry was conducted for one of the West Frisian Islands: Terschelling. This island achieved a significantly higher score amongst the Dutch population as a potential holiday destination. Terschelling may well be, in absolute terms, a better holiday base than the Lauwersmeer but the difference noted above could simply be a question of the images and the length of time they have been transmitted to the Dutch population. Again the conclusion is that further and more detailed market analyses are required.

CONCLUSIONS

These short descriptions of two cases of tourism market research demonstrate that their results require very cautious and critical interpretation. In the case of the leisure park a risk analysis should be applied to the implicit conditions that underlie the predictions of the expected number of visitors. These predictions need to be subjected to some form of sensitivity or robustness analysis. A critical reader of the report must be sceptical about the results, especially when the report notes at the beginning of the analysis: 'For the location Sexbierum all important concentrations of population are relatively far away'. Secondly, greater certainty about the market and therefore about participation rates could be obtained from a household survey among the most important groups expected to use the facility.

However, this experience confirms scepticism about the value of any market research. Would it not be more fruitful to concentrate on the creation of a unique and high quality product? Supply will then create its own demand through an appropriate marketing policy.

The second example discussed above sought to answer a different question: should provincial administrations go on stimulating tourism development in the Lauwersmeer region or is it fruitless because of its position in the market? The conclusion was positive: the Lauwersmeer can have a significant role in Dutch tourism. The inquiry therefore gives some clues for framing a more effective policy. The poor image of the region seems to be an important reason why plans for a capital intensive project have failed to find entrepreneurial backing. The positive results of the inquiry might help to convince investors of the profitability of tourism developments in the region. In addition planning of the merit leisure goods can be directed more specifically towards the demands of interested groups. In neither of the case studies, however, can detailed market analysis guarantee profitable project development and continuing success for a region's tourism industry.

REFERENCES

Ashworth, G.J., Bergsma J., & Schuurmans, F. (1984) Choice in water recreation: The Lauwersmeer dilemma, Leisure Studies, 3, 1-14

Bureau Kappelhoff (1984), Ontwikkelingsmogelijkheden en Inrichtingsplan Toeristisch Bezoekerscentrum Sexbierum, Bureau Kappelhoff, Breda

Friskus, J. & van der Knijff, E.C. (1987) Toeristische Potenties van de region Lauwersmeer, PPD-Groningen/Afdeling Onderzoek Provincie Friesland

Heidemij, De Vries en Partners, (1984) Toeristisch Recreatief Ontwikkelingsplan Friesland, ETIF, Arnhem

Chapter 14

MARKETING THROUGH TRAVEL AGENCIES

Mark Radburn and Brian Goodall

THE ROLE OF THE TRAVEL AGENT

The travel agent acts as an intermediary between the holiday demands of consumers and the commercial suppliers of holiday opportunities. Travel agents are the 'retailers' of the tourism industry (Foster, 1985), although they do not carry a 'stock' of travel products for resale to the consumer as is the case with other shopkeepers. They 'market' the products of tour operators and provide a locally accessible point for the purchase of holidays and travel by acting as booking agents for tour operators and transport companies, as well as a source of information and choice on such services.

Travel agencies range from single independent establishments to large national chains. Where integration has taken place within the United Kingdom (UK) tourism industry a few travel agency chains are now part of tour operator/travel agency/airline groupings. Whatever their commercial organisation, the relationship between the travel agent and the consumer is fundamental. Travel agency is the one activity most clearly recognised by the general public as representing the tourism industry, indeed Lavery (1987) suggests that most consumers are unaware that the travel agent is most usually acting on behalf of a third party.

The travel agent, according to Lavery (1987) and Buck (1988), generally offers the following range of services:

(i) selling prepared inclusive tours (ITs), preparing individual itineraries, personally escorted tours and group tours;
(ii) arranging transport including car hire,

selling airline tickets, rail, coach and cruise trips;

(iii) arranging hotels, motels, sightseeing trips, transfer of passengers between airport or ferry terminals and hotels;

(iv) handling and advising on the many details involved in travel, especially foreign travel, such as travel and luggage insurance, medical insurance, travellers' cheques, visas;

(v) providing information and advice on airline, rail and coach schedules and fares, hotel rates and local taxes;

(vi) arranging reservations for special interest activities such as business travel, sporting holidays, religious pilgrimages;

(vii) interpreting and advising clients of the many complex and often discounted holiday and airline prices;

(viii) playing a supportive role in dealing with clients' complaints and insurance claims.

The range of services may vary between travel agencies. Not all of these services are available in every travel agency outlet, even though on-line database link-ups allow most travel agencies access to information to serve most potential tourists' needs. In most travel agencies, business is likely to revolve around two main areas of activity: the sale of ITs and the sale of airline tickets. These are the areas which generate volume sales, and therefore most revenue. This chapter concentrates on the travel agencies' role in supplying IT packages, since this comprises 80 per cent of their business (Key Note Report, 1988) and some 90 per cent of ITs are sold via travel agencies (Holloway, 1985; Goodall, 1988).

LOCAL OPPORTUNITY SETS

Travel agencies therefore dominate the supply of IT holiday opportunities available to consumers resident in a particular area. The range of IT holidays offered by any travel agency outlet or group of outlets located in an area will depend upon the relationships between travel agencies and tour operators. Thus the national industry IT opportunity set (see Chp. 2), which includes all ITs of all tour operators based in that country, needs to be disaggregated for each region or locality because ITs of every tour operator will not be 'stocked' by every travel agency in the region. Indeed ITs of some tour operators and particular IT products of other tour operators may not be offered in a given region. Therefore, the industry IT opportunity set available to consumers varies between different parts of the country. A **local industry IT opportunity set** can be identified which includes all IT holidays available through travel agencies in a given locality at a given point in time. In the same way as company opportunity sets can be defined for tour operators, the local industry IT opportunity set may be disaggregated into travel agency outlet opportunity sets.

The role of tour operators and travel agents in a local opportunity set

The extent of the local industry IT opportunity set will be conditioned by the actions of both tour operators and travel agents. Interaction between tour operators and travel agents and the structure of travel agency in a locality will therefore determine the choice of ITs available to local residents.

The maximum extent of the local IT opportunity set is conditioned by the range of IT holidays tour operators are willing to offer for sale at any given time. Most tour operators licence the sale of their ITs through travel agencies by means of an agency agreement or contract. As well as entering into a formal agreement with a tour operator, the travel agent is required to belong to the Association of British Travel Agents (ABTA) if they are to sell the ITs of tour operators who are themselves members of ABTA. The majority of tour operators and travel agencies are therefore members of ABTA. It has been the policy of tour operators to sell their ITs throughout the entire network of ABTA travel agents (Holloway, 1985) - in which case local industry IT opportunity sets would not differ between parts of the country and, indeed, IT opportunity sets for individual travel agency outlets would be identical. In practice this is not the case: the actual local IT opportunity set will not be as extensive as the maximum described above and there will be differences between outlet opportunity sets.

First, differences in local industry and, especially, outlet opportunity sets may arise as a

result of the actions of tour operators. Some tour
operators issue different brochures for different
regions of the UK in which special ITs or a
different range of ITs are offered to consumers in
a particular tourist-generating region. This
shows, for example, in the varying range of
destinations accessible from regional departure
airports. Increasingly tour operators have adopted
a policy of limiting outlets retailing their ITs on
the basis of outlet productivity - the relatively
unproductive outlets are dropped. This is a policy
which mass tour operators have adopted consequent
upon an analysis of sales which revealed that a
large number of travel agents were producing few
bookings while 90 per cent of bookings were
achieved through some 100 very productive outlets
(Holloway, 1985). Also small tour operators (i.e.
companies licenced to sell less than 10,000
holidays per year) cannot afford to distribute
through the national travel agency network and have
to develop a policy of choosing key agents to
support or to restrict distribution of their ITs to
travel agents in just one or two regions of the
country. Therefore, in terms of tour operators
represented, local industry IT opportunity sets and
even more so, outlet opportunity sets will differ.
The same applies to the range of destinations
available within these IT sets.

Second, the role of the travel agent will
influence the outlet opportunity set. The local
travel agency outlet is either unlikely or unable
to stock all tour operator brochures and be even
more selective of the tour operator brochures which
are to be displayed prominently. Travel agencies
are therefore selective of the ITs they 'stock' and
recommend depending not only on what they believe
to be in the consumers' interest but also to be in
their self-interest as well. The latter will
reflect factors such as the commission levels
payable by tour operators, the efficiency of the
tour operators' reservation systems, and any
personal relationship or goodwill which exists
between travel agent and tour operator. Size and
structure of travel agency is also important:
differences are to be expected between independent,
single outlet travel agencies and national agencies
with many branches. The national industry IT
opportunity set is therefore filtered through
travel agencies to generate local industry IT
opportunity sets which again vary between parts of
the country and outlets within a locality.

The local industry IT opportunity set is an aggregation of travel agency outlet opportunity sets available in that locality. This local opportunity set is likely to be constrained, compared to the national set, as demonstrated above by the distribution policy of tour operators and the structure and operation of travel agency. There is, of course, considerable overlap between the outlet opportunity sets of travel agencies located in a particular area: a proportion of the local opportunity set is likely to be available in all of the area's travel agencies, e.g. national and regional chains as well as independent outlets are likely to sell ITs offered by a selection of the UK's 'top ten' tour operators. Travel agency outlets of the national/multiple chain 'holiday shop' type are likely to offer the most restricted range of holiday opportunities because they concentrate on high volume sales by selling ITs of mass tour operators to the (local) mass market. Independent travel agencies are more likely to have broader opportunity sets covering a wider proportion of the national set. In terms of destinations, certain resorts, such as the popular Spanish Mediterranean ones, will be available in all outlet opportunity sets but other destinations, Iceland for example, are likely to appear only in independent outlet opportunity sets. Indeed the latter may specialise in holidays to particular destinations or certain types of, say, activity holidays. The range of products encompassed by a local opportunity set may be viewed as a determinant of the awareness of the potential consumer of the range of holiday opportunities and the result of the travel agents' interpretation of what consumers in the locality want.

A case study: the Reading area local opportunity set

A local IT opportunity set for 'summer sun' holidays was established by recording the range of tour operators' brochures displayed in travel agencies in Reading, Bracknell and Wokingham (Radburn, 1988). This local opportunity set, in which 857 tour operators are represented, is shown in Table 14.1. Travel agencies which are part of national, regional and local chains or are independent are identified and the number of brochures displayed in each agency is indicated.

Table 14.1: The Reading area local opportunity set for 'summer sun' ITs

Travel Agency	Type	No of Brochures Displayed
Reading		
AA	N	41
Brooking Travel	I	101
Carters Travel	L	38
Thomas Cook	N	51
Co-op Travelcare	N	62
Exchange Travel	L	35
Harvey Thomas	N	108
Hogg Robinson	N	68
Hogg Robinson	N	75
Lunn Poly	N	74
Pickfords	N	60
Pickfords	N	38
British Airways	I	56
Horsemans	L	59
Keith Bailey	I	99
Meadway Travel	N	59
British Rail	N	4
RUSU Travel	I	15
Wokingham		
Eton Travel	L	224
Hogg Robinson	N	72
Pickfords	N	82
Bracknell		
A.T. Mays	N	175
Thomas Cook	N	50
Exchange	N	63
Hogg Robinson	N	21
Ian Allan	R	68
Pickfords	N	66
W.H. Smith	N	95

No of tour operators represented in:	
Reading	659
Wokingham	162
Bracknell	132
Local opp. set	857

Note: key to travel agency type, N = National chain, R = Regional chain, L = Local chain, I = Independent

Table 14.2: Differences between travel agency types in brochures displayed

Travel Agency Type	No of Outlets in Opp. Set	No of Brochures Displayed Average	Median
National chain	20	65.5	62.5
Regional chain	1	68	68
Local chain	5	79	41
Independent	4	68	77.5

These brochures are a tangible representation of the local opportunity set and act as the primary source of information about holiday opportunities available to customers who visit agencies to, at least initially collect or, browse through the holidays on offer. The wider the selection of brochures available, the broader is the opportunity set available to consumers. However, the displayed brochures in each agency are those which the agency perceives will generate most sales (it is accepted that displayed brochures represent only a proportion of the total holiday opportunities bookable through each agency).

Differences occur in the number of brochures displayed in national, regional and local chains and independent agencies with the widest choice in independent and local chain outlets (see Table 14.2). More surprisingly differences occur between outlets within the same chain as demonstrated by the 37 per cent variation in number of brochures displayed in Hogg Robinson's two Reading branches and the 80 per cent difference between Hogg Robinson's largest Reading branch and their Bracknell branch.

Representation of tour operators also differs between travel agencies in Reading, Bracknell and Wokingham. Table 14.3 identifies the top 20 tour operators in each of the towns and in the area as a whole on the basis of frequency of occurrence of their brochures in travel agencies. The local industry IT opportunity set is dominated by a relatively small number of 'brand names' owned by an even smaller number of mass tour operators. Even so only one tour operator, Thomson, ranks in the top 10 and a further two in the top 20 for all three towns; 13 tour operators appear in the local opportunity set of just two of the towns but most

243

Table 14.3: The Reading area opportunity set as defined by its top 20 tour operators

Reading		Bracknell		Wokingham
1 Thomson	1	Club 18-30	1	Thomson
2 Intasun	2	Skytours	2	P&O Car Ferries
3 Global Air	=	Wings OSl	=	Best of Greece
4 Horizon	4	Brittany Ferries	4	Horizon
5 Cosmos	=	Sunmed	=	Wings(Horizon)
6 Enterprise	=	Falcon	=	Club 18-30
7 Sunmed	7	Enterprise	=	Club Cantabrica
8 Lancaster	8	Wallace Arnold	=	Club Med.
9 Sovereign	=	Iberian	=	Pan World Hols
10 Wings OSL	10	Thomson	=	Scan Tours
11 Falcon	11	Jetsave	=	Skytours
12 Speedbird	=	Crystal Hols	=	Sol Hols
13 HCI	=	Flair	13	Intasun
14 Kuoni	=	Global Air	14	Tradewinds
15 Club 18-30	15	Rainbow Hols	15	Cosmos
16 Yugotours	=	Sally Tours	16	Kuoni
17 Skytours	=	Silk Cut Travel	=	Best Travel
= SwissTravel	=	TravelSmith	=	Australasia
= Manos	=	Wardair	19	Pan Am Hols
= Flair	20	Lancaster	20	Pegasus

Overall

1	Thomson	=	Kuoni
2	Intasun	12	Club 18-30
3	Horizon	13	Yugotours
=	Cosmos	14	Wings (Horizon)
5	Sovereign	15	Skytours
6	Global Air	16	Global Tours
7	Enterprise	=	Wallace Arnold
8	Wings OSL	18	Poundstretcher
=	Lancaster	19	Select Hols
10	Falcon	20	Flair

tour operators in the top 20 lists appear for only one town. Whilst only a quarter of Reading's top 20 tour operators are not represented in either Bracknell or Wokingham, half of Bracknell's and nearly three-quarters of Wokingham's top 20 are unique to those towns.

How important are these differences for the potential holidaymaker? No consumer is likely to visit every travel agency in their locality before making a holiday choice. Choice will be made from only part of the local opportunity set and, indeed, may be restricted to a single outlet opportunity set. The Reading area travel agency survey suggests that, on the basis of both numbers of brochures displayed and tour operators represented, the range of holiday opportunities which the consumer will become aware of depends on the travel agency outlet(s) visited. The variation, which is most marked in the case of the 'top 20' tour operators, is not simply the result of travel agency-tour operator interaction but also reflects differences in the socio-economic composition of the market: Bracknell, for example, is a new town with a high proportion of blue collar manufacturing workers whilst Wokingham is a fashionable market town accommodating London commuters and employees working in the high-tech industries of the M4 corridor. Travel agency outlets obviously have to respond to such local market variations if they are to succeed. Whilst variation between the Reading, Bracknell and Wokingham opportunity sets can be in large part explained by different market composition, the differences between agency outlets within such local opportunity sets is a result of spatial filtering of holiday opportunities consequent upon travel agency-tour operator interactions.

SPATIAL FILTERING OF IT OPPORTUNITY SETS

The travel agents' commission

Commission rates offered by tour operators to travel agents vary. This rate variation will, in certain circumstances, affect the travel agent's willingness to sell a particular tour operator's ITs. This has consequences for both the outlet and the local opportunity sets. However, the popular IT brand names of the mass tour operators achieve sales figures which travel agents, whatever their size, cannot ignore, even if the commission rates offered are less than those paid by other tour operators. Therefore, certain ITs are likely to appear in all local industry opportunity sets and in the majority of travel agency outlet opportunity sets.

Some tour operators offer a fixed rate of commission to all travel agents, while others differentiate between travel agents (rewarding those who achieve high volume sales with a higher rate of commission). Commission rates are normally confidential, but in general 10 per cent of the holiday price can be taken as a guideline. In the competitive UK tour operator sector of the industry, where increased market share through volume sales has been an important objective, the travel agent's basic commission per holiday has for a number of years been higher than a tour operator's expected profit on each holiday sold (around 2 per cent for mass market ITs).

There is a process of negotiation between travel agent and tour operator during which a commission rate is set. Travel agencies can be offered more favourable terms, known as **commission overrides**, than are 'normally' offered by a tour operator. Commission overrides are used by tour operators to reward travel agents' high sales performance. They may also be used to encourage a travel agent to stock a brand name brochure (either when a product is being launched by a tour operator, or when a tour operator is attempting a wider distribution of its products).

Typical commissions from mass tour operators during the 1987 summer season for an independent travel agent in Reading were as follows:

(i) Thomson Holidays offered a simple, flat rate commission of 10 per cent. This company appears to have a policy of non-negotiation and will not offer any overrides. As market leaders, they can afford to take this attitude.

(ii) International Leisure Group offered a basic 10 per cent commission plus an additional £3 for each holiday sold irrespective of any threshold sales level.

(iii) Falcon Leisure Group agreed a 10 per cent commission and negotiated a sales target with the travel agent, with a bonus of 2.5 per cent paid for sales over that target.

(iv) Redwing offered a basic 10 per cent commission and the following range of bonuses:

£3 per holiday for 61-100 holidays sold,

£3.50 per holiday for 101-150 holidays sold,

£4 per holiday for 151-200 holidays sold,

£4.50 per holiday for 201-250 holidays sold,

and £5 per holiday for more than 250 holidays sold.

Commission overrides encourage travel agency outlets to push a particular tour operator's products rather than those of a rival operator. Some filtering by a travel agent of the potential range of holiday opportunities is therefore bound to take place. The travel agent is more likely to display prominently and refer potential customers to brochures of operators offering a higher rate of commission. Commission overrides therefore act to restrict travel agents' opportunity sets and consequently, the local industry opportunity sets available to consumers. Certain destinations will also be favoured by such commission overrides - in particular the most popular summer sun resorts offered by mass tour operators.

The largest tour operators, with the highest levels of sales, offer the lowest commission rates. Thomson Holidays, the market leader, generally offers the lowest rate of all. It is inconceivable that travel agents would refuse to stock market leader brochures because consumers are likely to be aware of their availability as a result of national media advertising undertaken by those operators. Most travel agents therefore regard the relatively high number of sales they are likely to make by offering leading brand names as secure and predictable income. A given travel agency outlet, however, could be excluded from a brochure distribution schedule where a tour operator adopts a policy of selective support to outlets. Generally, as Table 14.3 shows, the filtering of the national IT opportunity set favours the brochures, holidays and destinations offered by the market leaders.

Rates of commission offered by tour operators may have a more significant role to play in the marketing of those holiday products which lie outside of the mass market IT opportunity set. These ITs from smaller tour operators emphasise specific activities or destinations which are not part of the mass market opportunity set, or present destinations which are part of the mass market opportunity set in a different way, e.g. by offering luxury accommodation. The sale of these holidays will depend not only on their being marketed by tour operators but also by travel agents. Given that, as Table 14.2 shows, it is only the smaller travel agency chains and independents which display a range of brochures very much wider than those of the thirty largest tour operators, it is important for smaller tour

247

operators that there exists a range of independent and local chain travel agencies prepared to stock and display a wider range of products. Small tour operators, however, cannot afford to produce and distribute brochures throughout the national travel agency network to the same extent as mass tour operators. They have to be selective, even where brochure distribution is limited to travel agency outlets in a particular region.

As a consequence the local industry opportunity set available to consumers in any given area will contain a core of mass market ITs which is common to all local opportunity sets and covers all popular destinations. Local opportunity sets therefore exhibit a degree of similarity because all mass tour operators are likely to be represented in at least one travel agency outlet in each area. Differences between local industry opportunity sets, and therefore the range of destinations available, arise primarily as a function of the degree to which the products of specialist and small tour operators are represented in travel agencies in each area. These operators are likely to be represented in varying numbers depending on the socio-economic characteristics of the resident population and on the business structure of travel agency in the area.

The structure of travel agency

The local industry opportunity set is also dependent on the structure of travel agency, i.e. the types of travel agency in a locality. The opportunity sets of national and regional chains and local or independent travel agents, as well as their relationships with tour operators, vary. Their sales and stocking policies, as demonstrated above, have implications for the local opportunity set. Consider each type of travel agency in turn.

National travel agency chains. These large travel agencies, with multiple branches throughout the country, are the least susceptible to tour operator pressure. Such national chains are large enough to compete with most tour operators on commercially equal terms. For example, Thomas Cook and Lunn Poly, two of the largest, seek to negotiate commission overrides before agreeing to stock a tour operator's brochure range.

Outlets of national chains occupy the better premises available to travel agencies - secondary central business district locations. They offer a limited range of ITs and concentrate on achieving a high volume of sales. They deal with the major UK tour operators, whose products are prominently displayed in modern, uncluttered retail space.

Their staff are trained primarily to be sales staff. They are not holiday experts and are normally ill-prepared to deal with consumer enquiries which fall outside the normal IT package. Staff knowledge and personal experience of holiday destinations are quite limited and they rely increasingly on the computerised reservation systems (in which national chains have invested heavily) as a source of information.

These national chains specialise in a particular product range - mass market ITs. This specialisation, together with investment in information technology is enabling these travel agencies to match general retailing trends. The 1980s have seen retailing in general moving towards offering product lines which reflect a brand image - an image which is standardised but identifiable by consumers as having certain quality attributes. Travel agency is now adopting better store design, based on the video screen rather than just brochure rackings and a shop counter, with the result that agencies such as Lunn Poly, Four Corners (British Airways) and Pickfords are creating an image which goes beyond the traditional view of a travel agent and attempts to develop the idea of a 'holiday shop'. As Bennett (1989) points out, travel agents are beginning to sell own-brand sun glasses, T-shirts, swimming costumes, etc. as part of a revamped holiday shop image.

National chains therefore represent the core of the industry IT opportunity set, i.e. the products of the mass tour operators, at the local level. They often supplement the discounts offered by tour operators with incentives of their own, e.g. free insurance or tangible goods such as Pickford Travel's offer of a 'walkman' radio with Cosmos Summer Sun 1988 holidays booked by 30 November 1987. Such actions are in keeping with the aggressive expansionary policies followed by these national chains who compete for a market share by extending their network of outlets. The likely consequence of this is an increasing similarity of local industry opportunity sets, especially in terms of the mass market core.

Regional travel agency chains. Much the same process appears to be taking place in regional agency chains. Again there is a dependence on volume sales of products supplied by major tour operators. There has been a similar high level of investment in information technology, and sales staff are again predominantly trained to <u>sell</u> products rather than have detailed knowledge of holiday places. Regional chains, however, are likely to have less resources to devote to investment in store renovation, computerised reservation systems, etc. and may occupy less favourable high street locations (often CBD secondary fringe or suburban shopping centre locations). Such regional chains are therefore often the target of take-over bids by the national chains, e.g. the 1988 take-over of the Ian Allan regional chain by W.H. Smith, a national chain. The opportunity sets offered by individual regional travel agents add little to the extent of the local industry opportunity sets available to consumers.

Local chains and independent travel agencies. The local travel agency may be either a small local chain, with a few outlets in two or three neighbouring towns, or an independent travel agent with a single outlet. This group is important to the filtering of IT holiday information to consumers in a locality because these travel agencies are likely to offer the widest range of holiday products, i.e. have the largest outlet opportunity sets.

The independent travel agency exists in two forms. The first competes directly with the high street national chain outlets for sales of mass market ITs. They compete by offering a caring service, claiming to understand their customers' needs better than the national chain outlet and so directing customers to the most suitable IT and destination (and not the one which maximises the agent's commission). Since they stock a few brochures of small tour operators their agency opportunity sets will be little larger than those of national chain outlets. They also attempt to supplement their activities by selling rail, theatre and coach tickets and their store design is likely to be based on maximising brochure display space.

The second type of local agency attempts to develop a market niche by offering a specialised service to its customers. These agencies offer a range of mass market products which dominate both the consumer's and the industry's IT opportunity set, but in addition they attempt to establish a reputation for a particular service to clients. They dispense the best advice on destinations and may specialise on particular destinations or holiday types or service to a particular type of client, such as locally based business travellers. Such local agencies, because they stock a wide range of brochures of smaller tour operators in addition to covering the core mass market ITs, have the most extensive outlet opportunity sets and cover the widest range of destinations.

It is this second type of agency which is most likely to survive in the face of increasing competition from increasingly dominant national travel agency chains. The independent agency or local chain which attempts to compete directly with the large travel agencies rarely has either the resources or the skills to make direct competition a success.

The presence or absence of the three broad types of travel agency discussed above therefore has an effect on the extent of local industry opportunity sets. It is clear that in nearly every travel agency, the consumer is likely to find those products which dominate the national IT opportunity set, but only in the case of local or independent agencies will an extensive range of other holiday opportunities be found along with supporting advice which places the customers' interests first.

Marketing activity of travel agencies

Travel agents, like other retailers, sell other firms' products. They are therefore heavily reliant upon tour operators to promote the IT product. Clearly it is in each tour operator's interest to create a brand image which implies quality and reliability (irrespective of the travel agency outlet through which the consumer makes a booking). This process of positive brand image creation by tour operators is independent of travel agency. Tour operators advertise and use national media opportunities to raise consumers' awareness of brand names and holiday opportunities. However, they also ensure that travel agents who stock their product ranges know how they would like the product to be sold. In addition to brochures, tour operators provide travel agents with marketing material including displays, posters, product familiarisation trips for travel agency staff and, increasingly, video tapes. The travel agent's role therefore has been, certainly in the past, that of reactive order-takers.

However, as the principal route through which ITs are normally purchased in the UK, travel agents might be expected to play a more positive role in marketing and sales promotion. Travel agencies can obviously influence the environment in which holidays are sold and, as hinted above, much is being done to improve shop design and layout, as well as staff and service levels. Well-designed and located travel agency outlets are not only critical for the individual outlet but also for travel agency as a whole if this branch of the tourism industry is to compete effectively on the high street with other retailers for consumers' discretionary expenditure. To date travel agency marketing activities have been limited. Indeed one-fifth of outlets in the Reading area survey undertook no promotional activity: most of the others confined their actions to advertising (not regularly) in local newspapers and less frequently on local radio or to talks to local groups. Such talks often deal with particular countries or destinations. Few had attempted, or even considered, door-to-door leaflet drops in their catchment areas. Major differences in promotional activity between the different types of travel agencies were not apparent in the Reading area study. In general travel agency promotional activity identifies the service available and emphasises the range of holiday types and destinations available rather than focusing on specific place products.

Change is to be expected as a result of the increasingly competitive nature of travel agency and the dominance national chains are achieving. Advertising by travel agencies may replace that by tour operators, reflecting the changed bargaining positions within the tourism industry. This is consistent with the normal evolution of retailer-supplier relationships in that the efficient large-scale high street retailer of goods is in a position to influence what is offered for sale. Brand loyalty will become increasingly the province of the retailer rather than the supplier and advertising will play an important role in this transfer of power from tour operator principals to

the distribution sector of travel agency (Holloway
& Plant, 1988). National travel agency chains
achieve high market profiles from their advertising
in national media and their willingness to offer
booking incentives, e.g. Lunn Poly and Pickfords
Travel. Cooperative promotions, such as the
Pickfords/Cosmos one mentioned above, may also be
pursued but only national agency chains will be
able to achieve such deals. Specialist independent
outlets may find an opportunity to grasp the
initiative in marketing destinations. Door-to-door
leaflet distribution by local travel agency outlets
to all households living within a given distance
may become more commonplace. The dominance of
national travel agency chains and their increasing
promotional activity is likely to bring about
greater similarity of local industry opportunity
sets throughout the UK.

CONCLUSION

The importance of the local industry
opportunity set as the basis of the consumer's
knowledge of the range of IT products and of
destinations should be emphasised, because, as
Middleton (1988) points out:

In marketing IT products, place does not just
mean the location of a tourist attraction or
facility, but the location of all the points
of sale which give consumers access to the
range of IT products on offer.

Marketing of ITs is still largely the
responsibility of the IT supplier, rather than the
travel agent (although this may be changing as
argued above). It is vital to the tour operator
that marketing creates the images necessary to
achieve volume sales. Volume sales are encouraged,
at least in part, by each tour operator offering a
range of packages with a high degree of
substitutability. Opportunities for comparison
shopping stimulate sales and this is what travel
agency outlets, both individually and collectively
in a locality, provide for tour operators' IT
products, i.e. comparative holiday shopping. It is
also apparent that travel agents have a role in
filtering IT holiday opportunities made available
at the local level and also, to the extent that
they channel information and give advice to

customers over and above that contained in tour operators' brochures, their activities are one factor influencing the perceived and awareness opportunity sets of consumers and ultimately the consumer's choice of destination.

For the travel agency sector, disaggregation of the local industry opportunity set on a destination place basis would demonstrate the importance of the independent specialist discussed above. For most travel agencies, sales of ITs based on the naive sun, sea and sand or winter sport images constitute the bulk of the outlet opportunity set because this is where volume sales may be achieved.

Many consumers are content to make use of the convenience and perceived reliabiity of high street travel agents. Most consumers purchase a holiday from a locally constrained opportunity set and most will consider the destination they visit only in terms of an overall package. Place is therefore a component of an overall IT package for consumers, tour operators and travel agents. Travel agents may, as suggested above, take the initiative in marketing destinations but at present their continued profitability depends on selling IT packages for holidays abroad. To get travel agents to promote domestic holiday opportunities to the same extent as they do foreign-based ITs would, for example, be a major achievement.

Place marketing is important for specific market segments, smaller tour operators, specialist holiday companies, and, of course, destinations. IT packages may or may not be marketed in a place-specific form by tour operators and where this is not the case travel agents may or may not emphasise the IT destination(s) as part of their sales pitch. Selling holidays is as important to the travel agent as it is to the tour operator. The local industry opportunity set consists of a largely homogeneous product range, and it is clear that if a travel agent cannot sell a consumer a particular holiday in a particular place, that agent will bring all persuasion to bear on selling a very similar holiday in a very similar place.

REFERENCES

Bennett, M. (1989) The impact of IT on travel agency, Geographical Papers, Tourism Series, 2, Dept. of Geography, University of Reading, Reading

Buck, M. (1988) The role of travel agent and tour operator, pp 67-74 in B. Goodall & G.J. Ashworth (Eds) Marketing in the Tourism Industry, Croom Helm, London

Foster, D. (1985) Travel and Tourism Management, Macmillan, Basingstoke

Goodall, B. (1988) Changing patterns and structure of European tourism, pp 18-38 in B. Goodall & G.J. Ashworth (Eds) Marketing in the Tourism Industry, Croom Helm, London

Holloway, J.C. (1985) The Business of Tourism, 2nd edition, Pitman, London

Holloway, J.C. & Plant, R.V. (1988) Marketing for Tourism, Pitman, London

Key Note Report (1988) Travel Agents and Overseas Tour Operators: An Industry Sector Overview, 7th edition, Key Note Publications, London

Lavery, P. (1987) Travel and Tourism, ELM Publication, Huntingdon

Middleton, V.T.C. (1988) Marketing in Travel and Tourism, Heinemann, London

Radburn, M.W. (1988) Market opportunity sets and the price structure of ITC products, paper presented at Leisure Studies Association 2nd International Conference, University of Sussex, Brighton

IV

SELLING TOURISM PLACES

Chapter 15

THE DYNAMICS OF TOURISM PLACE MARKETING

Brian Goodall

SELLING TOURISM PLACES

The theme of this book is that tourist destinations as place products have to be sold like any other product to potential customers, the holidaymakers. For the destination, success in selling its place product is vital to the commercial future of its tourism businesses, especially the many, often small, indigenous ones, and is also important to the buoyancy and development of the local economy, the more so if the area's 'exports' are concentrated in the tourism sector. The many tourist destinations are in competition with each other and 'brand loyalty' to any particular resort is low. Therefore, tourism place products do have to be sold!

Why should customers buy a particular place product rather than a product from one of the many competing tourist destinations? The answer appears deceptively straightforward - because that destination offers 'value for money' in the form of a superior place product. Such an answer assumes the potential tourist is fully aware of all possible destinations, their attractions and facilities; however, this is not so. If only because of the spatial separation of the tourist's normal place of residence and the places of consumption of holidays, potential tourists are likely to be aware, at any given time, of limited opportunities, as Stabler (Chp. 2) and Kent (Chp. 3) have argued. Indeed, Kent goes on to show that a tourist gives active consideration to a very restricted set of place products. The answer also assumes tourists view the place product in the same way as the destination's tourism industry. Nor is this necessarily true. Viewed from the destination the place product is the 'total product', even though it is properly recognised as a composite product comprising the destination's attractions and facilities. The tourist's view, at least prior to arrival in the destination on holiday, may be significantly different: the product may be as much 'the holiday' as 'the place'. For the tourist the product is again a composite one but now the 'total product' includes not only the place components but also the travel components. This applies whether tourists buy the total product as a package from a tour operator or assemble the individual components themselves or via travel agents. Having chosen a holiday and therefore a destination the tourist's perception of the place product may still differ from that of the destination tourism agency as de Haan et al. (Chp. 9) show with respect to the actual consumption of the place product.

The 'product' is also different things to the various businesses and organisations in the tourism industry (Foster, 1985). For some firms it is an individual component (attraction or facility) of the place product, e.g. for the hotel it is 'guest-nights', and for the theme park or stately home the number of visitors. For the destination tourism agency it is the composite place product, including common property resources such as climate. For yet other tourism businesses it is a component of the 'total tourism product', e.g. for the charter airline 'the number of seats or passenger kilometres flown'. For the tour operator producing, and the travel agent retailing, inclusive tours it is the total tourism product, i.e. number of holidays sold (irrespective of destination). Such complexities of interpretation of the 'tourism product' are at the root of the difficulties faced in defining and especially in selling tourism place products.

Furthermore, the tourism market is a dynamic one. The number and composition of the holidaying population, their socio-economic circumstances and their holiday tastes, are always changing. Both short- and long-term changes in demand ensue. For example, in the United Kingdom in early 1989 the high interest rates (stemming from government monetary policy) led to high mortgage rates, to lower holiday bookings and therefore to tour operators cutting back hard on the planned capacities of their summer sun inclusive tour programmes. Of longer-term significance in the case of North-West Europe is the ageing population: the youth boom is over and the 45 to 59 year olds are now a major target for the tourism industry (Wright & Wood, 1988). Similarly, on the supply side the comparative advantage of destinations is changing as a consequence of innovation, improvement and extension of transport networks, e.g. the proposed completion of the Channel Tunnel by 1993, or of new or revised legislation, e.g. deregulation of scheduled airfares and services, or of relative factor price changes, e.g. labour shortages in certain destinations. Destinations must repond to these changes - the place product must adapt. This may involve the expansion and improvement of existing place products to maintain market share and the introduction of new place products to capture a new clientele, as well as the demise of obsolescent place products.

To sell a tourism place successfully a link needs to be established between place product marketing and the tourist's holiday choice process. The tourist's decision to buy a place product is normally considered and planned over a period of time. Three phases have been distinguished in this choice process before the tourist actually goes away on holiday (Lundberg, 1985): first, a dream phase, involving speculation about the ideal holiday and destination; second, an information gathering phase to investigate a range of possible holidays and destinations, and third, the practical holiday decision phase during which a destination is selected and a firm booking made. Marketing of the tourism place product needs to be tailored to where the potential tourist is in this choice process: it must seek to change the tourist's attitudes, opinions, perceptions, image, desires, expectations, knowledge, awareness and inclination to buy in favour of that place product. Thus marketing needs to move the destination or place product through a sequence with the tourist which can be summarised - awareness, association, conviction, perceived value and action (Davidson, 1987). Repeat business may not be guaranteed for a destination, even where the place product fulfils all of the tourist's expectations, because either the tourist prefers a new destination for every holiday or there was dissatisfaction with the holiday experience as a result of something that happened outside the destination but as part of the total tourism product, e.g. flight delays or consolidations which affected the outward journey.

The two critical decisions for destination tourism agencies and businesses are to get their place products right and to identify the appropriate markets for those products.

GETTING THE PLACE PRODUCT RIGHT

Satisfied customers are good for business. If a place product provides a tourist with a highly satisfying experience repeat visits (purchases) are likely, when the tourist may well sample further components of the place product: at the very least the satisfied tourist is likely to recommend that destination to friends and relatives. But if the place product is not what the tourists want, no amount of advertising or price cutting will persuade them to buy (at least, not more than once). Hence the importance of getting the place product right.

Potential tourists must make comparative judgements of the anticipated worth of place products on the basis of indirect information. Even allowing for the individual's past holiday experiences, information pertaining to a future holiday is drawn from sources other than destination tourism agencies and businesses, even from beyond the industry's tour operators and travel agents in the case of opinions and experiences of friends and relatives and non-holiday-related information where destinations have been highlighted, because of political events or natural disasters, in the national media of the tourist's home country. There is ample opportunity for the place product to be distorted during this process of product formulation and transmission from tourist destination to potential holidaymaker.

Throughout this book, the complexity of the tourism place product as an amalgam of attractions and facilities has been emphasised. Attractions are place characteristics, often unique, e.g. natural environment or historic artefacts, or events, such as festivals and sporting occasions. Facilities refer to the destination's services which house, feed and transport locally the holidaymakers. Whilst it is the attractions which provide the initial 'pull' factor to generate tourist flows to a destination, the absence of, or limited facilities might well deter visitors, a point emphasised by Goodall (Chp. 4) in explaining tour operators' selection of French skiing resorts. Thus, in formulating a place product there is a threshold - the **generic** or **core product** (Kotler, 1984; Hymas, 1987; Middleton, 1988) which represents a lowest common denominator of components (attractions and facilities) which a destination must assemble before it can consider selling itself as a tourism place. This is recognised in the discussion of the historic city as a tourism product by Ashworth (Chp. 8), the 'product Languedoc' by de Haan et al. (Chp. 9), and the 'vital statistics' of skiing resorts considered by Goodall and Bergsma (Chp. 10).

Tourist destination product policy must give sympathetic consideration to the needs of potential holidaymakers since these will define an **expected product** (to which the generic product must at least match up). The place product actually marketed by a tourist destination will need to be more sophisticated and persuasive than the generic product: this **augmented product** (Kotler, 1984; Hymas, 1987; Middleton, 1988) will have a certain perceived standard or quality and will have been differentiated from the place products of other tourist destinations. Attractions are the primary distinguishing characteristic of places but differentiation can also be accomplished on the basis of facilities provided, e.g. luxury accommodation or, as Jansen-Verbeke (Chp. 7) demonstrates, leisure-shopping mix.

The destination tourism agency's augmented product combines those attractions and facilities which together provide distinctive benefits in that place product, not to be found in the place products of competing destinations, i.e. its USP or Unique Selling Proposition (Foster, 1985; Holloway & Plant, 1988). This is equivalent to identifying the destination's comparative advantage across a range of holiday activities and to determining where the destination's place product stands compared to the competition. USP may be based on:

(i)   the reliability of the place product, e.g. the snow record of ski resorts, so often missing from the 'vital statistics' quoted by tour operators as Goodall and Bergsma noted (Chp. 10);

(ii)   the quality of the place product, e.g. the more caring and personal service in small hotels stressed by Moutinho (Chp. 6);

(iii)   the good design or style of the place product, e.g. the layout and design of shopping malls discussed by Jansen-Verbeke (Chp. 7) or the availability of self-catering accommodation in Languedoc mentioned by de Haan et al. (Chp. 9);

(iv)   cheaper prices or added features at an inclusive price, e.g. the distinctions between package holidays to resorts in Malaga noted by Sinclair et al. (Chp. 5);

(v) the flexibility of the product, which allows made-to-measure holidays or visits, e.g. the 'tourist trail' in Groningen discussed by Ashworth (Chp. 8).

Product branding

Marketing of the place product may be facilitated by the use of a brand name or slogan, such as the unique destination label **Beautiful Berkshire** described by Pattinson (Chp. 12). Branding sets a place product apart from its competitors, e.g. **Beautiful Berkshire** from Bronte Country, Red Rose Country, White Cliffs Country, or The 1066 Country, etc.; acts as a 'cue' to potential holidaymakers, and, especially in the case of intangible products like holidays, helps consumers avoid risks, therefore encouraging repeat business and generating brand loyalty (Holloway & Plant, 1988). It is a key tool in market segmentation (discussed below) and becomes increasingly important as competition intensifies. The concept has been quite widely used in the tourism industry, but could be more effectively exploited by many destination areas.

The concept of branding applies not only to place products per se but can be applied equally to individual components of the place product. This is commonplace, for example, in the case of accommodation supplied by international hotel chains: brands like THF (Trust House Forte), Best Western, Holiday Inn, etc. invoke a product image of quality and reliability wherever the destination. Branding is also frequently used by mass tour operators for their inclusive tours, e.g. Poundstretcher for British Airways' long-haul holidays. However, the fragmentation of the destination tourism industry frequently results in the lack of a coherent product, and especially, brand image for both the general place product and certain of its individual components (the products of small tourism businesses).

Product life cycle

The competitive position of all place products changes over time: all follow the characteristic product life cycle, even though the exact duration of the cycle cannot be predicted. The early or introductory phase of the product life cycle corresponds to the introduction and adoption of a new product, such as the marketing of a new destination or place product about which potential tourists know very little, e.g. the recent introduction of Turkey as a destination for summer sun inclusive tours or the attempt to promote Spanish touring holidays in areas away from the Costas. As the place product becomes better known and establishes a positive reputation there is a growth phase during which sales steadily increase, e.g. skiing holidays to France from The Netherlands and the United Kingdom throughout the 1970s. At maturity demand has reached saturation level since all consumers likely to buy that place product have done so and sales even out: this is the situation that Zimmermann (Chp. 11) argues has been reached in the case of winter-sports holidays to Austria. Competition intensifies throughout the growth phase, as successful place products are copied by other destinations, until at maturity the destination has to fight harder to retain its share of a stagnant market. If newer products are thought to be superior then sales of the place product decline, the destination tourism economy suffers recession and tourism businesses cease trading, unless the place product is altered or replaced. Zimmermann (Chp. 11) acknowledges that, in the Austrian case, the product **Summer in the Alps** is no longer as competitive as previously and is attracting fewer visitors: this is one factor leading to the reorganisation of tourism marketing in the Austrian case.

For the destination tourism agency there is value in knowing where its place product lies with respect to the stages of the product life cycle because this will influence marketing strategy and product policy. In the early stages of the cycle the agency's marketing activities seek to inform tourists of the existence of the new place product; with the growth phase marketing's role switches increasingly to persuading more tourists to purchase that place product rather than one from the many competing destinations, and during the maturity stage emphasises and reminds tourists of the brand image and its 'low-risk' associations (Ashworth & Goodall, 1988). At some point during this latter phase attention turns to product policy since the place product needs to be found new

markets, revitalised or replaced. The destination
tourism agency is the best placed organisation to
monitor the place product's quality and its price
competitiveness in this context.

Changing the place product

Destinations rarely offer a single place
product and are therefore faced with decisions
about the mix of products to be marketed. The
place product mix comprises, at any given time, a
number of different product lines, i.e. the product
width, together with the number of variants within
each product line, i.e. the product depth (Holloway
& Plant, 1988). This may be illustrated in the
case of Austrian mountain resorts where their
product width embraces winter-sports holidays, both
downhill and cross-country skiing, and summer
mountain holidays, both sightseeing and activity,
and their product depth, for skiing holidays,
offers a choice of accommodation in serviced hotels
and chalets or self-catering apartments. The
product mix can be changed by altering both width
and depth.

Tourist destinations must take the external
factors which condition the level of demand in
tourist-generating countries for holidays abroad as
given and beyond their influence. But they do have
to respond to those changing needs and expectations
of their potential foreign holidaymakers. This
requires that destination tourism agencies and
tourism businesses continually re-evaluate their
place product(s) and their marketing strategies in
order to match them to the changing demands. Place
products can be altered, the way those products are
marketed can be revamped, and the prices charged
for package holidays or individual components of
the place product can be adjusted. Certainly, when
the place product has entered the maturity stage of
the product life cycle some modification and
rationalisation will be necessary.

Revitalising the place product. This is
essentially a change in product depth. If
attempting, in the face of declining demand, to
revitalise a place product it is first necessary to
establish why that demand is falling. Consider,
for example, the changing tastes with respect to
seaside holiday accommodation over the past 25

years where a major feature has been the switch to self-catering for reasons of flexibility and cost: if a resort has persisted with serviced accommodation, even where low priced, it will have lost visitors. Similarly within serviced accommodation there has been an increased demand for rooms with en suite facilities and if hotel accommodation has not been upgraded again the resort loses out. Likewise if the resort has not kept pace with new possibilities for water-based activities, such as board sailing, the decline in demand may be permanent. For any given resort, this will be the more likely if competing destinations have made appropriate adjustments to their place products.

It is therefore necessary to keep abreast of the additional features which competing resorts are adding to their attractions and facilities. The lesson is 'to keep one step ahead of the field', i.e. to revitalise the place product by adding new but different benefits in order to continue its appeal to its usual markets.

Repositioning the place product. Another reaction to falling demand might be to reduce the price of the place product and emphasise the value for money represented by the current product. A related line of action is to attempt to reach a new and more price-sensitive market, i.e. reposition the product to bring it within reach of potential holidaymakers who had not previously considered that destination or holiday activity. Increased advertising would certainly be needed to tap new markets, as would the introduction of new or the expansion of existing sales promotion campaigns, e.g. familiarisation trips for representatives of tour operators and travel agencies. For example, the response of the **Beautiful Berkshire** Campaign to overdependence on the North American market, and therefore the vulnerability of the area's tourism industry to fluctuations in the number of American tourists, has been to reposition its place product with respect to the European market, as described by Pattinson (Chp. 12).

Launching a new place product. This involves increasing the product width. It is the riskiest line of response for a tourist destination and begs the question 'what is a new place product?' How

267

the modifications suggested above as part
alisation creating a new product rather
ely extending the depth of the existing
oduct for the present market? This applies
particularly where it is the facilities of the
destination, rather than its attractions, which are
being altered. Certainly the introduction of fun
shopping, as proposed by Jansen-Verbeke (Chp. 7),
would represent a new product on the urban tourism
scene for most cities. Similarly, the AEOLUS
windmill park, described by van der Knijff (Chp.
13) is a new component in Friesland's place
product. Such developments therefore represent a
diversification or extension of the destination's
place product width.

Thus destination tourism agencies and
businesses need to monitor continuously the market
status of their place products and to adapt those
products as necessary to changing demand. But
getting the place product right is only part of any
success story - it is equally important to
understand the market for that product.

GETTING THE MARKET FOR THE PLACE PRODUCT RIGHT

A single destination cannot possibly serve the
total holiday market. It must identify those parts
of the market which contain potential holidaymakers
who are most likely to respond positively to its
particular place product. Tourist destinations,
and indeed the tourism industry in general, are
considered, however, to lag behind other consumer
product and business services in the use of market
research (Wertheim, 1988).

Place products need to be matched to
holidaymakers: formulating the place product
therefore has its mirror image in market
segmentation, i.e. positioning that place product
to serve a particular target market. The place
product is therefore designed and sold to satisfy
specifically the needs and wants of a particular
group of customers, e.g. skiing ITs aimed at 18-30
year olds or winter sun holidays for 'Glams'
(greying, leisured, affluent, middle-aged). The
place product, which is dependent in turn on the
destination's comparative advantage, is a major
factor determining which part(s) of the overall
holiday market that destination can attempt to
serve. Identification of the target markets or
market segments can be assisted by market-product-

competitor analysis (Mill & Morrison, 1985), which determines where, in this case, a place product stands compared to the competition in the eyes of the customer, or by SWOT analysis (Holloway & Plant, 1988; Middleton, 1988) in which the strengths, weaknesses, opportunities and threats relating to a place product are examined.

The strengths of a place product, as viewed by the holidaymakers, will be those attractions and facilities of the destination which match up to the consumers' requirements, e.g. for a summer sun holiday the destination must have reliable sunshine, warmth, a beach with clean sand and good bathing conditions; for an advanced skiing holiday the destination must offer a wide choice of challenging pistes, opportunities for off-piste skiing and an integrated lift system; for the cultural holiday in the historic city a range of historic artefacts, museums and events. Weaknesses may also be identified in place products, especially those well-advanced in the product life cycle, and these may often be associated with the destination's facilities, e.g. the destination lacks self-catering accommodation for low priced family summer sun holidays; or a capital city such as London is poorly provided with budget-price hotels for foreign tourists. Opportunities arise both from elements under the control of the destination's tourism industry, e.g. the development of pony trekking and other activity holidays in remote rural upland areas, and from changes in external factors which can be exploited to the destination's advantage, e.g. transport improvements which increase accessibility or the choice of that destination as the site of a prestigious event such as the Olympic Games. Threats also arise from both internal factors, e.g. a deterioration in the quality of the destination's attractions as has happened at many seaside resorts where bathing waters have been polluted by local sewage effluent, or external factors, e.g. usually increasing competition from other destinations but exchange rate fluctuations, acts of international terrorism, etc. may also deter tourists.

In targeting part of or segmenting the market a tourist destination seeks to reduce the competition faced by its place product. Markets may be segmented according to a number of principles, the most usual of which are:

(i) Socio-economic or demographic segmentation in which the market is subdivided on the basis of multivariate criteria covering income, education, occupation, and family life cycle (itself a surrogate for marital status, age, number of children). Tour operators practice this type of segmentation where they produce inclusive tours aimed at particular age groups, e.g. young adults or senior citizens and destinations would be doing likewise in targeting family groups where they provide holiday camps or villages complete with accommodation and on-site attractions, amusements and entertainments.

(ii) Product-related segmentation based on variables such as type of activity, use of equipment, length of stay, etc. This type of segmentation can apply particularly to destinations in the sense that their place products are based on a comparative advantage for a particular holiday activity such as downhill skiing, and markets are targeted in neighbouring regions or countries which lack suitable physical environments for the practice of that activity. It is a form of segmentation common in other parts of the tourism industry as well: tour operators use it when producing different brochures for summer sun, winter sun, and winter-sports holidays, as also do the producers of individual components of place products, e.g. hotels distinguishing between corporate or business guests, group tours, individual holidaymakers, conference delegates and weekend breaks. Such segmentation, and therefore recognition that a place product can be sold in more than one market, is implicit in Pattinson's description (Chp. 12) of the five individual promotions which currently comprise the **Beautiful Berkshire** Campaign.

(iii) Psychographic segmentation, which is based on the attitudes, interests and opinions of holidaymakers, is the most recent form of segmentation and one which is not, as yet, widely used in the tourism industry. Kent's discussion (Chp. 3) of the importance of people's preferences in their choice of holiday destinations and the differences in attitudes and behaviour revealed in the survey of Languedoc visitors by de Haan et al. (Chp. 9) suggest the future importance of this type

of segmentation for tourism, whilst van der Knijff (Chp. 13) demonstrates the style of market research, in the case of the Lauwersmeer, undertaken in order to identify intentions to buy holidays in that region.
(iv) Geographic segmentation in which primary, secondary and even tertiary markets are recognised according to the proportion of actual visitors drawn from different areas. This is probably the most common form of segmentation practiced in the case of tourist destinations, e.g. in recognising local residents, day-trippers, domestic tourists and foreign tourists. Geographic segmentation is the basis of the market research for the AEOLUS windmill park described by van der Knijff (Chp. 13).

Having tailored the place product, on the basis of the destination's comparative advantage, and having identified who the best possible customers are, the two have to be brought together by effective marketing.

GETTING THE PLACE PRODUCT MESSAGE ACROSS

The carefully formulated place product still has to be sold to its target market, i.e. prospective holidaymakers who are normally resident in another country. The problem lies in communicating with these persons at an acceptable cost. The tourism industry straddles this spatial separation of tourist origins and destinations and tourism businesses may be based in either location. Obviously businesses supplying components of the place product must be destination-based but other businesses, supplying a total tourism product in the form of an inclusive tour providing travel to and from the destination, are usually based in tourist-origin countries. Wherever the 'tourism producers' are based there will be a need for a distribution system in the origin area, such as the retail travel agencies described by Radburn and Goodall (Chp. 14). Also, in the tourist destination, public or semi-public organisations emerge to oversee the general interests of the destination's tourism industry: these usually take the form of a national, provincial or regional, or local tourist office/board which acts for the destination as a whole even though it has no product of its own for sale. This latter type of destination tourism agency is particularly significant in marketing the destination as a place product.

How do destination tourism agencies communicate the existence of their place products to potential holidaymakers in tourist-origin areas? Do they adopt a direct sell approach, leaving holidaymakers to make their own travel arrangements? This might work for domestic tourists but would prove less satisfactory for foreign ones. Do they attempt to distribute their place product via the travel agency network in the tourist-origin country, with the travel agent handling holidaymakers' travel arrangements? This would be an indirect and complex way to contact potential tourists. Or, do they persuade tour operators based in origin countries to include their destination or place product as one choice in the operators' inclusive tour programmes? A destination's place products, as represented by its resorts, may not all be accepted into inclusive tour programmes as Goodall (Chp. 4) demonstrated for French ski resorts.

The individual tourism business in the destination, such as a hotel, is unlikely to be in a position to undertake a direct sell campaign to potential holidaymakers living in many countries. Indeed, few destination tourism businesses are large enough to fund marketing campaigns that have any real impact in the market place. Marketing of the destination as a place product is therefore usually undertaken by the destination tourism agency - the national tourist office (NTO) or regional tourist board (RTB) - acting in a facilitating role for the destination's tourism businesses.

Two levels of tourism place product marketing are usually distinguished (Burkart & Medlik, 1981; Middleton, 1988). First, that of the destination or place product as a whole, undertaken as argued above by the destination tourism agency, i.e. the NTO or RTB. Second, the individual components of the place product which are marketed by their individual producers within the framework of the overall place product campaign, as well as separately to tourists once the latter have arrived in the destination.

The marketing requirements of NTOs/RTBs would appear to vary from those of the commercial tourism trade because these organisations are not usually

trying to make actual sales. They are concerned
with promoting interest in the destination's
attractions, creating an identifiable image and
increasing acceptance of that destination as a good
holiday base. Historically the role of NTOs/RTBs
was confined to such narrow promotional activity
but now they focus increasingly on targeting
specific markets and on their facilitating role for
destination tourism businesses. Indeed, as
Zimmermann (Chp. 11) notes in the case of the
Carinthia Tourism Company, they may be able to take
an equity interest in such businesses. Whilst they
organise and coordinate the external marketing of
the destination the extent to which they exercise
influence over the destination tourism industry as
a whole may be limited because only a small
proportion of destination tourism businesses have a
formal relationship with the NTO (Middleton, 1988).

Although destination tourism agencies usually
have no place product to sell (in the sense that
hotels have bed-nights for sale) the marketing
tools needed to transmit the place product image to
the potential holidaymakers are no different from
those used by commercial firms. To promote its
place product the destination tourism agency must
take raw information about that product to encode a
message which is channelled, via various media, to
recipients who decode the message and respond
accordingly (Ashworth & Goodall, 1988). This
process of transition from raw information to
received message may suffer from distortions,
ambiguities, fragmentation, inaccuracies, editing
and bias, as Goodall and Bergsma (Chp. 10) showed
for the representation of ski resorts in tour
operators' brochures and Radburn and Goodall (Chp.
14) showed for the availability of inclusive tour
place products through travel agents.

Promotional activities of destination tourism
agencies encompass the usual range of advertising,
personal selling, sales promotion and publicity
techniques. It is important to remember that the
destination tourism agency is marketing the place
product to at least two sets of 'customers' - the
ultimate holidaymakers and the intermediary
businesses of the tourism industry, especially tour
operators. Links with the tourism industry in the
tourist-origin countries are especially important
and frequently involve the NTO/RTB (Kosters, 1987;
Middleton, 1988; Mill & Morrison, 1985) in:

(i) establishing 'overseas' offices;

(ii) visits to tour operators and travel agents in target markets;

(iii) organisation of workshops to bring together representatives of all the main components of place and tourism products in both generating and destination countries;

(iv) sales seminars to familiarise the generating country's travel trade with the place product;

(v) study tours or familiarisation trips for selected managers of tour operators and travel agencies;

(vi) regular direct mail shots to the generating area's travel trade, including newsletters, destination travel trade manuals, etc.;

(vii) promotional events.

Pattinson (Chp. 12) has described the use of most of these techniques by the **Beautiful Berkshire** Campaign. In addition the NTO's/RTB's facilitating role may involve joint marketing schemes with destination tourism businesses, the advantages of which for small firms are expounded by Moutinho (Chp. 6). Such destination tourism agencies may also administer government grant schemes to assist local tourism development.

NTOs/RTBs also address their marketing to the potential holidaymakers by means of general advertising (to communicate with consumers whose identity is unknown and with whom no direct contact has been established) and sales promotion (where the consumer's identity and home address is known from a previous visit), as well as by servicing potential holidaymakers' enquiries, participating in tourism fairs open to the general public, sponsoring local promotional events, and supplying window displays about the destination for travel agencies. There is a further side to consumer contact associated with the needs of the holidaymaker once the latter has arrived in the destination: here the NTO/RTB may provide a welcoming or reception service, a local tourist information service to promote individual attractions and facilities, and even provide the casual visitor with assistance in booking accommodation, etc.

The marketing message encoded for a particular place product has to be continuously adapted in order to keep abreast of the competition, to reflect the stage reached in the product life cycle, in the attempt to tap new market segments, and especially to capitalise upon improvements to the place product. Destination tourism agencies must therefore keep their marketing strategies under constant review - the theme of their marketing message, the frequency and timing of its use - in order to promote the destination as effectively as possible within the budget available.

GETTING THE PLACE PRODUCT PRICE RIGHT

Pricing the place product, let alone determining the right price, is an almost impossible task. As Ashworth and Voogd (Chp. 1) pointed out, destination tourism agencies are currently attempting to market an unpriced product in largely unknown quantities. This is because the place product is an amalgam of components: some of which may be assembled by tourism businesses, such as tour operators, for purchase by the holidaymaker before arrival in the destination, e.g. accommodation; others of which may be purchased individually before or after arrival in the destination, e.g. excursions, and yet others which can only be purchased in the destination, e.g. holiday souvenirs. All components may be purchased separately and in different combinations by different holidaymakers visiting a destination. Casual visitors will make all their purchases in the destination. But not all components are priced in the conventional sense. Those that are - hotel accommodation, restaurant meals, car hire, theme park entry, etc. - present least difficulty but some components are 'unpriced', e.g. the sunny clime of the seaside resort, and yet others are priced in some places but not in others, e.g. car parking, or viewing a natural feature, such as a waterfall, or an historic building, such as a church or cathedral. What price, therefore, can be put on the place product?

Most discussions of pricing in the tourism literature (Burkart & Medlik, 1981; Foster, 1985; Holloway & Plant, 1988; Middleton, 1988; Mill & Morrison, 1985) deal with the pricing of individual place product components or the determination of a price for a tourism product, such as an inclusive tour. Where priced components are purchased as a 'package holiday' the collective price is less than the aggregate of the prices of the components if purchased individually. No single unique price can therefore be put on the place product. Holidaymakers get what they pay for - quality products command a higher price, as confirmed by Sinclair et al. (Chp. 5). Not only does price convey something to the holidaymakers about the quality of the product but it also regulates demand and raises revenue for the producers, whilst holidaymakers' willingness to pay in turn highlights their preferences. Pricing remains the crux of voluntary exchange in a competitive market.

Undoubtedly tourists are sensitive to price considerations. The price of any given place product is constrained by its substitutability by other place products, i.e. for many tourists one summer sun destination is readily substitutable for any other summer sun destination. In all such cases pricing policy can be used to achieve marketing objectives. Suppliers of individual place components determine their prices independently of each other but with regard to the reactions of their immediate competitors: they set prices in one of three bands - premium prices, i.e. above the general market level to convey a superior product; value for money prices, i.e. a middle range price with the stress on 'fairness'; or cheap prices which attempt to lead the field.

It remains impossible, however, to put an accurate price on the place product consumed by each holidaymaker because that place product is an assemblage of place components unique to that person and comprises different combinations of priced and unpriced components. Social marketing, of unpriced and even unpriceable place products, therefore best describes the functional role of destination tourism agencies although their activities do, and could to an even greater extent, include the distribution of information on prices of place product components. An element of 'overall pricing' of the place product might be introduced (following certain principles of provision of public goods) via direct taxation of tourist activity in the destination, such as the tourist tax on Austrian bed-nights referred to by Zimmermann (Chp. 11). This may be a more equitable method of ensuring funds to cover a destination tourism agency's marketing activities than the voluntary subscriptions of participating members, as largely relied upon to fund campaigns such as the **Beautiful Berkshire** one described by Pattinson (Chp. 12).

DESTINATIONS AND MARKETING CONTROL

Tourism businesses, whether based in tourist-generating or destination areas, are primarily concerned with the short-term profitability and growth of their own business and not with the long-term development of a well-balanced tourism industry in the destination. They therefore produce what sells and this means the destination adapting to the holidaymakers' needs, not the other way around. These businesses have shown an increasing willingness and an improving ability to use the tools of marketing for the future good of their individual firm. Increasingly, as tour operators have grown in size and power and vertically integrated systems of place product distribution have been established, destinations have grown more dependent upon organised flows of tourists (Mill & Morrison, 1985). It is the marketing and bargaining power of the tourism trade intermediaries which appears to dominate although the social marketing activities of destination tourism agencies have probably compounded the situation. The destination tourism agency, despite its command of marketing techniques, cannot exercise a large measure of marketing control in tourist-generating countries.

Destinations and place products need not be 'pawns' in the market place. Many destinations have learnt their lessons from mass tourism the hard way: in as competitive an industry as tourism changing tastes and circumstances can quickly erode established markets. Destinations must protect the integrity and attraction of their place products and guard against the actions of competing destinations: this will entail joint ventures between tourism businesses within a destination and even cooperation between destinations. Resorts in a destination and suppliers of product components must be aware of their contribution to the tourism place product. Since tourism development is not 'all benefit' to the destination, suppliers of place products, including destination tourism agencies, should acknowledge a responsibility not only to the holidaymaker but also to the host population and the destination environment - the aim should be to produce 'human tourism' (Krippendorf, 1987), or 'gentle tourism' as described by Zimmermann (Chp. 11) or environmentally sensitive tourism as described by Moutinho (Chp. 6). Destination tourism agencies

277

can make a significant contribution to this by
providing authentic information to 'partners' in
tourist-generating countries and refraining from
clichéd advertisements. A societal marketing
approach should be adopted in which destinations
market their place products to satisfy tourist
needs whilst respecting the long-term interests of
the community (Mill & Morrison, 1985; Murphy,
1985).

REFERENCES

Ashworth, G.J. & Goodall, B. (1988) Tourist
     images: marketing considerations, pp. 213-238
     in B. Goodall & G.J. Ashworth (Eds) Marketing
     in the Tourism Industry, Croom Helm, Beckenham
Burkart, A.J. & Medlik, S. (1981) Tourism: Past,
     Present and Future, 2nd edition, Heinemann,
     London
Davidson, T.L. (1987) Assessing the effectiveness
     of persuasive communications in tourism, pp.
     473-480 in J.R. Brent Ritchie & C.R. Goeldner
     (Eds) Travel, Tourism and Hospitality
     Research, John Wiley, New York
Foster, D. (1985) Travel and Tourism Management,
     Macmillan, Basingstoke
Holloway, J.C. & Plant, R.V. (1988) Marketing for
     Tourism, Pitman, London
Hymas, R. (1987) Marketing business travel
     services, pp. 107-134 in A. Hodgson (Ed) The
     Travel and Tourism Industry: Strategies for
     the Future, Pergamon, Oxford
Kotler, P. (1984) Marketing Management: Analysis,
     Planning and Control, 5th edition, Prentice-
     Hall, London
Kosters, M.J. (1987) Tourism research in European
     national tourist organisations, pp. 129-143
     in J.R. Brent Ritchie & C.R. Goeldner (Eds)
     Travel, Tourism and Hospitality Research, John
     Wiley, New York
Krippendorf, J. (1987) The Holiday Makers,
     Heinemann, London
Lundberg, D.E. (1985) The Tourist Business, 5th
     edition, Van Nostrand Reinhold, New York
Middleton, V.T.C. (1988) Marketing in Travel and
     Tourism, Heinemann, London
Mill, R.C. & Morrison, A.M. (1985) The Tourism
     System, Prentice-Hall, Englewood Cliffs, New
     Jersey

Murphy, P.E. (1985) Tourism: A Community Approach, Methuen, London
Wertheim, M. (1988) Using market research, pp. 41-43 in The Tourism Society, The Tourism Industry 1988/89, Tourism Society, London
Wright, T. & Wood, M. (1988) Key marketing issues, pp. 40-41 in The Tourism Society, The Tourism Industry 1988/89, Tourism Society, London